Peter Sellers

Other books by Alexander Walker:

Sex in The Movies
Stardom: The Hollywood Phenomenon
Stanley Kubrick Directs
Hollywood, England: The British
  Film Industry in the Sixties
Rudolph Valentino
Double Takes
Superstars
The Shattered Silents: How the Talkies
  Came to Stay
Garbo: A Portrait
Joan Crawford
Vivien

PETER SELLERS

The Authorized Biography

ALEXANDER WALKER

WEIDENFELD AND NICOLSON
LONDON

Contents

Picture Acknowledgements

The photographs in this book are reproduced by permission of the following:

Associated Newspapers 1; *Tom Blau/Camera Press* 6 above; *Brian Connon* 1; *Lynne Frederick* 4 (below), 7 (above), 8; *Hulton Deutsch Collection* 1; *Kobal* 2 (below); *National Film Archive* 3 (above), 5; *Popperfoto* 2 (above), 3 (below), 6 (below); *Rex Features* 4 (above); *Alexander Walker* 7 (below)

Acknowledgements

'It is obvious that writers of their own lives possess evident advantages over other biographers.' So wrote Peter Sellers's ancestor, the boxer Daniel Mendoza, in the opening sentence of his own *Memoirs*, published in 1816.

It anticipates the apology I must make. My first debt is a posthumous one – to Peter Sellers himself. No doubt he should have written his own 'life' – no doubt he would have – but a cruelly premature death determined otherwise.

I knew him personally, as well as in my role as a film critic, for some twenty-five years. Several times he encouraged me to consider writing this book. Not in any vainglorious spirit, I think, but out of a genuine desire to see if others could give a meaning to a life that often baffled and distressed him. I cried off, protesting that it was too soon. The day came, however, when I had to write not a life, but an obituary; and this book is partly a reaction to my bitter realization that it was then too late. Too late, anyhow, to draw directly on Peter's own vast reservoir of recollections, enriched by the mimicry which he employed to turn time past into present mirth. 'I feel safer with an accent than an anecdote,' he used to say; but the trepidation of the performer wasn't evident in the performance. When the mood was good, he was a born narrator of his own life-story.

An American critic has borrowed the jazz term 'riffs' to describe Peter's inspired improvizations. That is indeed what it was like: I wish my powers of notation had kept up with them.

But much more of this book comes from the customary hard grind of biography which takes one to the vast number of people who knew Peter Sellers – or thought they did, as I myself thought I did, before the interviews convinced me that I did not really know Peter at all – or, rather, did not really know all the 'Peters' he contained. I finished writing this account of his life with a feeling of incredulousness that so many contradictory and combative selves should have been crammed into it.

The names of many who helped me are recorded below; a few people asked for anonymity, and I have respected this request without any lessening of gratitude.

I especially thank Peter Sellers's widow, the actress Lynne Frederick. She encouraged me in the project with very practical help, yet in no way sought to influence what I was writing in her late husband's favour, or indeed in anyone else's. I made my own interpretations, reached my own conclusions.

Just one more point: it concerns the limits of a biographer's judicious re-creation of events. Some of the people I interviewed were themselves dramatically forceful characters. They talked, naturally and even compulsively, in 'dialogue', recalling conversations of many years before as if they were still hearing the people who once spoke the words. In such instances, when I felt they could be trusted, I have set the words down this way, too. In other passages, such as the thoughts in Peter's mind on that last day of his life, I have used what those closest to him at the time reported as his preoccupations. Likelihood is one of the licences of biography.

My thanks are due to the following who consented to being specially interviewed for this book: Lynne Frederick, Woody Allen, Elwood A. Rickless, Sue Evans, Michael Jeffery, Mrs Vera Marks (Aunty Ve), Mrs Dorothy Elmore (Aunty Do), Bryan Connon, Joy Parker, Mark Primhak, David Lodge, Graham Stark, Blake Edwards, Stanley Kubrick, Shirley MacLaine, John Boulting, Roy Boulting, John Redway, Dennis Selinger, Canon John Hester, Hattie Stevenson, Penny Heath-Brown, Dimitri de Grunwald, Wolf Mankowitz, Bert Mortimer, Lord Snowdon, Rev. Br. Cornelius, Rev. Br. Hugh, Martin Baum, Theo Cowan, Bryan Forbes, Sir Peter Hall, Douglas Hayward, Joe McGrath, Mo Rothman, Sanford Lieberson, Jules Dassin.

For their insights into Peter Sellers gained over the years of acquaintanceship or chance encounters of more recent date, I thank: Spike Milligan, Harry Secombe, Michael Bentine, Jerzy Kosinski, Victor Spinetti, Satyajit Ray, Richard A. C. Boyle and Jocelyn Stevens.

Since I believe the work of any great artist should be reflected, in a judicious measure, by what other critics besides the author have written about him, I thank those critics and journalists who are quoted in the text.

ACKNOWLEDGEMENTS

For seeing this book through its many stages to publication, I am indebted to John Curtis of Weidenfeld & Nicolson, my editor Alex MacCormick, Michael Paul for his copy-editing, and Richard and Hilary Bird for the index.

I acknowledge the services generously offered me at the British Film Institute, the British Museum Reading Room, and the Margaret Herrick Library of the Academy of Motion Picture Arts and Sciences, and the assistance of Paul Heeb at the Hotel Schweizerhof, Davos.

The passage from *The Teaching of Buddha* is reprinted by permission of Bukkyo Dendo Kyokai, Tokyo (Kosaido Printing Co. Ltd, Tokyo, Japan, 1980); the quotations on page 24 are by permission of Beatrix Miller, editor of British *Vogue*, and The Condé Nast Publications Ltd; and those on page 65 by permission of Harry Secombe from his book *Goon to Lunch* (M. & J. Hobbs & Michael Joseph, London, 1975).

Alexander Walker
Davos and London, 1981

Preface by Lynne Frederick

Nothing about Peter Sellers or his life was simple, either for himself or for those around him, and the four-and-a-half precious years we shared were no exception. It was a relationship that had to be nurtured twenty-four hours a day, with someone who often – sometimes contritely and sometimes proudly – described himself as one of the most complicated men in the world. It was a relationship that had to be renewed daily, kept fresh, kept young, and above all kept together; and so it was, except for one brief interlude of separation fifteen months before he died – a wound which we both knew would be healed, for when I went to an analyst for advice at this time, he listened to what I told him, then looked at me and said, 'You know, it's as if you and Peter are obsessed with each other.' We were. After every argument, every trauma that the film business can breed, it always ended by his saying to me, 'You're the person who knows me best. Nobody understands me the way you do.' By then, I hope, he was right. There was very little Peter did that I couldn't relate to or comprehend, though the learning process had sometimes been hard and painful.

He was a terribly vulnerable person: people could 'get' to him, hurt him, more woundingly than you could ever imagine. Peter never learned to shield himself, despite his long years in the film business. People might think he was the toughest nut around, but he wasn't: he had no protective shell. One word could destroy him. Even saying 'Hello' the wrong way could put him off his stroke. A well-meaning friend once said to him, 'Peter, how well you look – you've put on a bit of weight.' For days afterwards, he didn't touch his food.

That is the way Peter was. It was up to me and a few other close companions to share these problems with him and to protect him from himself, as far as we could. There is no concealing the fact that he was frequently his own worst enemy, but once you understood him, you could forgive him.

When I met him, he spent the first six months of our relationship telling me horrendous stories about his earlier life, the marriages, the girlfriends, the children, the movies, all the intimate details, night after night, day after day. I suppose it was rather like an amateur analysis session – a thing he would have hated and feared had it been thrust on him by others even for his own good, but which he volunteered with an unconscious need to tell all when he had someone to lend a sympathetic ear. When he had completed his revelations, I felt: 'Well, I know everything about everyone else in your life. All we have to do now is to get to know each other!' It had not been merely a recounting of the past; in a very real sense, it had been a recanting of it, too.

I drew from this experience: it gave me the key to him. When you're about to play a role in a film, you construct the character in your mind. I put Peter together in the same way, one piece of self-revelation after another, until I had a picture of him that was like an in-depth study for our life together. I felt I was ready to take my PhD. in my chosen subject, 'The life and times of Peter Richard Henry Sellers'. I not only felt I knew what his feelings were at any time, I also tried to anticipate what was going to upset him before it did – and if possible prevent it. (Not always, I might add, with total success!)

Whatever his behaviour, I would try to find a reason for it and an alibi for his own use. 'Isn't it a bit stupid to be doing this?' he'd ask me, nervously, when he was spending a fortune on some strictly unnecessary bit of pleasure. And I'd reply: 'Why not, darling? I suppose it is, a little, but then life's not that long.' I knew it couldn't be very long for him; even so, I'd no idea it would be cut quite so cruelly short.

At the time of his death, I think he was coming into his finest hour as an actor. It was vital to try and instil in him the confidence that he could do anything. Some people may think it odd that he needed this constant reassurance, but Peter was convinced – and, by this time, he was a very sick man – that all he was fit for was playing Inspector Clouseau for the rest of his life. When I first met him, he used to say, 'I was quite talented once.... Now all I can do is fall over.' What overcame this was his success in *Being There*, which was his creative pinnacle. I felt he was moving more into straight roles, more into subtle humour, and thus realizing the size and nature of his true potential.

It is no compensation for the loss of living, but knowing Peter, I am relieved he never had to read the notices of his last film, *The Fiendish Plot of Dr Fu Manchu*. The reviews were not unfair – it was far from being a good film – but the criticism would have conveyed to him the feeling of being unwanted again. He would have thought that *Being There* was just a five-minute wonder. Even the success of *Being There* was double-edged. After finishing it, he went through a series of suicide threats, which were really cries for help. He felt that he had achieved the utmost within his powers. It was not the most he could have done had he been a healthy man, maybe; but he had certainly transcended his debilitated condition and touched genius again. However, it was then that he started to say last thing at night, 'Pray I won't wake up in the morning. Just pray that God will take me.' I'd say: 'Darling, you don't mean that.' But I realized that in one sense he did mean it. When shooting finished on the film, he was quiet, unnaturally silent, sitting there in the same room as myself, but seeming light years away. I'd ask him: 'Darling, are you all right?' And he'd say, 'I don't feel anything. I've done what I wanted to do. I've fulfilled my ambition. Apart from you, I've no reason to go on living.'

There is an observation in this book that success acted on Peter like a depressant – it is true. He was a genius, but he lacked the creative energy to maintain his self-confidence, though, when something inspired him, he'd get enthusiastic, the adrenalin would start pumping and he could forget about the unstable condition of his heart. He could certainly never have given it all up. At the Cannes Film Festival, in May 1980, I was asked by people who were appalled at Peter's haggard, almost cadaverous appearance, 'Why don't you persuade him to retire?' I'd reply: 'But what would he do? He would die much sooner of inaction and boredom than if he works to the end.' The industry that he loved and hated kept him going.

When I met Peter, I already had some sense of the industry, which came from my own involvement with films. I had a sense of what it could do to stars like Peter Sellers and also, to be honest, what *he* could do to the film industry, as Alexander Walker's account of his life sometimes makes horrifyingly plain. It was a balance of advantages: sometimes the advantage was Peter's and life seemed good to him; sometimes it was the opposite and then life seemed bleak, with no future for him at all. When he was at the fulcrum, the pressures on him were intense and very destructive. He took everything so much to heart – and I am aware of the tragic *double-entendre* in that last phrase.

With few exceptions, he always did what he wanted, sometimes succeeding magnificently, sometimes failing lamentably. Occasionally he yielded to the temptation of huge fees, then bitterly regretted it when he saw how he had exposed himself to working on subjects unworthy of his talents. At other times, he battled for years to win the power to do something he wanted – and then h valued the result.

I think this book reveals the remarkable range and incredible resilience of Peter's career, which spanned twenty-five years and two continents, and encompassed slapstick comedy, dazzling satire, Goonish surrealism, inspired improvisations and impersonations, and the most delicately shaded revelations of human nature. He made the name 'Peter Sellers' mean something to those who enjoyed him in his lifetime; and other people, discovering Peter's art years from now, will understand how he succeeded, at terrible cost to himself, in making a part of film-making his own for nearly three decades.

Because we had no children, I was able to stay closer to Peter and his career than I could otherwise have done. In some ways he was like a child himself; it was a curious reversal of age and circumstances. He was happy when he knew where I was, which was generally near him. On a film set, he'd look across the studio to me after a take for a sign, a nod of approval or an opinion like, 'Well, I think you could do it better.' But this wasn't criticism: it was guidance and moral support. It came from someone he trusted not to deceive him; if he felt he wasn't getting sufficient guidance and support from the director, he'd look to me for it. I understood his occasional rages and the way his conduct made other people angry. And because I knew the people he was dealing with, I could try to be a go-between. Being married to Peter didn't mean closing your eyes to his faults – it meant constantly adjusting to them and shielding him from their consequences.

It is difficult for me to read this book objectively, but there are several of Peter's qualities that I hope shine through. I hope that readers will appreciate his sense of humour – he could never have entranced the world without it. I hope that readers will realize that his magnetism – albeit volatile – was easier to experience than to describe. Also, readers will see that perfectionism, however admirable, is a brute to live with. It is not so for those around the perfectionist – forget about us – but, above all, for the perfectionist himself.

I'll always remember Peter for a side of him that he only showed to those he totally trusted: it was a sort of sweet innocence. He had one phrase that sticks in my mind, the phrase 'I'm only a little thing', which he used to resort to when he couldn't cope, or when he felt people were out to get him, or when he blamed himself for something that had momentarily gone wrong. By being small, by making himself into a little boy in his own mind, he hoped to soften the enemy and deflect his rage – for how could a seven-year-old be expected to understand? It was as if he were saying, 'She's my mother ... she'll take care of me.' So, when people called him about something that might spell trouble for him, he'd say to me, 'Lynne, you talk to them, you know what to say. I'll get into such a muddle, you know, I'm only a little thing.' It was an intensely vulnerable and disarming characteristic. You had to pardon and love him, whatever he had done.

In those moments he could touch you with his pain, just as he touched the lives of so many millions of people with laughter. He deserved a little more of this last precious quality in his own life.

Lynne Frederick

Peter Sellers

Once upon a time, a man was travelling alone. He came to a vacant house towards the evening and decided to spend the night there. About midnight, a demon brought in a corpse and left it on the floor. Shortly, another demon appeared and claimed the corpse as his and they quarrelled over it.

Then the first demon said it was useless to argue about it further and proposed to refer it to a judge to decide the possessor. The other demon agreed to this and, seeing the man cowering in the corner, asked him to decide the ownership. The man was terribly frightened, for he well knew that whatever decision he might make would anger the demon that lost and that the losing demon would seek revenge and kill him, but he decided to tell truthfully just what he had witnessed.

As he expected, this angered the second demon, who grabbed one of the man's arms and tore it off; but the first demon replaced the arm with one taken from the corpse. The angry demon tore away the man's other arm, but the first demon replaced that with the other arm of the corpse. And so it went on until both arms, both legs, the head and the body had been successively torn away and replaced with the corresponding parts of the corpse. Then the two demons, seeing the parts of the man scattered about on the floor, picked them up and devoured them and went away chuckling.

The man who had taken refuge in the deserted house was very much upset by his misfortunes. The parts of his body which the demons had eaten were the parts his parents had given him, and the parts that he now had belonged to the corpse. Who was he, anyway? Realizing all the facts, he was unable to figure it out and, becoming crazy, he wandered out of the house. Coming to a temple, he went in and told his troubles to the monks. People could see in his story the true meaning of selflessness.

THE TEACHING OF BUDDHA

Prologue

He had flown into London so unexpectedly the day before that his favourite hotel was unable to give him the suite he usually occupied. As things turned out, it was just as well. The Harlequin Suite was no place for a clown to die. Instead, the Dorchester offered him a suite, at £200.00 a day, on its sixth floor, overlooking a Hyde Park that was beginning in this summer weather to assume the slightly overblown look of a West End green space at the height of the tourist season. *Green* ... at least that colour, which his superstitious nature led him to believe was an ill-omen, wasn't a feature of the suite's decor. In that respect, this unfamiliar room was reassuring to the man of fifty-four who opened his eyes and awoke, alone, around seven o'clock on the morning of Tuesday 22 July 1980.

'I could live here all my life,' he used to say about the Dorchester. He liked the attention he received, the service always to hand, a little anonymous maybe yet suited to his own restless disposition.

As usual, he hadn't slept much – hardly at all – despite the heavy medication he was taking, but a man trying to face up to the most perilous decision of his life would not have been surprised by his insomnia.

Peter Sellers was aware that he was gravely ill, perhaps mortally so, and that he might not have much time left. It was in this frame of mind that he had resolved on one last hazardous attempt to prolong the time remaining.

From his chalet in Switzerland a few weeks earlier he had called his London lawyer, Elwood Rickless, and told him that now he was ready to undergo the operation which had been recommended by his physician in Los Angeles. It was an angiogram, an exploratory operation to determine whether Sellers was strong enough to withstand the shock of major heart surgery. The doctor had called it the last hope, but 'hope' was hardly the right word. The operation itself was known to be a dangerous one: it could well precipitate another heart attack.

How many of these had he already suffered? He recognized the major crises: there had been the one in Hollywood in 1964; the indisposition aboard the plane from Nice in 1977, which had led to his first pacemaker implantation; and the collapse en route to Geneva from New York in 1979, just before he began work on what he regarded as the film of his career. That last hospitalization had been the best-kept secret of his life – lest the film go ahead with someone else in the role he had dreamed of for himself. But he had suffered so many aches and pains that felt potentially lethal that he had almost given up counting. His physician had urged that it was essential to know for certain the amount of damage done to his heart and that he be authorized to operate during the course of the angiogram or immediately afterwards. No one outside the immediate circle of his wife Lynne, his lawyer and his personal assistants knew that his transit-stop in London was fraught with such imminent risk of mortality. That secret, too, had been well kept.

Those who did know he was in England believed it was solely for his own enjoyment. That night he was going to a reunion supper with two of his oldest friends, Spike Milligan and Harry Secombe, who had shared many *Goon Shows* with him in the days that now seemed dearest to him – the days before it all began.

Peter Sellers was the screen's greatest comic actor and one of the world's best publicized stars. Though people had been shocked in recent months to see his almost cadaverous condition – the skull beginning to show too clearly through the thin skin which covered it – his features had retained their familiar definition and could flick through characters and emotions with the skill of a card-sharper making sure that his hand held the winning combination. His voice could still, almost eerily, be that of anyone he chose to impersonate, parody or seemingly incarnate. He was in a pensive mood that morning.

Being There ... at least he had lived long enough to do that film, the one he had worked seven years to set up. Its story of a man who had been made famous by what other people saw in him, or imagined they saw, seemed in some bizarre way to offer comfort to an actor who had declared, time without number, that he could be all things to all men, but did not know who he was to himself. Two months earlier, he had been mortified to see the Cannes Film Festival pass him over for a prize, for reasons that jury-room indiscretions suggested had nothing to do

4

with the merit of his performance. But at least *Being There* and his role in it had assured his artistic reputation, just as his inspired creation of Inspector Clouseau, the walking disaster-area of the *Pink Panther* films, had made him rich and popular.

Rich ... this was another word that carried its own omens. People imagined a superstar like himself must be enormously rich and, indeed, if he survived the operation, he would be. There was a bulky script in the Dorchester suite entitled *The Romance of the Pink Panther*. It was going to be his next picture. Once that was behind him, he would be at least three million dollars richer. And there were films already slated for production after that which would make him richer still. Yet money was something Peter Sellers had never really stopped to count. He'd always assumed it would be there – and generally it was. But few people knew of the time, not so many years earlier, when his business adviser had told him the scarcely credible news that after years of good films, high fees and what he had thought was a secure financial future, he had almost no money left. Disappointing investments, extravagant living, a run of poor pictures, loss of faith in his 'bankability' – all these had stripped him of his financial assets and professional credit. He would have been broke, if it hadn't been for the lucky Pink Panther.

He wondered whether he should wear, for this evening's reunion, the shirt which bore this mischievous animal's cartoon likeness. He cheered up when he thought of Harry and Spike. It was their annual bean-feast, the occasion that used to give them a six-month hangover because they enjoyed themselves so much. It was Harry who had arranged it: 'We'd better have it while we're still around to do something about it,' he said in his brusque Welsh way. Peter had always kept the avenues leading back to the past unobstructed by any of the bitter recriminations which had terminated more recent friendships. Such avenues were escape routes to the blessedly simple days. He sometimes wished he could flee down them, like a refugee from his present, and never come back.

He decided against the Pink Panther shirt and his mind turned to the wardrobe of creams, beiges and navy-blues which his wife Lynne had helped him choose for Cannes. Lynne always had a good eye for what suited him. He was happy to let others take such decisions. He judged that Lynne was at that moment preparing for bed in their Hollywood home, where he was going to join her before checking into the clinic. He missed her intensely and wished she were in London with him. Of all his four wives, she was the one who had most given him the security of her company – and much besides. He had more than once talked of her 'extrasensory instinct' – her perceptiveness in deciphering his needs. It reminded him of other people he knew who seemed able to read his thoughts or forecast his future.

This set him wondering about his mother, Peg. The first thing he had done after arriving in England yesterday was to pay a visit to the garden where a rose tree and a plaque commemorated Bill and Peg, his father and mother, near the spot where their ashes had been scattered in the crematorium grounds. He had flown over from Geneva yesterday morning, travelling in his customary private plane, accompanied only by his personal assistant, Michael Jeffery. They had landed at Stansted Airport, because the Customs men there were his friends, whereas at Heathrow Airport he felt they were all petty-minded bureaucrats who saw him coming. He *hated* dressed-up authority. Besides, when one looked as ill as he did, it was a blessing to escape the ever-vigilant Press men – and this, too, was easier at an out-of-the-way airport like Stansted.

He had several times wanted to go and see the commemorative plaque which he had had placed on the wall in Golders Green garden of remembrance. Once, he had even started out on the journey, but had turned back before he was half-way there, unwilling to revive the trauma of separation that death had precipitated – in his mother's case, before he had had the time (or the courage) to get to her bedside. He would see both of them again in the next world; of this he was confident. Indeed, he had been to 'sittings' where Peg had 'spoken' to him and assured him that, when it was time for him to give it all up, she would let him know ... his mother would tell him.

Yesterday, as if he had somehow guessed he might not have another chance to make the journey, he had ordered the limousine to drive him and Michael Jeffery out to that sad area of North London, and he had even joked, as they entered the crematorium gates, about each of them smuggling in a red rose of remembrance to a garden where many roses grew, but where the 'unofficial' ones were frowned on by the authorities. He would be cremated there himself one day. He chuckled as he thought of the surprise in store for the friends attending the service – he'd spring his last joke on them, his posthumous prank.

Jokes. ... His mood had lightened with the brightening day and he recalled the pranks that Michael Jeffery and he had played on each other, in that very hotel, usually about this hour. Both were supposed to be observing a strict diet, but sometimes Sellers would call room service and stealthily order Michael's breakfast to be delivered to him in his room across the corridor. 'Yes,' he would blandly tell the astounded

Dorchester kitchen, 'for Mr Jeffery ... yes, all of it.' And so Michael Jeffery, trying to pace Sellers on the calorie-cutting count, would find a relay of breakfast trolleys being wheeled in, bearing fifty orders of fried eggs, fifty slices of bacon, fifty sausages, fifty tomato slices, and so on.

It was good to start the day with a laugh, if one could, Peter decided. It made one more alert. And he needed to be alert on this particular day, despite the haze of medication which usually cocooned him when Lynne wasn't there to steer him clear of pharmaceutics which he swallowed like sweets, in order to put the finishing touches to some family business which his lawyer had in hand.

His family.... He knew his children weren't at the centre of his affections, but then he wasn't close to theirs, either. He hadn't been a bad father to Michael and Sarah, his children by his first wife, Anne Hayes, or to Victoria, his daughter by Britt Ekland, though he had once done the unpardonable thing of asking his son, when he was much smaller, whom he preferred – Daddy or Mummy? One should never ask a child that kind of question, especially in view of the answer he received. At this stage of his life Peter felt closer to Michael than he had for many years, due to the careful diplomacy of his present wife, Lynne, who smoothed over the resentment that a neglectful parent felt for children who, he believed, had never paid him due respect. Once, he'd drawn Victoria's attention to what someone was saying on television about his movie *Being There*. Yes, the child had seen it: it was quite good. Her casualness had irritated him, and his rebuke had caused a flare-up. In many ways Peter Sellers was a child himself, and no child likes to feel unappreciated by other children.

When his lawyer came with the documents, he would feel easier in his mind, for the last piece of business which he was to transact that day, which was in fact to be his last in the world, concerned his youngest child, Victoria.

At about eight o'clock, after he had showered, shaved and put on a navy-blue track suit, he had ordered breakfast to be sent up: coffee and melba toast this morning. He'd considered having that curious article of English breakfast food, a kipper. Kippers had always amused him. He'd once done a vaudeville act in which he pretended that his lines were written on this brown, smoke-cured, filleted herring. The audience had simply been perplexed and he had shown his contempt for them so obviously that, although they missed the point of his surreal farce, they had sensed his feelings and the curtain came down in resounding silence. Remembering those days suddenly depressed him again.

He telephoned Michael Jeffery's room. Jeffery, a young man of patience and cheerfulness when both were needed, recognized the despondency in the voice. He resolved to do all in his power to get the boss in a better humour.

Peter decided he would have a massage. Lack of sleep had given him no respite from the psychosomatic tension which exhausted him even on the days when he did nothing more arduous than tinker with his cameras, video-recorders or some other plaything. A masseuse was sent up to him, and Michael Jeffery took the opportunity of her presence with Peter to slip back to his own room to telephone Peter's secretary, Sue Evans, in her Pembroke Place home.

'Sue, come over. Say you'll stay to lunch. P.S. is in one of his moods. It's "happy faces" time, dear.' (When Peter's aides were talking to him, and often when they were talking about him, they never called him 'Peter', but always 'Mr Sellers' or 'P.S.')

Sue was ready for Peter's usual call to her. It came at about nine o'clock. She'd be at the Dorchester in ten minutes, she said.

The massage was just ending when she arrived and, while Peter took a nap, she and Michael Jeffery discussed the phone calls she had received the day before. Any that might distress Peter were kept from him, to be dealt with by Sue or Lynne. He was due to fly to California on an airline which had first-class seats that converted to recliners. His reservations were checked and confirmed. If only Concorde flew to Los Angeles – it was the quickest and therefore his favourite means of transport. But changing aircraft at Kennedy Airport, supposing he crossed the Atlantic by Concorde, would tax his strength and might expose him to the scrutiny of the media or the harassment of some petty official, which would do his heart no good at all.

The two young people succeeded in cheering Peter, so that by the time Elwood Rickless came to the hotel with his lawyer's document case, Peter was happy, smiling and boasting of how fit he felt. Rickless, a tall American with a deceptively relaxed manner, who had law offices in London and Los Angeles, admitted to himself that Peter had a good tan and a ruddy complexion – perhaps the massage had helped his circulation – but he looked painfully thin, rather like someone who has overtrained for an event.

Left alone with him, the lawyer told Peter his affairs were all in order except for this one small matter – establishing a Trust for his child Victoria, then aged fifteen.

Peter had told Rickless on an earlier occasion that he did not want a lot of money to be inherited by his children upon his death. As the lawyer saw it, this attitude wasn't prompted by malice or rancour over real or imaginary hurts which his children might have caused him; he simply felt it was wrong to spoil children by endowing them with sudden wealth. He had earned his money by his own efforts. Although huge amounts of it now seemed to appear out of nowhere, the lawyer knew all about the cost in emotional and physical terms that living in the world of the wheelers and dealers had inflicted on Peter.

Peter had felt he ought to give each of his three children a twenty-first birthday present of a lump sum for 'a start in life'. Consequently he had already given £20,000 to Michael and Sarah, who were by this time twenty-six and twenty-two, but the documentation setting up a Trust for Victoria had still to be completed. In the normal way, Rickless felt, he would simply have said, 'Well, no matter – I'll give her the cheque myself when she's twenty-one.' But now both of them sensed he might never live to see Victoria's twenty-first birthday. Hence the urgent need to establish the Trust and ensure that the £20,000 was not included in the bulk of the estate which he intended should go to his wife, Lynne Frederick.

After Rickless had explained the brief terms of the Trust indenture, Peter signed it. He looked relieved. They remained together for a few minutes more, sipping their coffee and gossiping. Peter was keen to start work on *The Romance of the Pink Panther*, because he wanted to show he could do a *Panther* film without the originator of the series and its customary director, Blake Edwards. It was the new challenge he had set himself after achieving his ambition to make *Being There*. He wanted to show that the success of the earlier *Panther* films had been due more to his own acting talent than to the director's contribution. Rickless knew both men well enough to realize that it was a partnership in which each brought out the best of each other's talents and sometimes the worst in each other's tempers. Peter was aware that his latest film, *The Fiendish Plot of Dr Fu Manchu*, which was almost ready for release, had not fulfilled his hopes of showing what he could do by himself without Blake Edwards. The new *Panther* film would give him a second chance.

Elwood Rickless shook hands and left for his practice, Rickless & Wolf, in St James's. Michael Jeffery and Sue Evans asked Peter what he'd like to do. How about a walk in the park? St James's Park was his favourite area of London greenery – he'd even filmed a scene for *The Magic Christian* near the pond where he liked to watch a variety of birds waddling and wading. No, he decided, this wasn't a day for walking.

He engaged them in his usual banter, speculated about the latest film gossip, made some excruciating funny-bad jokes and then said, 'What about lunch?'

It was about 12.30 p.m. when a waiter wheeled in a trolley through the suite's service kitchen. They had ordered a simple meal of grilled plaice with a green salad. Peter had asked for a double order of plaice. 'They don't give you much of the fish at the Dorchester,' he said. No one drank wine, only Perrier mineral water. Peter had a little cheese after the fish.

Shortly before two o'clock, Michael Jeffery went into Peter's bedroom to lay out the clothes he might want to wear for his supper with the Goons. They had decided on one of his characteristic black outfits: black trousers *à la* Fu Manchu, a black shirt, a black-and-white check casual jacket and black lizard-skin shoes.

Sue Evans was preparing to go over to Rickless & Wolf with some documents when Peter suddenly said to her, 'Sue, don't go yet. Sit on for a bit and talk to me.'

She looked at him closely as she sat down. Suddenly he said, 'I do feel faint ... I think I shall faint.'

She reached out and felt his brow. It was covered with sweat. 'Better go and get into bed,' she said. But before he could get to his feet and do as she suggested, she saw his face beginning to change colour. It turned a dark shade of purple, and then it went very pale. He gasped and closed his eyes.

'Michael,' she cried in the direction of the bedroom, already lunging for the sitting-room telephone, 'get a doctor.'

ONE

What Pete Wanted, Pete Got

The man was naked except for long satin trunks which stopped below the knee and were caught up into short silk stockings. His hair was luxuriantly thick: it fitted the Iberian oval of his face. The nose was strongly defined and sensual. And although the man's arms were raised in the traditional stance of bare-fisted pugnacity, to match the boxer's crouch of his torso, his figure had an air of serenity – or sadness.

In the days of his youth, when he was quite a pudgy lad, and in his penultimate film, when he had deliberately put on weight and washed his face clean of all inner traumas for the role of a Holy Innocent who has celebrity thrust on him, Peter Sellers resembled the ancestor he most revered – Daniel Mendoza. An engraving of the great eighteenth-century pugilist, poised for action, usually hung in Sellers's office or home. His image was going to be the logo for a film company he planned to set up at one time – it was short-lived – in order to retain the profits from his own productions. The man was Sellers's great-great-grandfather. A Portuguese Jew, born in London's East End, he became the heavyweight champion of England, and he raised more than his fists: he raised the status of all other Jews. He neither denied nor proclaimed his Jewishness; yet his prowess in the ring reflected on to his co-religionists, then a lowly and despised sect in England. It's unlikely that Peter Sellers worshipped this aspect of Mendoza. It is interesting, though, that when Kenneth Tynan interviewed Sellers in 1961, seeking the motive force for the ambitions he was then groping his way to express, the critic concluded that it was 'his hatred of anti-semitism'. Tynan continued: 'In scholars, lawyers, doctors and vaudeville comedians, Jewishness is tolerated. In legitimate actors, much less often. . . . Hence [Peter Sellers's refusal] to be content with the secure reputation of a great mimic and his determination to go down in history as something more – a great actor, perhaps, or a great director.' Sellers

certainly inherited a variety of Jewish characteristics: curiosity, restlessness and a chameleon's talent in the art of protective coloration that
often assumed an independent life of its own. But crusading for his
Jewishness wasn't among his personal priorities, whatever he may have
persuaded himself that Tynan wished to hear. He was always far more
fascinated by Mendoza's other 'religion', which was show-business.

Daniel Mendoza was a celebrity in the modern sense of being as
much a victim as an idol. He projected a personality as well as a punch;
he could fill a theatre as well as a boxing ring. Showmen wanted him: he
earned £50 for a demonstration bout, and generally did three per week
at the peak of his career. In 1785, when only twenty-one, he was being
paid £1,000 a fight, an enormous sum in those days. Royalty took him
up, just as later members of the same ruling family would invite Sellers
to be their guest, friend and entertainer. Mendoza taught the Prince of
Wales the rudiments of fisticuffs. And when King George III summoned
him to Windsor Castle in the royal carriage, he walked and talked
publicly with the monarch on the castle terrace for over an hour – one of
the earliest occasions on which a Jew was so signally honoured.

As well as being a socialite who enjoyed the distinguished company
he kept – a trait that Sellers, who abhorred being made to 'sing for his
supper', assuredly did not inherit – Mendoza was a tireless self-
publicist, and a literate one. His book on *The Art of Boxing*, published in
1787, was so popular that it quite eclipsed in news value the storming of
the Bastille and drove reports of this event off the front pages of the
public prints.

Mendoza used his wits as well as his fists to provide himself with a
living. Outside the ring he played a multitude of parts. Though they
were 'social roles', unlike the cinema ones his descendant accepted,
their variety was converted by Sellers into a tenet of psychic faith when
he began to explore what he conceived to be his own past history of
reincarnation. Mendoza was in turn publican, process-server, recruit-
ing sergeant, greengrocer, tobacconist's assistant, tea-shop waiter and
glazier. He even issued his own banknotes backed by the collateral of
his enormous reputation.

Like Sellers again, he loved masquerading. He loved dressing up in
another's identity. Once, he and his friends donned matelot outfits, and
narrowly escaped arrest by the press-gang for suspected desertion from
their ship. At a much later date, Peter Sellers also put on uniforms to
which he wasn't entitled; but he was already in the services and merely
usurping a more prestigious rank than the one he bore himself. However, the two men had the same fondness for mischievous deceit.

Mendoza let success go to his head, all too literally. He allowed his abundant hair to grow abnormally long in the foppish fashion of the time. This proved a fatal mistake, for when he came to fight John Jackson in 1795, the no-nonsense American boxer seized the English champion by his handy locks, held him down like a tethered Gulliver, and thumped the life out of him. Upon recovery, Mendoza shaved his skull, as much out of contrition as wisdom after the event, though when he came to write his *Memoirs*, in 1816, vanity got the better of him – he didn't once allude to the shaming event. He seemed to think that if one dismissed it from one's mind, it had never happened. It is a way of dealing with unco-operative reality much favoured by those who suffer from the precarious fluctuations of stardom. Peter Sellers was quite frank about his own débâcles; what *he* closed his eyes to was seeing the consequences of his actions. Mendoza ran through several fortunes and saw the inside of the debtor's prison more than once before he died in poverty in 1836 at the age of seventy-three. He had been improvident in the manner of latter-day film stars who never quite come to terms with their own worth, but endlessly overspend. His widow and eleven children inherited precious little, except pride and resilience. His true legacy was to British boxing. By training London slum kids, he enabled a long line of battling young Jews to escape from the ghetto streets and re-assert their ethnic self-esteem in the ring.

Peter Sellers could on occasion work himself into a towering rage, which astonished those who witnessed it and terrified those who received the force of his displeasure. But in general his skill lay in the subtler transformation of character through art, not aggression. Yet if one is seeking the origins of his peculiar genius, they are lodged in the inheritance of Daniel Mendoza.

The talents which Mendoza bequeathed to his immediate descendants were less violent. His grand-daughter, Sellers's maternal grandmother, was a lady called Welcome Mendoza. She was a vigorous Jewish matriarch who married a London merchant and speculator named Solomon Marks at the age of forty-four and proceeded to have ten children by him. Eight were boys: George, Harry, Chick, Alfred, Lewis, Dick, Moss and Bert – not a Peter among them. Two were girls: Cissie and Peg. Welcome had a good business head and, with such a brood, she needed one. She also had a family penchant for public spectacles. She put the two together at a family council meeting in their home at Cassland Crescent, Hackney, and out came the idea of a theatrical touring company. Welcome put her sons and daughters on the stage as artists and managers, touring under the banner of Ray

Brothers Limited – she herself changed her name and became known as Ma Ray. By 1911, she had forty vaudeville companies performing the length and breadth of England.

Ma Ray was credited with bringing the first Continental-type revue to Britain. She was sold the 'concept' by a German entrepreneur who had discovered a way of presenting pulchritude in an unexpectedly exotic element many years before Esther Williams demonstrated that to be wet was to be a star. The revue was called *Splash Me!* It consisted of a large glass tank on the stage into which girls dived and in which they swam, frolicked and occasionally performed some esoteric and vaguely erotic act like consuming a banana while submerged. Ma Ray preserved the show from the disapproval of the local authority, whose licence she had to obtain, by the simple expedient of darkening the water in the tank until it matched the hue of local prejudice. Sometimes the swimsuited chorines were almost lost to view in towns with a reputation for prudery. The First World War was of great help to Ma in one respect: she added translucent dyes of red, white and blue to bathe the intermeshing limbs of her bathing belles, and then dared the Watch Committee to ban the prismatic patriotism of the show.

Ma's favourite child was her daughter Peg, and together they devised another stage act which defeated the prudes without disappointing the prurient.

Sellers himself has recalled how Peg – for she was to become his mother – used to stand behind a curtain in flesh-coloured tights and a leotard. The curtain rose slowly, revealing Peg inch by inch and turning what had been a silhouette into a reasonably titillating simulation of a naked lady. 'For the 1910s, that was brazen,' he said. 'But no sooner had the audience caught its breath at the apparent nudity than my Uncle Bert would project on to Peg's contours a series of lantern slides that "dressed" her in one costume after another. She would turn into Florence Nightingale, Britannia, Queen Victoria, Elizabeth Tudor, the Statue of Liberty. . . . I remember standing in the wings, looking at this woman becoming a multitude of different people and hearing the applause of the audience for each transformation. The colour and the magic and the sound of appreciation – I never forgot it.'

Four of Ma Ray's sons went to fight in the war in Belgium and she grew to rely increasingly on willing young Peg. The girl was forced to give up her 'speciality poses' for the time being and take to less elaborate rôles, like an amorous charlady or an unfaithful wife in the naughty playlets that preceded the aquashow. Peg spent most of her off-stage hours with Ma, too. When the troupe travelled they did so in comfort, in reserved carriages on provincial trains. Ma supervised the dressing of the chorus and maintained an inflexible etiquette backstage – through what went on in the back alleys was another matter. Ma had a tolerant morality where sex was concerned, so long as it didn't interfere with business or break up the family, but she could see that Peg, now twenty-four, was lacking something for a girl of her age, namely a husband.

Whoever Ma Ray preferred for her cherished daughter had to be capable of serving mother as well by driving the huge car (a Ford some say, others an Austin) which ferried the flamboyant impresario and her daughter between their theatre shows and advertised Ma's presence inside the building by its own scarlet-coloured coachwork stationed outside.

One day in 1921, Ma arrived at Portsmouth, where a new edition of her show, entitled *Have a Dip!*, was being presented at the King's Theatre. It was in every sense a lighter-toned version, befitting the post-war mood of relief and revelry: this time the girls dived into clear water, splashing the musicians in the orchestra pit with the overspill. Ma and Peg were taking tea in a Lyon's Corner House café when they heard that year's hit tune, 'I'm For Ever Blowing Bubbles', being played on the piano in the corner.

'That sounds good,' Ma said and, turning round, she took in the amiable-looking young fellow at the keyboard. 'He can really play.'

'Not bad looking, either,' she added for Peg's benefit. 'What's your name, luv?'

'Sellers ... Bill Sellers,' said the young man, with a touch of flat North Country in his voice.

'What places have you played in?'

'Bradford Cathedral ... I was assistant organist there, sang in the choir, too. I'm musical director for the orchestra here at the Corner House.'

'Well, Bill,' Ma told him, 'I need a piano player as good as you for my show. But I also need a chap to drive my car. Think you can do both?'

Bill Sellers came of the sort of country stock that always lent a hand to the neighbours in season. He had the look of a farmer's son, he was good-natured and he also did as he was bid. He liked the casual conviviality that went with providing the patrons of the *thé-dansants* with undemanding and mellifluous music, but he was also attracted to the glamour of touring theatricals. Ma Ray had picked intuitively and shrewdly for herself and her daughter.

Bill Sellers quickly agreed to Ma's proposal and found the proximity of Peg an agreeable bonus for his labours. As for Ma, she found Bill's Protestant faith to be no bar to the growing relationship between him and Peg. Mixed marriages were commonplace in theatreland. Jewishness could – and still can – be an additional allegiance between the folk who work there, but it has always tended to take second place to the freemasonry of talent.

Bill and Peg were married at Bloomsbury Registry Office, London, in 1923, the bride being whisked off by her mother immediately the brief ceremony ended to play the amorous charlady in a Ray Brothers revue, while the groom changed into a stiff-fronted shirt to play the piano in a stage act comprising a Russian refugee who played the balalaika, a coloured drummer and a lady violinist. The newly-weds set up home in a few rooms in a house in Highgate, North London, which was rented to theatre people. Ma moved in with them, too. It is not surprising that with two such formidable women in the domestic vicinity, Bill Sellers tended to move into the background. Fortunately, it was a position he never complained about occupying; life was easier in the background.

Peg experienced the first labour pains of her pregnancy while she was playing in one of her mother's revues at Southsea. At this point in Ma's business, times must have been tough, because no understudy was available and Peg was told to carry on as long as she could. She overdid it and Peter Sellers nearly came into the world in the wings of a theatre, but, as it was about to happen, Bill popped Peg into the back seat of the scarlet car and got her back to the flat which the family occupied over a corner shop selling picture postcards. And thus, at 'Postcard Corner', on 8 September 1925, a certain Dr Little delivered Peg's son. A week later the mother was back in the show; two weeks later, the baby was carried on stage by the number one comic, Dickie Henderson senior, father of the present-day comedian, who wished the baby well and called for a chorus of 'For He's a Jolly Good Fellow' from a willing audience overwhelmed by this sentimental entr'acte. It is recorded that the child immediately gave vent to a long howl and a flood of tears, and prolonged the attention that later, in more subtle ways, he would demand from audiences and entourage.

From the very beginning, everyone agrees that Peter Richard Henry Sellers was an outrageously spoiled child. 'He was a little monster,' recalled his Aunty Ve, wife of Uncle Bert; while Uncle Bert said, 'He had far too many people worshipping him. A good smacking would have done him the world of good, but Peg would never hear one word of criticism against the child. He was a little horror.' However, it wasn't simply the fact that any mother, and particularly a Jewish mother, might be expected to dote on her first-born son that accounts for the excessive adulation poured over young Peter. There was another reason, never alluded to publicly by the family: the truth is, Peter was not the couple's first child. Peg and Bill had had a son within a year of their marriage. The baby died, apparently before it could be christened. The shock was traumatic; it had to be put out of mind. 'We were told that we were never, never to refer to that child,' said Aunty Ve, her voice holding a note of hushed obedience over fifty years later. 'It was as if he had never existed.' But of course he had, for a few, painfully few hours or days in the affections of Bill, Peg and Ma Ray. The severity of the loss, and the fear that she might never bear another child, impelled Peg to cherish her second son with the strength of affection that struck virtually everyone who knew her in years to come as dangerously indulgent.

Even so, the baby took a back seat to the demands of the stage. Peg couldn't be spared from the show to become a housewife and she probably didn't want to be; for she was a businesswoman rather than a home-maker. So, while Peg and Bill toured with Ma Ray's companies all over England, their baby lay in a basket in the wings where the other acts could keep an intermittent eye on him. Small wonder that he contracted bronchial pneumonia during the first bitter winter of his life while his parents were playing in a revue called *The Sideshow* at the Keighley Hippodrome, in Yorkshire. His life was saved by the night-long ministrations of a black doctor who had been brought over to England to complete his medical studies by a 'mission to the heathen of foreign continents'. Peg regarded it as divine intervention. On and off, over the next five years, Peter continued to tour with his parents and, when they left him at home, Ma Ray and Aunty Cissie fussed over him. Bill Sellers had little say in this matriarchal nest, which the child, like a large, demanding cuckoo, grew adept at manipulating. A howl, a tantrum or a show of love, depending on the mood and the object of desire, soon taught him how to elicit the indulgences he took for granted. Peg had ambitions for her son: she wanted him to follow her and Bill on to the stage. She believed one could never start a child too early on such a career and so, when Peter was just two-and-a-half, she took him to the theatrical tailors who dressed Ma's shows and had a minute suit of white tie, top hat and tails made for him. Looking as if he had emerged from an outsize Christmas cracker and further burdened by a silver-knobbed cane, he was taught to stand on stage and sing the ditty 'My Old Dutch', which Albert Chevalier had made famous. He hated it and one day stamped on the top hat. Peg persisted. 'I longed for Peter to be able to carry on when I had to leave off,' she used to say. 'It was only natural.' She enrolled him in Miss Whitney's Dancing Academy in King's Road, Southsea; but he proved such an undisciplined pupil that she had to shelve her ambitions temporarily.

Peter was happier in the company of his Aunty Ve, being introduced to a world of make-believe in which the restrictions of daily life did not apply – or, at any rate, did not apply to him. Before he was three, he would say, 'Come on, Ve' – he called parents and relatives by their straight family names, in precocious equality with the adults in the Sellers household – and the two of them would trot down to the sea front, where a gorgeously-uniformed band played in an ornate pavilion on the Ladies' Mile for the summer season. 'He couldn't read the clock at that age,' Ve said. 'How he always knew the time to go is a mystery to me.' Dressed in a silk shirt and well-pressed shorts, Peter would dance to the popular tunes. Occasionally, to the amusement of the deckchair crowds, he was allowed to conduct the band. 'He was the attraction, not the music.'

He was not a tranquil child. There was a streak of bravado in him that could lead to nasty accidents, to himself or others, because he never took into account the consequences of some impulsive action. One day Ve took him up to London to see *Peter Pan* at the Shaftesbury Theatre. 'When it was all over, Peter said to me, "Ve, I could fly like the boys in the show."' They were sitting in the Royal circle – the tickets had been provided by a family friend in the box-office – and Peter started to get out of his seat and reach for the balcony rail. Ve snatched him up and both of them 'flew' from the theatre before Peg's son could nose-dive into the stalls. Occasionally he was just mischievous. One day Peg called in the doctor to treat her for some minor ailment. When the consultation finished, the physician reclaimed his tall hat and cane from the hall table and, as he left the house, Peter was observed hanging out of the upstairs window.

'What are you doing, Pete?' Peg asked.

'I spitted in the doctor's top hat when he left it on the hall table and I want to see it run down his face.'

The first professional fee he earned was at the age of four or five. Cyril Lawrence, a family friend and business associate of Ma Ray's, learned that Mazda, the electric light bulb manufacturers, wanted a child model for an advertisement. He quickly recommended Peter. The fee was £5 for the photo session. 'Peg and Bill were over the moon,' Ve recalled. 'Cyril thought the child had a big future as a model and was all set to become his manager. They all thought, "This is where we sit back and Peter will make us a fortune." ' But Peter hated the posing, the helplessness of having to take orders from the photographer. A restless child at the best of times, when he wasn't enjoying himself he became a fractious and destructive one. When it was all over he refused point-blank to do another modelling job, ever. Again, Peg took it badly, but she had discovered the strength of her son's resistance. He was not only spoiled; he was stubborn.

These were the years that developed in him a deep loathing amounting to irrational anger at being bidden to perform to order. He hated the exposure, either as a baby in a wicker basket or as a tiny-tot performer, to vociferous, smelly audiences in cold, insanitary music-halls. Even though the patrons applauded his parents on stage, covering the watching boy with a warm glow from this tangible appreciation (until his own critical eye came to see, in later years, the shabbiness of Peg's costume 'poses'), Peter Sellers never overcame his revulsion at the backstage squalor, the communal dressing-rooms impregnated with the stench of oil lamps or gas globes, cheap greasepaint and stale food, and the sweat of the artists packed into the wings while waiting for their entry on stage. When his parents took him on tour with them, he had to suffer the lonely neglect of bedrooms in theatrical boarding-houses or the active dislike of the drudges who were the miserable servants in such establishments. Later on, he attributed his anxiety to know where his loved ones were at any given moment to this childhood experience of abandonment among strangers.

In later years, when he was overwhelmed by the pressures that came with success, Sellers was sometimes urged to seek the help of an analyst. He always refused, very firmly. But on one occasion, when he was seeking a cure for smoking, he yielded far enough to consult 'quite a kindly' psychiatrist. It was deeply distressing. As he lay on the couch and talked, all the pathetic memories of a 'not so happy childhood' surged up in him.

'Most of my childhood seemed to be spent curled up on my mother's lap in the back seat of a car, going from town to town, theatrical digs to theatrical digs. Into the car, out of the car, suitcases out of the trunk, clump, clump, clump up the stairs of some third-rate boarding-house.' Then came the smells. He never forgot the dozens of odours that permeated his childhood.

'Every place we stopped at had its own peculiar smell, usually of aspidistras in airless parlours, leaking gas, dirty sheets, bad plumbing, greasy cooking . . . the odours depending on the landlady's nationality.'

He used to return to some of these places when he was famous, stand on the threshold of the tawdry, cramped rooms – and sniff. The memories this stirred in him overcame any desire to 'enquire within'. 'The bedrooms where I spent so much of my time while Peg and Bill were on stage were all alike: marble wash-stands, cold-water taps, brass beds, and mattresses like ploughed fields. I'd lie on the thread-bare coverlets and stare at the ceiling and think to myself, "Oh God, I wish we had one home to go to."' As a result of these poky little dwelling-places, Sellers developed a curiously converse phobia: he hated living in lavish and spacious homes, so that the backgrounds against which film stardom presented itself tended to depress him quickly. When he was making *Being There* on location at the 10,000-acre Biltmore estate belonging to George W. Vanderbilt in North Carolina, one of the mansion's huge rooms was turned into the star dressing-room for Sellers. After one look at its museum-like dimensions, he retreated to his trailer parked outside.

'Those days bred a great determination in me never to be pushed around, if I could help it. There was no magic in them, only dinginess.'

Ma Ray died in 1930. She had had the organizing zeal and, without her, business momentum faltered and, one by one, the touring companies were run down too. Talking pictures were anyhow going to curtail vaudeville's appeal – and audiences. The uncles began taking more fixed employment in show-business; so did the Sellers family. They had moved to London from Southsea because Ma Ray had decided she should be nearer her offices in Cranbourn Street – ones later occupied by the impresario Val Parnell. They lived in a flat over a furniture shop in Upper Street, Islington; and after Ma's death, Peter and his parents moved to another flat over the Bedford Music Hall in Camden Town. They were a family who always seemed to be 'living over' something. Aunty Cissie 'lived over' them. From this point on they moved so frequently around London that a record of their progress is impossible to keep. This was chiefly because, with Ma's passing, the money supply became erratic and it was often cheaper to move than to pay the rent. Bill Sellers had settled, as amiably as ever, into a different routine from his vaudeville one – he cleaned out the grate and put on the dinner. What brought him back to the halls again was the need to replenish the family kitty. He teamed up with a fellow trouper called Lewis in a ukulele act and this left Peter increasingly in his mother's company.

The child's wilfulness had taken a disturbing turn. One day he was teasing the two cats, Hildegarde and Kitty, and one of the creatures, tormented beyond endurance, scratched him. Peter placed the cat in the 'Fold-U-Up' sofa to punish her: Fortunately Peg heard her crying and released the animal before a permanent crease had developed in her feline form.

Peter was also revealing a talent for the odd absurd remark that anticipated the Goon Show's milder examples of logical zaniness. One year he had to have his tonsils out – in those days a far more hazardous and expensive (if privately performed) operation than is the case today. Peg sold many of her small personal valuables to pay for the surgeon and the private clinic, for it was unthinkable that Peter should go into a public hospital ward.

'Well, my boy,' said the surgeon, arriving to see his convalescing patient, 'I've taken your tonsils out.'

The little boy in bed looked back at him grimly, and without a trace of gratitude on his face, he said: 'You have, have you? Then you know what you can do. You can put them back in again.'

Peg no longer appeared on stage; but she found opportunities to activate her dormant talent when Britain went off the gold standard in 1931. She developed a freelance operation which she called 'golding'. This involved the family driving out of London (where they might have been too well known in certain neighbourhoods), usually using Uncle Bert's car, and mounting a door-to-door operation in some provincial town. Peg devised the patter for her husband and brother to follow.

'Good day, Madam,' they would say when their polite but re-assuringly firm rap on the door had been answered. 'We wonder if you have any articles of value in your possession, particularly gold ones. If you have, we're prepared to quote you top prices. We're from the London Gold Refiners Company Limited.'

Peter often went with his parents on these 'golding' expeditions, but they kept him well out of sight – the presence of a child didn't increase business confidence. But he later talked about his relish of Peg's brazen impersonation. He could sometimes hear her improvised repartee as he lurked in the car parked by the kerb. It made him feel that an enterprise of greater distinction, if more dubious intent, was afoot than the costume 'posing' stage acts which ultimately exposed Peg to the cruel rebuffs of the more sophisticated audiences at that time. As he listened to the various accents she put on, and the to-and-fro of the bartering, the element of drama was percolating through his childish conscious-ness; and his imagination was being fed the raw material of impersona-tion that would one day create a character or fatten a part in a radio show or a film script.

Aunty Ve recalled going with the party sometimes. She and Bert would work one set of streets, then pick up Peg and Peter by arrangement, usually at midday outside the local post office. Hauls would be compared: then the gold prospectors would drive off to lunch, its nature and cost depending on their trawl. The afternoon followed a similar pattern. Barnstaple was one of the places where the takings glistered most satisfyingly and sometimes they would take the afternoon off and go to the beach.

'One day the two old dears who owned the Marigold Café at Croyde Bay, where Peg had come golding and done very well, thank you, suggested we have one of their cream-cake teas. Peter was cream-cake mad. And as Peg was complimenting the proprietresses on their baking, he demanded another pastry.' Peg said, in a refined voice, 'No, Pete, you've had quite enough' and rolled up her eyes at the old dear as if to say, 'Boys will be boys.' Peter glared at his mother. Then he said, loudly and deliberately, 'You bugger . . . you *bugger!*' Ever ready for an emergency, Peg said smartly, 'Did you say you wanted *sugar*, Pete?' Peter moved swiftly to grab a cake off the plate. Peg moved it even more smartly out of range. Peter lunged at it. The plate skidded across the polished table and Uncle Bert received its contents, plus a few cups of tea, bang in his lap.

'The old dears just stood there horrified,' Ve recalled. 'Peg grabbed Peter. His feet never touched the ground until they were both out of the café, in the street and round the corner. Bert just sat there, contemplating the mess in his lap, waiting for me to do something. I was hysterical. One of the old dears went straight to the door, opened it, looked at us, and said, "Out." I'm sure we didn't pay the bill. Bert was itching to get his hands on Peter; and the silence between Peg and her son could have been cut with a cake knife.' The real damage, though, was to Bert's one and only respectable suit. It had to go to the cleaner's, which meant that London Gold Refiners Co. Ltd had to suspend operations for a week.

However, by about 1933, even Peg began to realize that Peter needed a more regular kind of life than that provided by the magpie opportunism of door-to-door collecting for the London Gold Refiners Co. Ltd, or by trailing after her and Bill when they did the occasional music-hall appearance.

Peter was by this time seven or eight. Peg rented a small flat at 43b Park Street (now Parkway), Camden Town, in North London, opposite a pet shop and above Heals the builders. With what Bill Sellers sent back from his Friday night pay-packet as part of the Sellers and Lewis ukulele act, and what she made by her own mysterious devices, she was able to enroll Peter in a fee-paying private school called St Mark's Kindergarten in Gloucester Road (now Gloucester Avenue), near Regent's Park. If Peter was glad to escape from the endless moves from one music-hall to another, and the loneliness resulting from such short-lived habitations, he didn't show it. His first reaction to the unaccustomed discipline of schooling was typically obstinate. 'Well, Peg,' he said, when his mother turned up at the gates to bring him home after his first day, 'I've been to school, haven't I?'

'Yes, darling.'

'Well, that's it, then. I've been to school, and I don't like it, and I'm not going back again.'

It took all Peg's persuasiveness to get him to return to class. Even then, he had his own way of dealing with unacceptable reality. 'If Peter disliked any of the lessons,' Aunty Ve recalled, 'he simply closed his eyes and pretended to go to sleep.' If such attacks of timely somnolence occurred in the mornings, Peg would be asked by Miss Penn, his teacher, not to keep little Peter up so late at nights; if inattention gripped him in the afternoon, Miss Penn put it down to a heavy lunch and asked Peg not to feed her son so much at midday that he couldn't keep his eyes open afterwards. Classes were small at St Mark's. Miss Penn's handbell kept the children orderly. There was a garden to play in during the break, not a hard-surfaced school yard. As schools go, it was a gentle induction to more regular habits and should have soothed some of the insecurities that Peter was nursing. Yet it was here that he ran full tilt into the kind of character that, in later life, he learned to spot like an alligator coming at him down river: the impresario, the entrepreneur with an eye to the main chance but a way of presenting it as though he were doing the victim a favour.

Sir Malcolm Campbell had recently broken the land speed record in his racing car Bluebird. One day, reluctantly en route to school, Peter spied a model of the azure automobile being tenderly placed in a toyshop window among the licorice, sherbert and water pistols. 'It was the most glorious thing I'd ever seen in my life, with real rubber tyres and a body made of lead, not plastic, as it would be today.' Passing the shop window every day was a moment of dreadful but exhilarating suspense – would the car still be there, or would some over-endowed possessor of pocket-money have already snaffled it? In such agonizingly anticipatory visions lay Peter Sellers's later preoccupation with, or mania for, covetable novelties, especially if they were the life-size cars on four wheels which became such a well-publicized trademark of his restless extravagance. Bluebird was certainly the first 'car' he owned; it cost him much less than many a later acquisition: 7s. 6d, to be precise, though this was a fair sum for Peg to spare from her weekly income of five or six pounds. But Peg never refused Peter anything – and the child used all his tricks of cajolery, affection offered, withdrawn and then lavishly restored, to overcome her initial hesitation. He bore the car to school concealed beneath an old jumper and impatiently awaited the liberating tinkle of Miss Penn's bell to announce playtime. Then he unwrapped it to a gratifying chorus of 'Ooohs!' and 'Aaahs!' that were, as he put it many years later, 'like teenyboppers at a pop concert'.

He demonstrated the car's seductive innards by detaching the coachwork and then found himself shoved up against the classroom wall by an eager rush of junior *cognoscenti*. All except one boy, who hung back.

'I noticed a small spotted thing with thick glasses and protruding ears silently edging his way along the wall to my left ... I remember thinking this was quite an ingenious manoeuvre to get closer to Bluebird. He looked up at me and the car. His breath made the shiny paint dull each time he exhaled. I resolved to hit him if he came any closer.'

Then the boy bent forward conspiratorially. Hoarsely, but urgently, he whispered, 'Can I be the man who sees no one touches it for you?'

Peter's scholastic backwardness didn't attract any great attention in the playtime curriculum of St Mark's. But despite his father's occasional tutoring at home or on tour, his deficiencies showed up painfully when Peg moved home a couple of miles north to Muswell Hill Road, Highgate, where she rented a tiny cottage, and put Peter into St Aloysius College, Hornsey Lane. St Aloysius was a Roman Catholic school staffed by a teaching order, the Brothers of Our Lady of Mercy, founded in Belgium in about 1879. Its motto was 'Blessed Are the Pure in Heart'; its uniform, a green blazer with dark red trimmings and a breastpocket monogram 'S.A.C.'. Green was a colour from which Peter Sellers pathologically shrank in later years. He believed it very unlucky; he wouldn't tolerate anyone with a touch of green in their attire anywhere near him. But at the age of eleven his worries were more commonplace. The child's lack of attainment was distressingly obvious and within a few days he was demoted from Form II to Form I. 'Naturally he was upset at the fact that he had to go to a lower class,' his teacher, Brother Hugh, recalled. 'He was a little older and bigger than the pupils in his new form.' This is an understatement. Peter was well over five feet, a big boy for his age, and clumsy-looking into the bargain, showing signs of the overweight physique which he was to lose quite dramatically once his romances became the staple gossip of the media in the 1960s. 'However, I reassured him that he had no reason to worry,' said Brother Hugh, 'and that we were all a friendly lot in Form 1. Years later he told me that these words of welcome and comfort were just what he needed at that difficult moment in his school life.'

The fact that his school life was difficult, though, was due to more than his excess growth and his deficient learning. In selecting St Aloysius as her son's school, Peg had set aside considerations of her own Jewish faith. It had no prior claim on her where she scented a bargain in a different wrapping, and as education went, St Aloysius was a very good 'buy'. In any case, Peter was by no means the only non-Catholic boy; the school, which was for boarders and local day-boys, admitted all faiths. One of Peter's classmates was Bryan Connon, a Presbyterian from Scotland, whose father had chosen the school because its theology was middle-of-the-road and its teaching was value for money. Connon, now advertising and publicity manager of the National Westminster Bank, is one of the best witnesses to Peter's development at this sensitive stage. He was also the boy's only close friend.

'It was a surprisingly cosmopolitan school for those days,' Connon recalled. 'There were lots of Irish boys, some foreigners from the Continent, even a few Americans. One of my pals was from the Deep South – his father had "started" a religion.' For a boy whose own accent was 'perfectly ordinary London', Sellers suddenly found the air around him humming with exotic intonations. It was easy to pick them up, if he wanted. Indeed he had no choice. 'Early on in life, I found sounds fascinated me,' he said. 'I didn't talk much. I listened. And people thought I was shy and/or intelligent or stupid.' He listened because he also felt 'remote' from the other boys. He attributed this in later years to the confusion he professed to feel about being a Jewish boy at a Roman Catholic school. There is a more straightforward explanation for his feeling an 'oddity'. The truth is, Peter was rather unpopular. 'He wasn't much liked,' Connon said. 'He never behaved the way boys are expected to do when thrown together. In some ways it wasn't his fault. He stuck out physically. He towered above most of us.' One of Peter's masters, Brother Cornelius, commented: 'At the age of eleven, he looked more like fifteen or sixteen. In the group photo of the class he was placed immediately behind me because he could see over my shoulder.' Boys also tend to pick on the chap who calls attention to himself by his stupidity and Peter was too shy to make a joke out of being considered the form dunce. Even more unforgivable was the general opinion of him as a 'mother's boy'. 'Peter was always the boy who had a bit of extra pocket money to spend in the tuckshop,' Connon said. 'He never needed to eat in the school dining-room, he rarely brought sandwiches. Peg gave him the money to bus himself home for lunch, then back to school for afternoon classes. He hadn't much chance to mix and showed even less inclination. He was excused games and not given corporal punishment. Boys notice this and resent it.'

Peter was never caned at school, according to Brother Hugh. After his first day he had reported back to Peg that naughty boys got two strokes of the cane on the hand for talking in class, three for cheekiness and six for some absolutely unspeakable offence. Peg acted before retribution of this kind could overtake her darling. She forbade his form master ever to lay the 'weapon' on any part of him. The compromise was giving him 'lines' to write out for any delinquency. Not that he misbehaved very much. Brother Cornelius, whose class he entered the year before the war, said, 'One always remembers the troublemakers. But Peter, we didn't notice him at all.' Not quite true. Boys who were not Roman Catholics were excused prayers and religious instruction if their parents expressed the wish. Evidence of Peg's *laissez-faire* attitude to her own faith was Peter's presence at both. He was even complimented by Brother Cornelius, who was exasperated by another lad's halting recitation of the Catechism. 'Sit down, O'Brien. Stand up, Sellers,' he ordered. Peter rattled off the articles of faith in a flash. Brother Cornelius turned to the class. 'The Jewish boy knows his Catechism better than the rest of you.' Actually the 'Jewish boy' did more than know it – he had intoned the responses precisely the way he had heard the Brothers recite them in chapel. He was rapidly discovering his talent for mimicry.

Sellers in later life was reticent about his schooldays. But emotional ties had been formed that surprised even him by their durability. Brother Cornelius, who was a convert to Catholicism and therefore a more forceful proponent of the faith than some of those who had grown up lapped in its folds, reappeared in an odd way just at the moment Peter Sellers's star was being acclaimed as the brightest in the cinema's comic firmament. Sellers was standing in front of a mirror working up his characterization of a Church of England vicar for the Boulting Brothers comedy *Heavens Above*, in 1963, when he suddenly realized that he had involuntarily copied the wise owl of a face, the spectacles, and the hair that was brushed stiffly up at the sides – his old teacher was staring back at him!

He also sent for Brother Cornelius's comforting presence at several times of crisis in his life. That he felt the need for priestly authority, in lieu of the parental model, is a supposition confirmed by the way he frequently turned in later life to all manner of faiths, seeking the 'truth' about himself in the philosophy of each godhead. His debt to the Catholic teachers of his boyhood stuck particularly close. At the time Peg lay dying, in the 1960s, the first call he put through from abroad for information and comfort was to St Aloysius. He may have passed through its classrooms virtually anonymously until his later fame jogged a few memories – unlike the school's other celebrated comedian, Ronald Shiner, who was well remembered. But the school remained a fixed point for spiritual comfort. Perhaps it is not surprising that he made it expensive gifts when he could afford to. More revealing was the arrival, late one afternoon in the early 1960s, of a pale, red-eyed Peter Sellers requesting to see the priest-in-charge of St Aloysius. He and his first wife had just parted. He wanted to talk over the situation. An eyewitness said, 'He looked very, very distressed.'

'Perhaps in those early days he wanted to become an actor,' Brother Hugh said, 'but he was too timid and reserved to speak about it. Or do anything about it, either. St Aloysius had a vigorous drama and choral society: it did a couple of ambitious productions a year, including a *Macbeth* in which the murdered Duncan and Banquo exuded enough blood to eclipse the Catholic martyrs whose gory fates permeated the religious instruction classes. But Brother Hugh cannot remember Peter Sellers ever appearing on the stage; Bryan Connon is sure he never took part in concert or chorale. 'Nor did he ever use his talent as a mimic to amuse the rest of us or ingratiate himself with his classmates,' Connon said. 'He seemed to have no need of friends. The retreat home to Peg was always open to him – it was the one he preferred to take.'

Sellers later called these 'my lonely years'. To them he attributed his inability to forge strong friendships. From them, he said, came the melancholia that often overwhelmed him. Yet he added: 'Not that I ever worried about being on my own. Sometimes I felt glad not to be too close to people. I might have been happier, I suppose. On the other hand, I never had much luck with people over the long run.'

The one relationship that approached anything like intimacy was with Bryan Connon. Connon was two years his junior – 'and at that age, it matters to boys'. But they had a powerfully shared interest which closed the gap: they delighted in the radio – 'the wireless', as it was then called, a name that now seems quaint, but in those days denoted the magic quality of the sounds that were filling many middle-class British households. The wireless meant the British Broadcasting Corporation, which possessed – and retained for nearly three more decades – the monopoly of education, information and entertainment. The standard week's mix that Sellers and Connon listened to was low-key and middle-brow. There was popular music, but not Pop – the term 'teen-agers' had not yet been invented. *Children's Hour*, staffed by reassuring 'aunties' and 'uncles' with names one expected to find in the birth-announcements column of *The Times*, monitored the young. There was a huge miscellany of comedians and comedy shows – not the hard-line situation comedies familiar to American listeners with their gag-lines and wisecracks, but a more modulated and infinitely more polite over-spill from the variety stage which Ma Ray's forty touring revues once dominated. There were artists like Robb Wilton (as Mr Muddlecombe, a bumbling country magistrate); Ronald Frankau and Tommy Hand-ley (as Mr Murgatroyd and Mr Winterbottom, a pair of comics who were respectively upper- and middle-class patter-men poking light satire at institutions like the Derby or the Boat Race); Arthur Askey and Richard Murdoch (pioneering a short-lived but 'absurdist' series called *Band Wagon*); Will Hay (usually doing his act as a none-too-scrupulous teacher at a run-down boys' academy); Harry Hemsley (with his imaginary family of kids); and a dozen others. There was a wide spread of 'speciality' acts – and especially 'voices'. To Connon and Sellers, radio was the middle-class boy's audible comic strip. The comedians whom radio established had their own weekly pantheon in the picture comics like *Radio Fun*, a product of the air waves which had emerged as a competitor to the screen's *Film Fun*. Peter Sellers's earliest heroes were the caricatured celebrities of the strips. Radio had given them the glamour of showbusiness without the drudgery he had had to suffer when his parents dragged him round the provinces.

The two boys particularly enjoyed and became compulsive listeners to one radio show: *Monday Night at Eight* was a calculatedly 'light' mixture of songs, music, entertainers and a 'puzzle corner' requiring pencil and paper. 'As we walked home together from school,' Connon recalled, 'Peter got endless pleasure imitating the people in *Monday Night at Eight*.' He soon realized his classmate had more than a retentive memory and a talent for mimicry. 'He had a gift for improvising dialogue. Sketches, too. I'd be the "straight" man, the "feed", and all the way up Archway Road I'd cue Peter and he'd do all the radio personalities and chuck in a few voices of his own invention as well. In hindsight, the *Goon Show* was a logical development of that sidewalk "show". I think I even heard Peter trying out a thin, reedy voice, very like the famous Bluebottle character who was so often "deaded". What

Peter discovered when he met the other Goons, Milligan, Secombe, and Bentine, was that they were all overgrown schoolboys, just like him, all hooked on the "Golden Age of Wireless", all at their happiest when they were fooling around for their own amusement and not an audience – though, for recording sessions, a studio audience had to be there. But they weren't mindful of the larger listening audience – just as Peter and I were blissfully unmindful of any passers-by who might have been mystified by the two schoolkids endlessly chatting each other up in funny voices.'

Peter's home was reached before Connon's parents' – after a twenty-minute walk. 'Once outside his cottage, it was a complete and sudden cut-off. Peter said goodbye. Then in he went – never an invitation to go with him – and that was that till school next day, when he would have resumed his self-imposed isolation.' Peter never lingered at school after lessons. It was as if he had to 'report in' to Peg.

'His mother was a very possessive sort of body, hostile to a friend of Peter's like me. I got short shrift any time I appeared with him. No one ever said "Stay to tea." So far as I recall, Peter never came to our house to play. That kind of camaraderie never existed between us, or between him and anyone else his age at that time.'

Peg had opened a small business beside the cottage. It ambitiously advertised itself as an antique shop. Closer scrutiny of its darker corners might have qualified it as a junk shop. Peg, officious, vigilant and fiercely clad in fire-engine red trousers, furnished it with the stock she bought on the cheap – and on the doorstep – from her domestic calls, rooted out on street stalls even cheaper than her own sales counter, or simply 'retained' from the earlier addresses she and her family had occupied. Connon and Peter once were in the shop when Peg's back was turned. Peter picked up an antique coin from some trumpery collection Peg had purchased, laid it on his pal's palm and made as if to douse it with a bottle of acid which Peg used to burnish newly bought metalware. 'First it cleans the coin,' Connon remembered him saying in one of his 'voices', 'then, heh-heh! it cleans your hand!' Years later Connon heard that voice again, in the mock-sinister tones of Dr Fu Manchu, the last role Sellers played on the screen.

'Sellers,' said Connon to his mate on one of their walks – St Aloysius boys always addressed each other by their surnames – 'do you know about girls?' Sellers later told a mutual friend that, 'I said "Yes" very firmly and Connon didn't open his mouth again for the rest of the way home.'

Peter Sellers was backward at his books, but where sex was concerned he was an early starter. Curious about the opposite sex well before he reached his teens, he quickly became audacious enough to carry his speculation into pleasurable experiment. He had witnessed the promiscuousness of backstage life, where 'good companions' behind the footlights turned into furtive and sometimes desperate comforters of each other after lights-out. He once recalled lying on the bed in the boarding-house, when his parents were performing at some nearby theatre, and hearing through the cardboard-thin walls of the room a couple engage in sex next door. He had his first pubescent crush on a classmate when he was still in kindergarten. The affair continued when he went to St Aloysius. The object of his affection was a girl with auburn hair, worn in flirtatious ringlets, and eyes that earned her the nickname of 'Sky Blue' from her thirteen-year-old admirer. Unfortunately his love wasn't reciprocated. As little Peter Sellers, he just did not rate a glance. Perhaps ... perhaps if he were not himself, but someone else, he reasoned, his luck would turn. And so, as he later confessed, he began to experience the utilitarian, not to say enjoyable advantages of masquerading in a more secure and glamorous identity than his own. His podgy figure he couldn't change, but he could practise mannerisms, and, adopt inflections that would associate him in his girlfriend's thoughts with her own heroic and romantic preferences. 'I found that "Sky Blue" had a movie hero, Errol Flynn. I'd seen him in *The Dawn Patrol*, and that was good enough. The next day I put on his voice, his accent, his mannerisms. I even threw in a background of aeroplane and machine-gun noises for good measure. All to impress "Sky Blue".' Alas, the spell didn't work: she didn't appear in the least bit interested. 'She'd switched her affections. Now she was a fan of Robert Donat's. So I went to any Donat films I could find playing – fortunately for me, he was a prolific actor – and went through the whole act again with his voice. No luck this time, either.'

It occurred to Peter that such film heroes as Flynn and Donat had one incalculable advantage over him that couldn't be so readily grafted on to his personality: they were all adults. He was still in short pants – a visible drawback to the amorous persona which his vocal craft, though junior-sized, could nevertheless stretch to cover. So Peg found herself besieged by Peter with pleas for long trousers. ' "No" was a word you didn't say to Peter,' Aunty Ve commented. Soon he was swanking around Muswell Hill in wide-bottomed white ducks. 'Sky Blue' was sufficiently impressed to invite him to have tea at her parents'; but such was Peter's impatient anticipation, coupled with his bashfulness at asking where the loo was when he needed to go, that the new trousers suffered a minor but humiliating accident that even Donat and Flynn would have had trouble in mustering enough confidence to dismiss with one of their devil-may-care shrugs.

Sellers's pursuit of 'Sky Blue' lasted until he was into his twenties and his circumstances, as well as his sexual experience, had enlarged his view of the world – without, however, giving him the gratification he still hankered after as far as this covetable Annabel Lee was concerned. A few years later the consequences for both of them were to be less than nostalgic.

Meanwhile he conducted sporadic but instructive flirtations with other girls, though it was frustrating to lack the opportunity to take them further than the early stages of reciprocal but fairly passive declarations of passion. 'I found out how much I liked girls and how much they liked me, or said they did,' he later said, adding a pensive rider to his intimations of early sexuality. Whether or not Peg knew about her son's would-be liaisons, it is unlikely that she had any power to curb him. Her hold over Peter was an emotional one; it didn't deflect him from the egoistic pursuit of his own satisfactions, then or later, and so far from 'scooping him out', as one of the film-makers who directed Peter and met Peg would remark much later on, Peg wasn't able to make a mark on the hardening rind of his self-esteem. She had to rely on the heart to relay its obligations to Peter's conscience. It was a situation which, in years to come, was bound to breed conflicts of extreme affection and remorseful resentment in her son and lead to both embarrassing exhibitions of filial love and tantrums of unbelievable reproach. In later years Peg would say, 'Pete never really liked school. He preferred being at home with me.' Then she would turn to her husband and, like someone rehearsing an adept budgerigar in a line of domestic dialogue, she would add, 'Peg never left Pete and Pete never left Peg, did we, Bill?' It wasn't the whole truth.

On some occasions, this had a pitiful consequence. For Peg's great love, next to her son, was a comforting succession of brandies at the local public-house, the Wellington, on Highgate Hill. She and Bill ensconced themselves at the bar there, along with the other regulars, and theatrical people like themselves drifted in and out with news of 'the profession', in which Peg's brothers still earned their bread as managers or stage entertainers. Children then, as now, were not allowed to accompany parents inside premises licensed to sell alcohol, so several nights a week Peter would be left to hang about wretchedly outside the Wellington's saloon-bar door while Peg and Bill (if he wasn't performing elsewhere) downed their brandies and beers inside.

He was given a large glass of lemonade to slake his thirst and told not to get into trouble. Sellers hardly touched alcohol in later life, the memory of those empty hours in the vicinity of a full saloon bar put such a stamp of misery on him. He felt excluded by more than the licensing laws. 'He'd play a little game,' Aunty Ve recalled. 'He'd have a bet with himself that his parents would be the next ones to come out of the pub. He didn't often collect his winnings. Peg and Bill were usually the last ones to leave.'

When the war broke out in 1939 St Aloysius was one of the earliest London schools to be evacuated to a safer country area. Wisbech was its chosen re-location, a Cambridgeshire town, in those days about two-and-a-half hours by train from the metropolis, but Peg wasn't going to let even a war separate her from Peter. He was then just fourteen, the age up to which the law said a child's education must continue. One day Peg took her son out of class and that, for all practical purposes, concluded Peter Sellers's years of formal instruction. Mother and son hung around Muswell Hill for the next few months of the winter. Peter helped out in the antique shop. Both of them grabbed blankets when the air-raid sirens began to sound their soon almost nightly warning of a coming blitz and hared across the road to dive into the subway shelter, there to bed down in reasonable, if claustrophobic security at the bottom of Highgate underground station. Eventually, however, even the resilient Peg could take no more of the bombardment, which had caused some slight damage to the Sellers's home, so she put the social disruption that ensued to shrewd use. One night she and Peter cleared out of the rented house, loaded the 'antiques' from Peg's shop into the back of a stage van belonging to one of her brothers, and headed south-west to Ilfracombe, a Devonshire coast resort on the verge of Exmoor, where another of Peg's brothers managed the Victoria Palace Theatre. The Highgate community soon forgot them, including the traders whose bills they (as usual) hadn't settled before their flit, though one lady who had been imprudent enough to trust Peg with an 'antique' copper kettle to sell for her never saw it again and remembered Peter Sellers by that purloined object. Otherwise, the couple left few marks on the locality or on the memories of neighbours. Bryan Connon completely lost sight of Sellers; he didn't even receive so much as a postcard from Devon.

Ilfracombe gave Peter his first deliberate nudge into a show-business career. Along with a boy of his own age called Derek Altman, he was given a job in his uncle's theatre. He was at first a 'gofer', a general dogsbody, sweeping the stage, ushering the patrons in, selling tickets, and gradually working his way up to a glorified assistant stage manager and lighting man. 'To start with, I got ten bob a week,' he recalled. 'It was better than doing dead-end tours in pre-war days. Now the shows came to us. I got a real kick seeing the works from inside. I remember the young actor who was playing Danny, the charming maniac who chops off old ladies' heads in Emlyn Williams's *Night Must Fall*. I manipulated the limes pretty effectively for him – I was intrigued by his voice, very deep and throaty for his age. His name was Paul Scofield, he was playing opposite Mary Clare.'

The first time Sellers appeared on stage, of his own volition, was in 1941. 'Derek Altman and I had worked up a double act – twanging ukuleles, telling funny stories, that sort of thing. We opened our act singing, 'We're Altman and Sellers, the younger generation,/ We always sing in the best syncopation,/ And we hope to make a big sensation/With you-ooh-ooh!" All the choruses in those days seemed to end with an "ooh-ooh!" We did our number as part of a Saturday Night Talent Contest, to encourage the other entrants; but we'd previously told the folks who bought tickets from us at the box-office whom they should vote for. We must have been persuasive, for we won the £5 prize.'

Ilfracombe offered other excitements. 'The girls were a strange lot Not as sharp as London girls, more impressionable, just as desirable. One day I put on a trench coat, the kind Bogart was wearing in the gangster movies, a trilby hat like William Powell's and a Clark Gable moustache. I was only about 17, but I looked twice the age. I'd let on I was a talent scout for the Saturday night shows. I'd take the girls out to Bull's Point, opposite the lighthouse, and get them to audition for me – songs, patter, dances. The ones who "won" were generally those with the most talent for being friendly. Surprising how many fell for my line, especially when I put on my Robert Donat voice that came out like slow treacle. I enjoyed the impersonation for the feeling of power it gave me. Nobody paid that kind of attention to plain Pete Sellers.'

Another friend of Sellers's was a boy called Terry Roberts. His mother, Estelle Roberts, was a medium. She was said to break off conversations with people and address the empty air near her with 'What are you saying?' Peg had dabbled in spiritualism, in the chatty backstreet circle of friends and acquaintances who met in the parlour to establish contact with the dear departed and compensated for an empty evening with drinks and a gossip. But Estelle Roberts had a far more serious approach: she had a philosophy. She believed the amount of matter in the world remained the same, and was reputed to insist that nobody ever died, but that they simply assumed spirit form and lived lives that were parallel to the mortal folks' down to having gardens, flowers, food, and even whisky. It wasn't till well after the war that Sellers started consulting mediums with any regularity and seriousness – and then it was to Estelle Roberts that he turned, first of all suspending his doubts and then swiftly, and increasingly, pinning his faith to the benevolent guidance of the spirit world, where he was convinced he had once lived, in so many forms, at so many periods, playing a multitude of parts. Inside Peter Sellers, he began to appreciate, even at that early stage, there might be more than just one Peter Sellers – there might be crowds of him. The idea was intriguing, and terrifying.

At least one new Sellers had emerged at Ilfracombe. The 'younger generation' of Altman and Sellers had broken up before it could win many more first prizes on the nights set aside for talent. (Altman went on to become a prosperous hairdresser.) One week a band called Joe Daniels and his Hot Shots was booked into the theatre, and Peter suddenly 'went wild' about the drums. 'I spent hours hanging around the wings watching the great drummer Joe Daniels in action. I was regarded at school as an awkward boy – my size made me clumsy. I observed the dexterity Joe used to beat out the rhythms and decided it was just what I needed to put myself out in front of the field.'

One day Sellers sneaked into the half-lit and empty auditorium, unveiled the drummer's kit 'and let myself go'. He was right in the middle of his impromptu session when Joe caught him. 'He was more flattered than offended. He saw me as a fan with the ambition to become a drummer's apprentice and there and then he gave me coaching on the skins. Before the band left for its next engagement, I was sitting in with it, courtesy of Joe Daniels, drumming away like a man possessed.'

Finding his son's enthusiasm didn't go off the boil, as was all too often the case in other things, Bill Sellers got him a local tutor. For half-a-guinea a session, Harold Leedings continued Peter's education as a drummer, and Peg and Bill were delighted and relieved that Peter's energies were now absorbed by something both in the family tradition and readily convertible into supplementary family income. They also pressed Peter to take piano lessons. He did so for a time, but the keyboard lacked the high, tribal excitement of the tight-stretched skins. He could lose himself in his drumming in a way he couldn't on the white or black notes. The sound was both trance and stimulus. When he beat out the rhythm, he felt he was himself – no one else, certainly not any of the rapidly multiplying and quickly confusing identities in which he would manifest himself on screen and off. As he sat on the stage in the ensemble of the orchestra or singled out as a soloist by the spotlight, Peter Sellers found warmth and contentment, and achieved a perspective that life would obstinately deny him in the coming years of infinitely greater material rewards. In August 1980, when he was within weeks of his death and subconsciously knew it, Sellers was moved by memories of the past to speak of his early struggles and those days when he played the drums as a jazz musician. Musicians, he said half-wistfully to Janet Maslin of *The New York Times*, 'view life differently from actors. I guess I've always been a musician'.

When she came to write his obituary, tragically sooner than she could have anticipated, the same journalist commented shrewdly: 'Sellers could bring a musician's improvisatory sense to a role, teasing and stretching a character until it took off in the free-flowing slip of a jazz riff.'

Not wanting to let his headstrong son's passion cool, Bill Sellers swiftly formed a four-piece band of his own with Peter as the drummer. Soon he was picking up two guineas a night following his father round the gigs in North Devon. When Bill got bored with the local scene he went back to his own boyhood locales, in Lancashire, and Peter and Peg soon joined him at the summer resort of Lytham St Annes for the concert season. Peter brushed up his ukulele playing. 'He proved a wizard at it, too,' Bill said and he had a stack of business cards printed for his sixteen-year-old son, billing him as 'The Young Ultra-Modern Swing Drummer and Uke Entertainer.' He had no trouble landing a well-paid job – £8 a week was good money at his age in those days – with a Blackpool band, while his father joined ENSA, the army of entertainers assembled in wartime Britain to stage shows, serious as well as light, for the Forces and the civilian munition-workers. Bill re-assembled his quartet and included Ethel Formby, sister of the tremendously popular film comedian and musician, George Formby, whose mildly *risqué* songs in a Lancashire accent already formed part of Peter's well-polished repertoire of star impersonations. But Peg was reluctant to see her son move to Blackpool, beyond her eye and reach.

'Why can't you get Pete into ENSA, too?' she asked Bill.

So Peter was co-opted, and Bill, with some unexplained windfall, bought him a set of drums costing £200. Even his idol, Gene Krupa, would have drooled over them. 'They were the finest,' Peg said. 'They had to be. Pete wouldn't have looked at them, if they hadn't been. With Pete, everything had to be perfect, or it wasn't for him. And what Pete wanted, Pete got.'

35

TWO

Drumming Man

Bill Sellers's ENSA concert party provided his son with stardom of a kind. Peter enjoyed his drumming turn. His tireless search for what he called 'perfection', which he indulged in later on in life, has its origins in these times. But the wish to freeze the moment of pleasure in the acquired object of his desires was seldom again to be so satisfyingly attained.

It is almost unnecessary to add that wherever the group went, Peg came, too. She was not supposed to do so, but somehow they got her into the ENSA hostels where the group lodged for a few days in each place, doing a half-hour show for munition workers at midday, contributing to an hour-long show for the troops in the evening. Peg made her presence felt. 'She was a small woman physically, but you felt her domineering energy,' said Joy Parker, a member of another ENSA team which was usually a stop ahead or behind Bill's but occasionally shared the overnight digs. 'She would try and run the outfit. "That damn woman," people would say, "is *she* in the show?") It was clear to everyone that Peter was Peg's whole life. She'd grab his rations immediately their party arrived – the top ENSA rate then was £10 a week, out of which they deducted thirty shillings for food and board – and label his jam, sugar and butter and keep it as tightly under guard in little jars or bags as she kept Peter himself, or tried to.

'He was a well-fed boy, with this great mop of hair rising up in well-greased tiers of waves. He was very jolly. Between the shows we played cards or games and Peter always had a jokey line of fun. The way he presented himself, even when not on stage, had a sort of magic to it. He was a spoiled child, but you could forgive him for that because you saw how much his mother had been to blame. He even slept in the same room as Peg, while Bill slept outside. Yes, he was big-headed, but he had talent.'

He also had a sort of 'try anything' glamour. He liked to be with a girl and show he had the power to fascinate women, Joy Parker recalled.

His ukulele was used as 'bait' to gain a girl's attentions. In the twenty or so ENSA people, all lodging under the same roof, there were usually a few girls to return Peter's teasing cajolery and cuddle close to him while he instructed them in the fairly quickly absorbed technique of ukulele-playing. 'He would play one off against the other. I've seen the girls in tears sometimes. He wasn't all that serious. He liked his fun and was generally forgiven his flirtatiousness – male chauvinism was not then as well defined as it is today. "Why doesn't he get away from that bloody mother?" people would ask.'

It seems that, on occasions, he did. Bill's concert party banged around the country in a little van with a tiny ENSA piano strapped on the back and the entertainers squeezed into encouraging proximity to each other inside. Besides Bill, who played the piano, and Peter, on drums, there were three young ladies – Ethel Formby had by this time dropped out – who were respectively a dancer, an acrobat and a singer. It was in this company that Peter recorded his first experience of sex. The circumstances had an element of black-comedy to them.

One of the ENSA girls, slightly older than he, took a flattering fancy to him. During a stop-over in Taunton the group lodged with the ENSA area manager, who was known by the nickname 'Echo Organ'. He had another distinction: he was the local undertaker and did his embalming in the same house as the ENSA parties used as digs. The tools of his trade served equally the requirements of the living or the dead, for Sellers recalled his father being in desperate need of a screwdriver to repair their dilapidated piano before the curtain went up and 'Echo Organ' fetching him 'the biggest screwdriver I've ever seen – the size you'd use in pantomime if you wanted to raise a laugh'. Only this implement was for screwing down the lids of the caskets. At all hours of the day, and sometimes at night, the premises were visited by people with floral tributes – or bodies. Small wonder that the girl who had taken a fancy to Peter confessed to him one day that she was scared stiff of the adjacent intimations of mortality. She imagined she'd heard sounds in the night, too. Peter confided his own apprehensions.

'Well,' she suggested, 'if ever you get frightened, come and knock on my door. We can be together for company. I always sleep with my door open.'

'What about the other girls?'

37

'Don't worry about them. The dead wouldn't waken them.'

'I thought this was not only highly sensible,' Sellers said. 'it was absolutely irresistible. Although I was still pretty young, I was no stranger to the charms of girls but I'd never had an invitation issued to me in such plausible circumstances. So one night, in pyjamas and dressing gown, and armed to the teeth with Robert Donat accents, I found my way along to the girls' room. Feigning fear, and trembling with what I hoped she'd think was fright, I got into bed with her. The only mistake I made was that I didn't take off a stitch in advance – it was a far from ideal state for impetuous love-making. But years later, when I was making *The Pink Panther*, and playing the accident-prone Inspector Clouseau for the first time, I remembered the embarrassment I'd suffered struggling out of my nightwear so that I could get on with satisfying my barely containable passion. It made a good gag and consolidated the conviction I had about Clouseau that, in all circumstances, whatever boob he'd made, the man must keep his dignity – which gave him a certain pathetic charm that the girls found seductive. It all went back to the frustrations I suffered as a result of a lack of priorities in love-making.'

Funny or frustrating, it was an experience that Peter was only too impatient to repeat as soon and as often as possible. The trouble was that Bill Sellers quickly suspected what was going on. Fearful of the anger of Peg, who had on this occasion given up her escort duties, he acted promptly and one night, from a distant part of the war-time provinces, a sulky Peter arrived back at his mother's. And that was the end of ENSA – and romance.

So it was back to the bands again. He was still below the age when he could be called up for military service. A lot of professional musicians were already in uniform, or entertainers in ENSA, and a youth of seventeen like Peter, possessing demonstrable talents, a good set of drums and family connections, had little trouble landing short-term engagements with good orchestras including those of Oscar Rabin and Henry Hall (whose hesitant mannerism of 'This *is* ... Henry Hall', when introducing his orchestra on radio, became one of Peter's cherishable impersonations).

'For one band I even became a Bohemian. That was when I played with Waldini and his Gypsy Orchestra. Waldini was a Welshman, as far as I could learn, and I don't think any of us "gypsies" had ever slept where our caravans had rested. Our costume was Romany, all right, but again it was hardly the gear in which tinkers travelled the shires ... We wore coloured bandanas round our foreheads which kept slipping down over our eyes like blindfolds, and blouses with very wide-cut sleeves and frilly cuffs that used to catch in the accordeon or muffle my drumsticks.'

Looking back on the experience, which had the kind of zany imposture he loved, Sellers would smile wistfully. But his face invariably became hard-set when he spoke of the tedium that went with touring – and this time there was none of the camaraderie (not to mention the sexy opportunities) that went with a tight-knit ENSA concert party cracking the smiles out of tired munition workers or riding the badinage of servicemen on lonely bases. The bands played dates all over the country, at all hours of the day, in the densest black-out and the most cheerless conditions imaginable, sleeping two or three to a bed wherever they could find hotels not choc-a-bloc with rank-pulling military, subject to all manner of hazards and hold-ups. To Peter, it was like being back in the wretched insecurities of his childhood. 'Although I was on my own at last, I hated the life. I felt lonely. I felt trapped. I missed Peg, who'd always entertained me when things were black. It put the final seal on my dislike of show-business, of *having* to entertain. I thought to myself, "There must be less humiliating ways of being pushed around."' Peg didn't like it much, either: there was no room for her around the camp-fire of Waldini's gypsies. She worried about Peter 'getting into trouble'.

He had begun showing an increasingly erratic side of his character. The first news Peg had of it was when he telephoned from Brighton, where he had taken an in-between job in a cinema, and said he was getting married.

'Who to, Pete?' she screamed at him.

'My landlady's daughter. I proposed to her. So I have to marry her, haven't I?'

The entire Sellers family, Peg, Bill, Aunty Ve and Aunty Cissie, dropped everything they were doing and rushed down to Brighton to bring the boy back to his senses – and home. Hardly had he been rescued from that self-inflicted fate, and was working as a temporary busker in a fairground, than he impulsively proposed to a girl at an adjacent sideshow. Compulsive desire, it seemed, had now to be accompanied by instantaneous possession.

Like many theatrical people, Peg was superstitious. She found fortune-tellers irresistible and was forever visiting them, on impulse and, as if to ward off whatever the future might bring, to have a 'reading' or a 'gazing'. It was a sort of superstitious hygiene: she felt better afterwards, particularly if she specified, as she usually did,

'Don't tell me anything bad, life's difficult enough already.' Peter was infected early, and for life, by the same need for comfort and guidance. The war years created a boom in soothsaying: but it was to while away the hours in ENSA lodgings, where his father's concert-party was staying, that he had submitted his palm to a pretty Irish nurse volunteering to read the lines on it – after all, a palm was as effective a way of bringing boy and girl together as a ukulele! 'We're holding hands already,' he cracked.

'You'll become famous,' was her encouraging opening comment after scrutinizing the lines, mounts and declivities over a cup of tea. 'You'll become a household name.'

'Like Oxo beef-cubes or Lux soap flakes, you mean?' Privately, he confided later, he felt so despondent at this time that the only means he could imagine of becoming a 'household name' was to change his own name to 'EXIT' – then people would find their way to him easily enough.

The girl was continuing her forecast, in a more plausible line of country – the heart-line. 'You'll get married, in fact you'll marry ... Well, I don't know, but I seem to see four wives.'

'Will I live that long?' he remembered saying, jokingly.

'Yes, you'll live a long time. You'll live till you're 75.' She finished with a comforting prophecy: 'And you'll die in your bed.'

'As long as it's not in someone else's,' he quipped, and received a flirtatious wrist-slap.

Peter took the forecast lightly. Why not? It didn't look to him as if much in the way of fame or even four wives, despite his accelerated rate of marriage proposals, was going to come his way. But later on, in the years when he depended on the caveats or placebos of astrologers and mediums of much greater eminence, this unnamed Irish girl's prophecy came to shape his superstitious expectations more and more. In some respects it was amazingly accurate: in one fatal respect, it was to prove a cruel decoy.

Meanwhile, no prophecy was required to suggest where he was shortly going to spend the next few years.

It is uncertain if Peter Sellers was called up for National Service when he reached his eighteenth birthday, or whether he volunteered for flying duty with the Royal Air Force. Thoughts of Errol Flynn and *The Dawn Patrol* were still in his mind: now the sound-track noises from that movie were actually in the skies over Britain and needed no imitation to invest him with a borrowed derring-do. But he was turned down for pilot duties because of his eyesight. Peg had been horrified at the thought of her darling Peter vanishing into the blue beyond his mother's ken and she had industriously sought evidence of childhood ailments which, she hoped, would return him to civilian life again before any damage was done. His general good health, unfortunately, did not confirm the wilder suspicions of epilepsy and so on which she kept bringing to light as grounds for exemption. Peter was put into uniform as Airman Second Class, No. 2223033, Sellers, P. 'It was so lowly a rank,' he said, 'that it hid itself behind the initials A.C.H.G.D. – Aircraft Hand, Ground Duties.' It was indeed the dogsbody rating, applied to those who might be good enough to be 'aircraft hands', but, in case they proved to be pretty brainless, could be assigned 'ground duties'. Peter felt humiliated: the rank he was forced to display became a source of continuous hurt. His actual duties were those of an assistant armourer – he armed fighter planes. The trouble was, he was now bereft of sympathetic friends: all his comrades were men with a trade, worthy but dull fellows, uninspiring to a man who believed he could challenge Gene Krupa to a jazz riff.

Still, life had its compensations. The tenacious Peg held on to her son, undaunted by war-time distance or Government defences. Wherever Peter was posted, Peg moved too, taking lodgings in a town near the camp, wangling extra rations, buying black market eggs, butter and steaks, and cooking Peter his customary calorie-full supper after he had consumed his skimpy helpings in the RAF mess-hall.

Then she had a brainwave. Why shouldn't Peter put his talent as an entertainer to the service of his country? The Ray family's civvy-street connections got to work on behalf of the bored armourer's assistant. A thriving part of the RAF consisted of concert entertainments, which were organized quite brilliantly by Squadron Leader Ralph Reader, a power in the Boy Scout movement before the war and now an impresario in air-force blue whose self-contained concert units were known as 'Gang Shows'. Sellers came to his attention. And before too long he was re-mustered as 'drummer, pianist and general funnyman' – though not before he had had a narrow escape when Reader accidentally heard him trying out a voice that Sellers later described as 'like rich fruitcake and port wine.' Reader recognized his own tones, but he was not a man to bear grudges. Sellers later said that Reader brought him the consolation of feeling he was the only one in the Gang Shows who mattered to him. And though Reader refused to recommend Sellers for promotion to Leading Aircraftsman, he coupled the refusal with a flattering reference to Al Jolson – who also, he said, wouldn't have got to wear the proud propeller on his tunic sleeve had he asked for it – and although the immediate connection with the 'Mammy' singer was not clear, Sellers found it a comforting association.

There were solid advantages to any RAF unit that had Peter Sellers in its entertainment section. Aunty Ve's husband, who was Peter's Uncle Bert, managed the Garrick Theatre, London. He knew a lot of the established talents whose call-up had been cancelled or deferred because they were needed to cheer up the Home Front and make an occasional sortie to the front line. Soon these people found themselves commuting a shorter and less dangerous distance – to Peter's air base. The Ray family rallied round Peg's only child and gave his lowly rank a sizeable boost by the wealth of theatrical talent which the lad seemed able to attract, week in, week out, for his mates' entertainment. Frequently the entire Garrick company, which included such comedians as Robertson Hare, would move to the base on a Sunday accompanied by scenery and props from the West End show. And if Peg felt that Peter's talents weren't sufficiently featured in the concerts, she was never backward in informing the manager and making sure that her son's role was fattened up. It was like music-hall with more regular habits.

What brought it to an end so far as Peg was concerned was Peter's posting to India, Ceylon and Burma. He was then in Gang Show No. 10. The separation from Peg was at last complete, for he seldom wrote to his mother. He preferred telephoning her, but once in Asia, this was impossible. Besides, he found a fascination he had never suspected in that part of the world and its inhabitants. His overseas service gave him an intensive, close-up view of what has been called 'the Raj and its dependents' – i.e., the hangover of British India, the inexorable and frequently comic decay of the imperial traditions, and the diverting phenomenon of being able to observe Anglo-Saxon characteristics contained (but rarely) inside Indian skin and features. 'He is not an eccentric,' Kenneth Tynan wrote in 1961, 'he is a student of eccentricity. This makes him an actor rather than a clown.' Peter found eccentricity almost everywhere he travelled with the Gang Show in India. The Indian accent he was to adopt with devastatingly tender-comic effect in *The Millionairess* – it was described as 'the best contribution to race relations ever *heard* in England' – derives from this stimulating contact with what was still identifiably Kipling's continent.

'I was attracted by the placidness of the Indians,' Sellers said of that time, 'their child-like capacity for standing aside, looking at themselves and liking what they saw. I once heard an Indian batman say to himself as he was arranging the soap and razor for his master in front of the shaving mirror, "How are you, my good man?" I was a pessimist; Indians seemed bursting with optimism.'

Sellers's memories of his first overseas posting were lively ones even at the end of his life. He did an interview for the BBC's British Forces Broadcasting Service only a few weeks before his death and spoke, in almost longing tones, of the experience:

We became the remnants of the last of the British Raj. India [at that time] was rampant with majors and colonels, types we have used since. Spike [Milligan] was born in Quetta on the North-West Frontier – his father was in the Indian Army – and he picked up the so-called Bombay–Welsh accent, and I picked it up, too, just through being there. We subsequently used it in some of the Goon Shows before the Asians started coming over here.... I must be attracted in some way to them, whether it's to a certain tic or idiosyncracy, or the warmth of their personality or character. At the time I didn't realize I was picking up their sounds, their styles and their thinking. I was too young to realize the general sort of feeling for Indian philosophy. But in later life, of course I have....

But it wasn't only the Indians that gave Sellers cause for amusement and those inspired incongruities which became a rich part of his impersonations in radio, film or on disc. Events in war-time India were very like a Goon Show comedy. One man who found Peter Sellers's Gang Show following him around the sub-continent was Mark Primhak, who had been appointed manager of ENSA shows in India by Major Jack Hawkins. In 1943 Sellers saw one of Primhak's shows, in which the six-piece orchestra featured an Italian prisoner-of-war pianist, who had been recruited from a POW camp near Calcutta when the original British pianist succumbed to malaria and had to be repatriated at short notice. Giorgio had been trained as a classical pianist and Sellers roared with laughter at his struggles to convert his discriminating touch to the swing rhythms necessary to dash off a passable rendering of 'Kalamazoo' on the ENSA piano. Life for Sellers was forming itself, unasked, into patterns of absurdity that took on an additionally surreal coloration in that theatre of war.

A more important contact for his post-war career occurred when he met Dennis Selinger. Selinger had been under-manager at Peterborough's Embassy Theatre before the war: now he was an RAF gunner, enjoying a few days rest and recreation in Calcutta when he ran into Sellers, who had just got back from a show in the jungle. 'He was affable, easy, very funny when the mood was on him, at other times surprisingly withdrawn, uncommunicative....' The two got on well together and on their final night were entertained to dinner after a boxing match by Melvyn Douglas, fresh from his starring role with Greta Garbo in the 1941 film *Two-Faced Woman* and at this time a US Entertainments Officer. He was to play a major supporting role to Sellers in *Being There*. But some years before that, in the early 1960s, Selinger, who was then negotiating Sellers's film contracts, had arranged to meet Peter, his wife Britt Ekland, David Begelman, then an important agent, and *his* wife at the London show-business eating club, The White Elephant. As Selinger entered he spotted Melvyn Douglas at a supper table and re-introduced himself with that memory of being taken out to dinner twenty years before in Calcutta. Ten minutes later in walked Sellers. Spotting Melvyn Douglas, he re-introduced himself with that memory of being taken out. No wonder Douglas thought he was the victim of a practical joke.

It was in India that Sellers really began to appreciate his own spectacular power when he attempted a deception: 'It was the time I first discovered I could impersonate people well enough not to be recognized for who I really was.' He had had an appetizing sample of it the day he had darkened his face with brown make-up and covered his wavy hair with a Sikh soldier's turban, but he had been careful not to carry on the vocal masquerade in the hearing of genuine Sikhs – not yet, anyway. With the ranks and accents of his own countrymen he felt safer and became increasingly bold.

One witness of how Sellers's initial temptation to deceive grew into a compulsive masquerade was David Lodge, later one of the British screen's leading character actors and a friend of Sellers until his death.

Lodge described himself then, around 1943, as being 'in the real Air Force' but about to be drafted into the commandos until his commanding officer 'rang up Ralph Reader and I found myself transferred, on the strength of my reputation as "the comic about the camp", into one of his Gang Shows. There I met Peter, who was just back from his overseas stint. A big, soft boy. I was big myself, but I had muscle underneath! We generally had a pianist, trumpet, tenor sax, a jazz accordionist and drums. Peter on the drums was one of the best performers ever. "Drumming Man" was how he was billed. He closed the show. To see him do his jazz numbers was a show in itself, throwing up the sticks, catching them. Nothing could have followed him! He doubled as a comedian, sometimes in drag. He'd a good peaches-and-cream complexion at that time – I'd deliberately grown a moustache so I wouldn't have to appear in skirts. Peter made a very convincing woman.

'But I used to be surprised at the sudden tempers Peter could throw. He could work himself up into a furious fighting-mad state, particularly if someone got on the wrong side of him or his mate. There was a hint of anti-semitism about some members of our Gang Show. What I remember about Peter was the way he stood up for the little Jewish bloke on the receiving end of it. Another time he actually broke a chair up, very deliberately, piece by piece, to work out his aggression. I made a note, "If you get on the wrong side of this boy. . . ."'

Lodge was soon brought home to the Sellers's place — they had moved to a flat in Finchley High Road, still faithful to North London and some of the favoured Jewish residential enclaves. There he met the formidable Peg. ' "Dave," she said, "you're older than my boy." I was then about 24, Peter wasn't 21. "You keep an eye on him for me — promise." I promised, of course. I thought Peter's relationship with Peg was too close for comfort; yet she didn't cow him. That boy did what he wanted. He was already showing the traits of a spoiled only child. One day in Paris at the end of the war, when we were all flush with money from some black-market fiddle – the kind everyone was on at that time – we dropped into a tea-shop which hadn't heard of rationing. A plate of cream cakes was put in front of us. Very deliberately, Peter took a single bite out of every pastry on it – he was like an immature, undisciplined child who must cram himself with as much satisfaction as he can and as quickly as he can.'

Other traits were as wilful, but infinitely riskier than hogging the cream cakes. To Lodge's great alarm, Peter began assuming the uniform and rank which belonged to RAF officers far, far higher than his own low and resented grade. The penalties for impersonating an officer were stiff ones – several years in jail, at least, dishonourable discharge almost certainly. But two things helped Sellers in the deception. One was the organizational shambles of most of the transit camps in which the Gang Show appeared. No one knew for certain who was who, or even for how long so-and-so might have been around camp; so an unfamiliar face was invariably not called into question, especially if its owner wore a high enough rank. The other advantage was a large supply of officers' uniforms in the wardrobe hampers of the concert party. Sellers borrowed these shamelessly, seduced by the enormity of the impersonation and indifferent to the consequences of being caught literally 'in the act'.

He was in Assam and feeling sorry for himself when he first dipped into the quick-change hamper, came up with a flight-lieutenant's tunic and, ten minutes later, wearing the new uniform, sauntered into the

Officers' Mess for a gin and tonic. 'I found it far more agreeable spending a few leisurely hours there than having to rough it in the other ranks' canteen. I suppose I've always hated privilege. I felt vaguely that, in some way, this was getting even with the natural unfairness of life.'

Lodge remembered with the clarity of a near-escape the first time he ever saw Sellers pulling this trick:

'We were at Gütersloh, in West Germany, a camp once used by the Luftwaffe and then in the American sector. We Gang Show bods were put in an L-shaped room atop the barracks – two floors below us were the ordinary RAF blokes. I don't know what got into Peter, but suddenly he said, "I'm going to inspect the men," and got a squadron leader's uniform out of the props. George White, who'd been a trumpeter with Stanley Black's orchestra, cried, "Don't be a bloody idiot, Peter." I said, "You'll get five years in clink if you're copped." No good. You might as well have been talking to him under water. On went a false moustache. He parted his hair down the centre, dusted it with talc around the temples, smoothed the medal ribbons he'd awarded himself for campaigns he'd never been in – which was another five years, maybe – and clapped his cap on at the rakish angle which was how that sort of rank was expected to wear it. Then he went downstairs, me following white with apprehension. I noticed his walk had even got ten years older, and carried an authority I never imagined Peter could muster. He threw open the door of the men's bunk-house and waited a second before he entered – even then he'd a great sense of timing. The blokes were on their beds, writing letters, reading, cleaning their buttons. "Tention," barks a lance-corporal. "Stand by your beds. Officer present."'

Sellers waited while the servicemen, some jacketless, a few even in vests and underpants, dutifully swung off their iron double-deckers and lined up both sides of the room. Then he walked down the centre, eyeing them with quiet pride. 'How's everything?' he drawled – Lodge noted he was imitating impeccably the tones of a man unused to having his authority questioned. 'I'm here with the Gang Show chappies. But apart from entertaining you – and, by God, you're going to enjoy tonight's concert – I'm here to enquire into your creature comforts.' A pause. 'Well, how *are* your creature comforts, eh?'

'Terrible shortage of water, sir.' (There had been severe winter flooding in the vicinity which had polluted the drinking supply and necessitated rationing.)

'Really?'

'Food not all that hot, either, sir.'

46

'You don't say?'

Lodge swears that Peter Sellers's attitude at this point was like Royalty meeting loyal workers on the factory floor. He unbent without closing the distance.

'I'm glad you told me. I'll certainly see what can be done.' Then with a nod to the lance-corporal, who called the men to attention again, Sellers exited on the line, 'Well, carry on, chaps. You're not forgotten, I assure you.'

'Half an hour later,' Lodge said, 'we all queued up, knives, forks, spoons in our hands, alongside the same chaps Peter had visited so grandly. Not one of them recognized the "officer" who'd given them such a pep talk. If they had, they'd have lynched him.'

The Gang Show members had their own masquerade going for them most of the time. Discipline wasn't strict and more than rules were made up. Sellers got hold of some Canadian Air Force uniforms, then of a much superior cut and material to the RAF-issue, and teamed them with Van Heusen shirts that enjoyed the luxury of wide-spread collars and a more azure blue than was seen in British skies. Then, purloining two cotton-wool packs intended for dressing wounds, he sewed them into the tunic shoulders – 'He was a handy boy with the needle,' Lodge said – which gave the whole ensemble an imposing dash that drew salutes from slightly bewildered but cautious sentries wherever the Gang Show played.

Lodge never quite got used to seeing his friend appear in borrowed authority and being stood drinks by the squaddies or the sergeants in their mess in return for his condescending affability. At times Peter even tossed off 'a few little amateur impressions' of famous entertainers whom he had seen cheering up the chaps. No one ever questioned how an officer came to possess such talents. Occasionally Sellers would mischievously single out the shrinking Lodge for special favour, drawing him reluctantly into the limelight and the anecdotes, enjoying the inner squirming of the friend who feared that unmasking must be imminent. These impersonations became so frequent that it was like watching Dr Jekyll's involuntary transformation into Mr Hyde. Quite the boldest coup Sellers staged was dressing up one Christmas Eve as an Air Commodore. He presented himself at the Officers' Mess. 'Fortunately everyone seemed blind drunk,' he recalled. 'I found myself standing at the bar with my arm affectionately round the shoulders of an Air Marshal. In a hoarse, conspiratorial whisper, just as if we'd come from some secret briefing session, he asked me what the devil I thought Tedder was up to.'

As Sellers hadn't any idea who Tedder was, much less what he might be up to, he fell back on the strategy he had devised for just such a fix.

'Sorry, old boy, mustn't say. Intelligence, you know.' This was calculated to draw a grovelling, confused apology for his indiscretion from the other officer and Sellers beat a tactful retreat into the Sergeants' Mess, where he judged, correctly, he was much less likely to have questions about Tedder put to him. There he wished everyone a happy Christmas.

'They were very touched by my thoughtfulness. One of them, about my father's age, said in a voice thick with emotion and Scotch, "I'd like to tell you, sir, 'ow much we chaps appreciate you comin' dahn here into our mess. The compliments of the season, sir."'

' "Very kind of you, sergeant," I'd say, and bow myself out in lordly fashion.'

It was a good life in other ways, too. Wherever Sellers and his colleagues stopped, they chatted up the camp quartermaster and invariably came away with Service-issue soap, extra blankets, spare rations, even petrol coupons, which came in handy for buying the black market pleasures of life – and feminine companionship.

For Lodge it was a hard task sometimes to reconcile his promise to Peg to keep an eye on her Pete with the boy's own roving eye. When they were posted to Cannes, flush with francs at inflated exchange rates, they unearthed the cellars of champagne that had been hidden from the invaders, located black-market caviar and had orgies which turned out more Goonish than sexually gratifying. 'We'd have the girls pretending to be cats, lapping up the franc notes as if they were saucers of cream.' It was all part of the euphoria liberated by the war's end and the strange state of make-believe which Peter was by then indulging almost daily.

Sometimes he didn't recognize reality when he saw it. On one occasion the pair decided to quit their rather grotty Gang Show billet in a camp on the outskirts of Paris and seek better-class accommodation in the city. 'We were in the Pigalle area,' Lodge recalled. 'It was raining hard and we saw this hotel with "*Chambres*" in the window. "That looks plush," said Peter. We went in. It did look comfortable. We stood there impressed by the style, then began negotiating a price for a room.' They found it unusually stiff, even for the obvious comforts of the place, and asked for 'a double' in their halting French, instead of two singles. To their surprise, the price was higher still. Then they began to notice girls, unusually lightly dressed for the public rooms, beginning to collect just off the lobby and eyeing them with interest.

'Suddenly there were girls everywhere,' Lodge recalled. 'Without knowing it, we'd entered a brothel. Peter was in his element. This was like a fantasy come true for him. But I'd promised Peg . . . and besides, we'd seen those Army hygiene movies, and we knew what happened to poor innocent Servicemen who gave their love to loose ladies of the night.'

Thirty years later Sellers found himself in a Second World War film comedy called *Soft Beds and Hard Battles*. He played seven parts, one of them a Very Important Person who is asked to inspect 'a famous Paris landmark'. The landmark turns out to be a bordello – and the character is Adolf Hitler, who is not amused to find it so. Art in Sellers's case had a way of sometimes aping life, only not always so successfully.

Lodge had his hands full safeguarding Peter's virtue in circumstances where his womanizing friend would gladly have surrendered it. Sometimes the risk proved to be exaggerated. He and Sellers spent Christmas 1945 in Paris performing for the troops at the Théâtre Marigny. They had been told that as most Frenchmen had been called up, they'd have to put up with female dressers. Sellers found the concupiscent gleam dying in his eye, however, when two staid aunt-like ladies presented themselves at the couple's door – 'They'd even hold out your jockstrap for you to climb into it, and not turn a hair,' said Sellers. He wasn't having anything as off-putting as that, and sent the two *habilleuses* about their business elsewhere, with the consolation of some soap and food coupons. 'Pity they weren't young birds,' he mused, climbing into his jockstrap unassisted.

Another encounter might have been less peacefully settled. Lodge and Sellers were in Toulon at the time. 'Everyone had had plenty to drink,' Lodge recalled, 'and Peter was suddenly discovered to have gone missing.' It was a dangerous neighbourhood. Pimps kept a sharp eye on their ladies and a sharper knife at the ready for any man who mistook trade for love. Lodge took off at top speed and was lucky enough to pick up Peter's scent and follow it to a seedy apartment block.

'It was a lonely place. I was dead scared. An Allied uniform might make you welcome in daylight: it pulled no rank with pimps at night. Luckily George White, who was with me, had just bought a ceremonial SS dagger as a souvenir. I opened my RAF blouse and attached this bit of cut-throat exoticism ostentatiously to my braces, to suggest I meant business, and we threw open the door of the apartment to which we'd traced Peter. He was just getting his trousers off. We grabbed him and then ran like hell before the lady's protector could raise it.'

From wherever he was in Europe, Peter was adept at pulling strings or, rather, telephone wires, to get calls through to London – and Peg. According to Lodge, hearing him say goodnight to her was a painful experience which demonstrated the claustrophobic closeness between mother and son. Not incestuous, just infantile. ' "Goodnight, Peg," he'd whisper into the phone. "God bless you ... Yes, you too ... God keep you safe ... I love you ... Yes I do ... Yes, I love you, too" – and so on. He was totally unable to sign off with the "Night, Mum" that any other young man would have uttered.' At other times Lodge detected an almost resentful build-up of violence in his friend. When something arose which he couldn't solve, and wouldn't let drop, he changed physically – and it was frightening to see. It was even more obvious in later years when Lodge was playing a role in a Sellers film. His friend was now the man of power and would work himself into towering rages on the set.

'I remember one director saying to me, "If I'd a gun, I'd shoot the bastard."

' "You're joking," was all I could find to say.

' "I'm not," he replied, grimly.'

Detecting early symptoms of such stress, Lodge found himself counselling Peter to think of marriage when the war was over, hopeful that a family of his own might resolve the emotional dependence on Peg and absorb those sexual energies he couldn't channel into his relationship with his mother. Then, unnervingly, he would find Peg almost reading his thoughts when they next met and saying to him in tones of obliquely chiding vigilance, 'Dave, you're something special. *You* don't want to get married and leave your mother.'

Lodge was demobilized from the RAF some months before Sellers. They said goodbye on a snowy station platform in Schleswig-Holstein. 'Peter had tears in his eyes,' Lodge recalled. ' " 'bye, Dave, "I can hear him calling yet, in that plaintive little voice he used with his friends.'

Lodge made his way back to London, via the usual channels of demobilization, and a few weeks later called on Peg, who told him proudly, as if she personally had fixed it, that Peter had been promoted to Flight Sergeant. She expressed her gratitude to Lodge for all he had done for her son. Then she said, 'Now, Dave, I am going to make you get a good start in the business. You know the Garrick Theatre? Well, my brother Bert manages it. I'm going to get in touch with him and tell him you're coming round to see him. He'll take care of you. Dave, you can be the commissionaire.'

THREE

Those Crazy People

The day came when Peg Sellers's son was also demobbed from the RAF, along with a 'civvy' suit (pinstripe, double-breasted), two pairs of socks, a pair of shoes, fourteen days' emergency ration coupons for food and a warning against women who might have designs on his discharge pay. He tucked into his wallet a testimonial from his Wing-Commander: 'The above named ... is strongly recommended for any work to do with entertainment.'

But as far as Peter Sellers was concerned, unfinished business of a romantic nature had priority over finding a job. He had continued his obsessive pursuit of the girl whom he called 'Sky Blue'. Even when he was on the other side of the world, he wrote to her almost daily. She tolerated these yearnings, but left them unreciprocated. Sellers persisted – until the day he received a 'Dear John' letter from her in which she told him, fairly bluntly, that she had fallen in love with a sergeant in the American air force. He was beside himself with grief and anger and there and then, near despair, he dashed off a supplicating letter begging her to postpone any final decision until he could get back to England and talk to her. No sooner was he back with his parents than he rushed round to 'Sky Blue's' flat, which she was sharing with two other girls who worked like her for a Government department in Whitehall. He took her out to the most expensive dinner he could find in the West End. Later he confessed, quite impenitently, that he got her drunk and deliberately made her pregnant. The idea in his mind was that the girl would now 'have to' marry him. It was the act of a desperate, inconsiderate youth, by now accustomed to getting his own way and letting others clear up the mess. It was like taking a single bite out of each cream-cake on the plate. But the girl's resolution proved stronger than Sellers had anticipated. She refused his marriage proposal even when it had been confirmed that there was a baby on the way. By then, of course, the entire Sellers family had been mustered to pool their resources and extricate Peg's boy from the mess. The girl's family was co-operative, too, since illegitimacy at that time still carried a heinous stigma: they didn't wish 'Sky Blue's' relationship with the man she *did* love – fortunately in an overseas posting at the time – to be imperilled by her involuntary infidelity.

She had her baby, a girl, in an adoption society's nursing home: it vanished immediately into the secrecy of the adoption system for unwanted babies. Sellers never even saw the infant. Years later he tried to trace its whereabouts, only to find that the records had vanished in the disruption of the immediate post-war years. He kept quiet about the affair until the permissive atmosphere of the 1960s encouraged him to confess to a fault of a by then fashionably hedonist kind. 'Sky Blue' was long married to her American husband and settled in the United States – 'and somewhere in England,' Sellers would say, right up to the end of his life, 'is a girl who doesn't know she's my daughter'. He was wont to add, 'I hope her childhood was happier than mine.'

He was entering an extremely unhappy period. During the war, away from home, liberated from Peg and liberating himself from 'Peter Sellers' by the persistent impersonation of others, he had known a couple of years of enjoyment without responsibility. Now the trip was over. Peacetime was a sickening let-down. It seemed to him that he had returned abruptly to the terrifying insecurities of childhood – with this difference. Since he was old enough, at twenty-one, to step into his father's shoes, he suffered all the depressing experiences of facing strange audiences in dreary music-halls without having the refuge of his parents, or the placid temperament which armoured Bill Sellers against the indifference or derision of changing tastes in popular entertainment.

Not that work was exactly easy to pick up. All London seemed filled with ex-servicemen who played the drums and sought engagements. Once more the Ray family connections were milked. Bill Sellers hired a church hall in East Finchley and persuaded an agent to come and listen to his son at a special, one-man audition. Sellers recalled the discomfort of the occasion – the empty, exposed platform, the chairs ranged round the walls, the terrifying vacuum in the middle which he was to occupy with his drums and, far away, his Dad and the all-important booker. 'More like a firing squad than an audition . . . I clashed a final cymbal. They showed no sign of being impressed but simply strolled outside while I dismantled my gear.

'I asked Dad afterwards, "What did he say?"

' "He said he'll let us know in a week." '

A week later came an offer. 'Seven pounds a week and you're on in Burnley.' Burnley! As far as Sellers knew, they ate their babies in that godforsaken provincial town. His Dad told the agent, politely, that he thought his son could do better. Part of Sellers's trouble was that the style of drumming had changed since he had learned to play and the more sophisticated orchestras being re-formed after the war realized it and resisted the approaches of a flamboyant player unversed in the new beat. Now you had to use your hands and elbow-thrust, pressing hard on the drum-skin to bring up the tone. Sellers took an honest look of self-appraisal and realized he would never make a crack modern drummer. Despondently, he began accepting one-night stands, dance-hall engagements and, one time when spirits were at their lowest ebb, a fairground job offered by a friend in Norwich which was little more than that of a tent-flap barker with a line in patter.

'We're full up,' he was told when he called the Norwich hotel: at least the job had included accommodation. 'Full up, perhaps, to Peter Sellers,' he thought grimly, 'but not to some VIP, someone with a handle to his name, a title if not a rank, someone, say, like the Earl of Beaconsfield.' Why Sellers decided to impersonate a descendant of Benjamin Disraeli, the great Victorian statesman, Tory Prime Minister, and the first Lord Beaconsfield, is still not quite clear, though he always contended that Peg's side of the family, through Ma Ray being the wife of Solomon Marks, had a peripheral connection with the Jewish politician and novelist. Anyhow, he arrived in Norwich, marched up to the hotel and declared himself to be 'Lord Beaconsfield' and in need of a room. 'Yes, my Lord ... Certainly, my Lord ... Please sign the book, my Lord.' Two porters vied for the honour of carrying the 'Earl's' single rather run-down suitcase to his extravagantly proportioned room. Half-an-hour after checking in, 'Lord Beaconsfield' was crying 'Roll-a-ball-a-ball, a penny a pitch' at a coconut-shy stand. But on returning to the hotel, the welcome he got was not nearly so beckoning.

'Excuse me, my Lord, could I trouble you to step into my office for a moment?' said the manager.

'Lord Beaconsfield?' asked one of two unsmiling men who stood there.

'Yes.'

'Really?' said the man, in harder tones. 'Or have we the honour of addressing No. 2223033, Flight-Sergeant Sellers, Peter?'

'Equally appropriate,' Sellers bluffed.

During his absence at the fairground, the chambermaid had unpacked his case and discovered the 'Earl' travelled light – a pair of pyjamas, a long woollen robe and a crushed packet of Woodbines, then the cheapest smoke on the market. The address which Sellers had entered in the hotel register, '211b High Road, East Finchley, London,' his parents' home, was respectable but un-aristocratic. Suspecting he had a deserter from the Forces on the premises, the manager had called the police, who, in turn, brought two RAF Special Investigation Branch officers from the nearby Norfolk air base, coincidentally a scene of Sellers's Gang Show concerts. Once they had verified that Sellers had been recently and honourably discharged, their interest in his more exotic ancestry lapsed – and so did the management's on his proving that, with his fairground earnings, he could pay the largish bill which the 'Earl' had run up.

Sellers's use of this pedigree didn't stop there, however. Trying to get publicity for a holiday camp on the island of Jersey, where he had taken a summer job as entertainments officer, he represented himself as the 'Fifth Earl of Beaconsfield', which brought a 'stringer' from a London daily newspaper to ask why a member of the Peerage was employed to stir the *petit-bourgeoisie* from their morning slumbers with the cheery cry of 'Wakey ... wakey!' He backtracked out of Burke's reference book of titled Britons quite skilfully, but until he got the sack for unspecified sins, he was known from then on as 'the Fifth Earl'.

Throughout this depressing period he was supported financially by his family. The Sellers's fortunes had been materially improved by the war. Though by no means well-off, they had enough to meet their needs. Besides Uncle Bert, who managed the Garrick, other relatives had successfully speculated in the property market in blitzed buildings. The hat was passed round if any family member needed a temporary loan. Peter certainly wanted for nothing in the way of home comforts – and gave no sign of suppressing any desire if he had wanted. If something took his fancy, he had to have it – there and then. Aunty Ve recalled seeing Peg staggering down Finchley Road lugging a brand-new drum kit which Peter had 'bought' from a local shop on credit. Later on he would apply the same kind of thoughtless acquisition to bigger objects of desire like ocean-going yachts – which could not be sent back to the shop so easily. As one acquaintance said later, 'I don't think Peter ever spent more than a fleeting moment on considering his future, and only slightly longer on his past. He was totally absorbed by the present. I don't think he ever had a dream about himself which he wanted to realize. He was an "instant" man.'

He still loved novelty regardless of expense. He was the first to be seen walking down the street carrying a then rare portable radio with music issuing from it. David Lodge recalled, 'He even had a white telephone by his bedside. A white telephone in those days was pure Hollywood. If I wanted to impress a girl, I bought her flowers. Peter would present her with a new bike.'

If Peg minded about her son's promiscuous pursuit of girls, whom he sometimes brought home to the flat while the family were out, she couldn't do much to stop it. What she probably really worried about was Peter's forming lasting attachments – like marriage. Sellers's restlessness at this dreary nadir of his scarcely existent career seems to have been channelled into the compensating pleasures that the fraternization of Service life had accustomed him to seeking. 'We used to date the nurses at one big London hospital,' David Lodge recalled fondly. 'One of Peter's uncles gave him coupons for black-market petrol and lent him an old pre-war Wolseley – in our draped jackets we must have looked a right couple of "Flash Harrys". We'd take the girls to a show or movie, then return to the ground-floor wing of their hospital, and the party would go on from there, with us occasionally staying the night in cots that weren't occupied by anyone with more urgent physical needs than ourselves. We'd hear the girls come back in the morning, the chink of cups as they brought in our breakfast, and I'd say to Peter, "Let's do our slow wake." It became a catch-phrase in the years ahead.' Catch-phrases were the little secret knots that Peter used to secure the close friendships he formed in the days before his celebrity. They became very important to him as he moved into a show-business world and understood that nothing (and no one) could be relied on. Most of his intimates used them to promote a reassuring sense of interdependency. The Goon Show scripts eventually furnished a well-stocked store-cupboard of names and phrases that were passwords to the good old times. But one of the most arcane phrases, which always caused him to beam with remembered glee, came from his association with the actor and early buddy of his, Graham Stark.

They met in the RAF at the war's end. Stark, who had lost a family in the blitz, was then lodging at the Union Jack Club. 'A place where you put the bedposts inside your shoes at night to stop folk running off with them.' Peter persuaded a neighbour whose flat was below his family's to give Stark lodgings. On demob leave they would tour the Service clubs in search of 'talent' – 'talent' that had no stage connections, Stark, too, noted Peter's besetting delight in anything new, especially if it were some gadget whose possession was a status symbol.

'Long before they came generally on to the market, Peter had an automatic record changer. One of those phonographs where the arm came over, the next record clunked down, the needle descended with a thud, the music blared out. ... We'd go to the Nuffield Centre, chat up a couple of Waafs [members of the Women's Auxiliary Air Force], and bring them back. Bill and Peg would have already been given their marching orders – down to the pub. Peter would load the record changer. It held eight discs. If we hadn't got anywhere with the girls by the fifth, we certainly wouldn't by the eighth. This became a catch-phrase which Peter and I used to bandy about. "If you haven't made it by the fifth ...!"'

Stark saw immediately Peg's total obsession with her son. 'It was as if she saw a halo round him, as if he could walk on water. But it was genuine. She didn't live vicariously, however, trying to have a second career for herself through her son. She kept her distance, but worshipped his success.'

At that moment there was precious little success – and a growing distance between Peter and Peg as she saw him sink into black moods in whose bottomless depths even she could no longer 'reach' him. His mood shifted gears with disconcerting abruptness: one moment elated, the next downcast, though nothing had outwardly changed to affect him for the worse. He was living 'within himself' to an unhealthy extent. The Ray family had had a couple of 'eccentric' relatives who used to require therapeutic care in a 'retreat'. Peg worried that conditions might be pushing Peter along this road. It was at this time that he acquainted David Lodge with some of his personal fantasies. They centred round a Tolkien-like universe populated by Hobbit-type creatures christened by Peter 'The Toffelmen'. (It is interesting, in the 'family' sense, that when Sellers's friend and fellow Goon, Michael Bentine, broke away from the Show early on and went solo on television, part of his act consisted of little imaginary creatures called 'The Bumblies'. Imaginary worlds were the Goons' pocket-map to sanity.) A Toffelman who could count up to ten was a mathematical genius. A Toffelman believed the worst was always certain, but maybe wouldn't happen just now. A Toffelman had a personal star, but took care to hide it among the other bright bodies in the heavens in case someone put it out. Lodge recalled: 'He characterized these little beings in a thin, myopic voice I later recognized as that of Bluebottle' – the voice that Bryan Connon had been treated to even earlier on their peripatetic improvisations en route from school. There was an innate sadness to Sellers's creative side. It persisted throughout his life. His ad libs had sometimes the feeling of being winched out of some well of loneliness. Stark, speaking of Sellers's brilliant cameo appearance as a seedy Dickensian doctor in *The Wrong Box*, in 1966, using a plethora of handy kittens as blotting paper for his prescription sheet, remembered that Sellers, at the end of the shot, suddenly appended a line of his own to the script's dialogue. Looking at the tiny moggy he was holding by the nape of its unresisting neck he said to it in tones of wisdom born out of infinite sadness: 'It won't do you any good, you know.' To Stark it was like the testamentary judgment a deeply melancholic man was passing on himself.

Peg realized that Peter's career needed the bracing hand of someone 'not in the family'. An agent: that's what her boy should have. So one day, early in 1946, Dennis Selinger, who had gone into agency work after leaving the RAF, got a call from the mother of the youth he had met in Calcutta. Her son was tremendously talented and would be worth a fortune to some lucky person some day. Selinger sighed, but said 'Yes, bring him along.'

'Peg impressed me a lot more than Peter did when they arrived. He just sat there for the most part, cap on his lap, gloves in his hand, in a demob suit that looked as if it had spent the night before under a mattress having the creases put in it. His most striking feature was his pile of wavy hair.' Sellers was then out of a job, having lost his Jersey holiday camp 'filler'. He had worked up an act depending on funny stories, impersonations and a bit of drumming and uke playing. Peg had bought him band-part covers made of fine-grained leather with his name tooled in gold on the front, even though some bands in the music halls where he appeared hardly knew what to do with this luxury. 'He was generally the second spot on the bill,' Selinger said, 'the comedian's graveyard.' One early engagement proved how quickly you 'died' if they didn't like you. The catcalls from an audience at Peterborough, impatient for the star turn, singer Dorothy Squires, left Sellers shaking with anger and humiliation at the wincing sympathies shown by other artists on the bill, who included a Hungarian acrobat, a blind accordion player and a man with a performing dog. The dog stole the show. 'I was seething when I came off,' Sellers said. During the interval the manager entered the packed dressing-room, thrust an envelope in his hand and said, 'Go on. Get out. You're through. Here's twelve quid. You're not a bad comic, but you're no good for this lot.' Sellers, nearly suicidal, was packing his things when the star, Dorothy Squires, intervened, 'Come on. Give the lad a chance. This is a "Monday-night" house. He can stick it till Saturday.' The manager relented and Sellers, assisted by

Dorothy Squires, who suggested how he could prune and pace his act, lasted out the week. 'But I hated it. Worse still, I hated the audience.'

A place not noted for its humour was London's Windmill Theatre, run by Vivian Van Damm, an impresario whose boast that 'We never closed' during the blitz had been fondly perverted into 'We never clothed' by the fans of the non-stop strip shows for which its stage was famous. In those days, however, the girls were forbidden by law to move; the customers did the moving, shifting forward, ever forward, as seats became vacant, till the front rows were packed by expressionless men in drab raincoats. Hearing the theatre needed a new comic, though doubting if he'd get the job, Sellers applied – and got it. What he didn't know was that Uncle Bert had been busy on the grapevine. Even so, Vivian Van Damm was not a man to lay out £30 a week simply to render a service. The turn Sellers did on stage mattered more than the good turn to a friend. Sellers stayed for six weeks, rising to £40, for insinuating his act between the fan dancers and the nudes, who reminded him of a more curvaceous set of Pegs without the lantern-slide costumes that Bill used to project on his mother. 'About fifty percent of the audience stayed all day, moving forward as the bump and grind routines went on. When my turn came, I could almost feel their hot breath on my kneecaps.'

When Sellers left, Van Damm paid him a compliment that also reflected well on the revue-manager's instinct. Without waiting to see how his career might prosper, he had the name 'Peter Sellers' added to the bronze plaque on the wall distinguishing 'Stars of Today Who Started Their Careers in This Theatre'. It appeared right after the name of another hopeful star who would soon be an inseparable, life-long friend of Sellers – Harry Secombe.

The Windmill didn't endear music-hall to Sellers; but it hardened his talent by annealing it in an engagement that was lengthy enough to give him a more confident self-image than that of a week-long survivor. What he wanted now was more exposure, Selinger told him. 'I can't face touring,' Sellers said, firmly.

'You don't have to – there's always radio.'

The immediate post-war years saw an explosion of comedy shows based on either the catch-phrases and characters of service life or the domestic mishaps involved in re-establishing civilian life in a country still short of material pleasures. One of the most popular was *Much Binding in the Marsh*, set in a fictitious RAF base and starring Kenneth

Horne as the Commanding Officer and Richard Murdoch as his Number Two.

One day Roy Speer, a BBC producer of many of these situation comedies stocked with funny characters and catch-phrases, was informed on his secretary's inter-com that Kenneth Horne wished a word. 'Hullo, Ken,' he said, when the call was put through, 'what can I do for you?'

'Listen, Roy,' came the familiar plummy tones at the other end of the line, 'I don't want to take up too much of your time, but I've something I ought to pass on to you. Dickie Murdoch and I saw a fellow the other week at the Windmill we thought might be rather good for one of your shows – didn't we, Dickie?'

'Absolutely,' Murdoch butted in. 'First-rate chappy. Very clever with voices.'

'What's his name?' Speer asked.

'Peter Sellers.'

'Where can I find him?' Speer enquired, reaching for his note-pad. There was a pause long enough to make him think he had been accidentally disconnected. Then a third voice, an unfamiliar one, said, 'Actually, he's here at the moment.'

'Who's that? Who's with you, Ken?'

The strange voice said, 'Mr Speer. This *is* Peter Sellers. Actually, neither Mr Horne nor Mr Murdoch knows a thing about this call. It was me all the time. Have I proved to you that I can do impersonations?'

Sellers, sitting on the side of his bed in Finchley, holding his white telephone in one hand while Peg gripped the other encouragingly, always said he felt the next few seconds lasted a lifetime. He could *hear* Speer's mind working, reflecting on his deceit. Then came a chuckle.

'You're a cheeky bastard. I expect you know that, though. Well, you took me in, so I suppose I've got to see you.'

Speer found Sellers a radio spot, no more than five minutes long, on a variety programme of newish acts called, uninventively, *Show Time*. It was recorded from the People's Palace in Mile End Road, the stronghold of Cockney music-hall, and introduced by a compère from Australia called Dick Bentley. Sellers's turn was billed as *My Nightmare*, and was the usual ragbag of impersonations (including Horne and Murdoch) of other radio and film personalities. Peter and his father had hammered out the script on their kitchen table. 'Terrible stuff,' thought Sellers Sr, 'but Pete made it work.' It was memorable enough to get him his earliest 'rave' review. 'This Mimic Is Tops,' declared Leslie Ayre, radio critic of the *Evening News*, in his column on 10 July 1948: 'O. Henry once spoke of an actor who did "impersonations of well-known impersonators". Certainly many mimics give too little study to their originals. Peter Cavanagh [then famous for his mimicry under the slogan 'The Voice of Them All'] is an exception. And now in Peter Sellers radio brings us another really conscientious and excellent artist and a genuine rival to Cav. . . . His first broadcast in *Show Time* brought a scurry of agents and he's already fixed up a long series of Sunday concerts all over the country.'

Speer immediately booked Sellers for the first available return date in *Show Time*. Selinger, forgiving the columnist's excess of zeal which spoke of a 'scurry of agents', had the piece reprinted in *The Stage*, though he omitted the words '. . . and a genuine rival to Cav'. Not just out of the 'ethics' of the profession: 'but because I knew Peter was going to be more than an impersonator'. Work certainly beckoned Sellers from now on, testifying to radio's pulling power. He was on *Workers' Playtime*, *Variety Band Box* and *Ray's a Laugh*, a witty and fast-paced half-hour, thriving on the clichés of domestic strife between comedian Ted Ray and his radio wife Kitty Bluett, into which were fitted characters with the outlandish names – a rather immature characteristic of nearly all British comedy shows – of Al K. Traz, an American gangster, his moll Penny Tentiary, as well as a Russian called Serge Suit who never quite got his English vowels in the order laid down by the dictionary. Sellers played both male characters. Voices now came out of him, like verbal ectoplasm, on the demand of inventive scriptwriters, who sometimes took their cues from the colour he gave their creations. He showed his loyalty to his friends by telephoning George Innes, another BBC producer, and this time, with the waxing confidence of his radio exposure, recommending his friend Graham Stark in much the same terms as he had put into Kenneth Horne's mouth, only now it was definitely Peter Sellers speaking. Stark was soon doing four shows weekly.

Dennis Selinger had told Peter that 'after three or four years with the BBC, I'd get him booked at the London Pavilion' – then the accolade that publicly announced a new star of the variety stage had 'arrived'. 'I didn't handle many acts at that time, about eight, and, if they were any good at all, every one of them played at the Pavilion – but I didn't tell Peter that!' Sellers's ascent in radio mimicry was so swift that Selinger signed him for the Palladium in October 1949 to support the bill-topping Gracie Fields in a turn called 'Speaking for the Stars'. But he was paid an unrehearsed tribute that said more about his nation-wide acceptance when he had a lucky escape in a car accident shortly afterwards. Shaken, but unhurt, he gave his name to the policeman. The man was obviously a fan of *Ray's a Laugh*'s growing numbers of freak characters all played by Sellers. 'Careful, sir,' he said, 'or you'll be killing Crystal Jollybottom one of these days.' It was Sellers's earliest intimation of how his 'act' was starting to stick.

Radio brought him many concert bookings, all of which he did for the money, not the love. It was good money, too: about £100 a night. 'He was developing a comic character of his own,' Selinger said, 'a young idiot boy with Goonish undertones, but a bit more realistic, called Sappy.' Nothing, perhaps fortunately, was heard of this Goofy-like character's development; but what began creeping into Sellers's acts in the South Coast holiday resorts was a nascent surrealism. It was a danger sign, too, born not only out of irrepressible inventiveness but also out of an increasing contempt for audiences 'with two-thousandths of an inch foreheads' to whose vulgar desire for a belly laugh he deeply resented having to lower himself. Surrealist gags took shape around this animus. Once when fluctuating between depression and distaste he went on stage in a plastic 'Pakamac' raincoat with a trilby hat pulled so low over his eyes that the shadow rendered his face completely invisible. He did his whole turn cocooned in this womb-like integument. 'The odd thing was I got a rave review in the local rag,' he recalled. 'Or so I thought, till I found out the reviewer was the paper's egg-head writer who fell out with his editor every week over his *avant-garde* opinions.' Less enthusiastic about Sellers's quirky appearance was the theatre's owner, a London impresario, who told him he would personally see to it that he never again worked in one of his theatres. 'Bugger off,' was Sellers's reply. Years later when the comedian was ensconced in the nation's affections as a Goon Show clown, the same impresario asked him to name his price for appearing in a London pantomime.

'I once told you to bugger off,' Sellers said curtly. 'Who told you to come crawling back?'

'When Peter was bent on a quarrel,' said David Lodge, 'he didn't pick on little people. He took on men.'

Such experiences, however painful, were exerting a creative pressure on Sellers. They were pushing him into a withdrawal from the world of conventional entertainment. Emotionally at first, and then artistically, he was withdrawing into a corner formed by his own extraordinary angle of vision.

The Goon Show offered just such a refuge, not only to Sellers but to his closest associates, who, with the exception of Michael Bentine, had all been wounded in their war with provincial vulgarity and derisive or indifferent audiences. The Goons were like a little secret conclave of people who discovered a shared measure of protectiveness in each other's eccentricities. They would, as they were to put it, open the door (of their humour) and let in the room (the outside world of the orthodox). And such invitations, virtually untranslatable to any medium other than the infinitely spatial one of radio, were strictly on their own terms.

Sellers met Harry Secombe in 1949 and they immediately appreciated that they shared the same sense of absurdity. Secombe, who came from Swansea, liked the music-halls no more than Sellers, but with his fine tenor could save himself in a sinking comedy act by abandoning ship and breaking into a song. He already knew Milligan — they had both played 'walk-on parts' in the war. He often recalled how Lance-Sergeant Terence A. (Spike) Milligan, son of an Indian Army warrant officer, was serving in North Africa when his howitzer jumped off its base when fired and went over a cliff as a result of the artillery crew's fumbling its anchorings. At the bottom of the cliff, but fortunately not directly beneath the falling gun, was Lance-Bombardier Secombe in a wireless truck. 'I immediately began looking in my German dictionary for phrases for surrender,' Secombe has recorded. 'If [the enemy] were throwing things that big at us there was no alternative.' Suddenly the flap on the wireless truck was jerked open. 'Anyone here seen a gun?' It was Milligan. The two did Army shows later in Sicily, where Secombe was a ballet dancer as well as a balladeer, and perfected the comedy act showing how different people shaved which won him his Windmill booking. The Windmill was where he met Michael Bentine, son of a Peruvian scientist, educated at Eton and the Sorbonne, and then half of a drums-and-piano act called Sherwood and Forest. The camaraderie of service life was still at blood heat. London's theatrical West End was a warren of small drinking clubs where the hours spent at a loose end between rehearsals or auditions drew together, quite spontaneously, comedy teams of performers with like temperaments. They swapped experiences and the usual bush tele-graph information about possible openings, and re-discovered in their mutual enjoyment, and indebtedness, a comradely fusion of talents that was never to be repeated once peacetime had sorted them into first and second ranks. Secombe met Sellers at a radio show and introduced him to the other two, who were doing a show called *Soldiers in Skirts* at the Bedford Theatre, Camden Town.

With the exception of Sellers, they were all first-generation show-business; which meant they were blessedly free from the hoary traditions of the stand-up comics who came on with a burst of music, told a string of stories and went out on a song. The Goons-to-be found their temperaments were high-speed ones. Their shared backgrounds and mental wavelengths gave a telepathic patness to their banter. Picking up sympathetic vibrations was to become second-nature to them. And woe betide a guest-star who did not send back a reassuring vibration.

But if they took their keynote from anyone in the group, it was from Milligan. He was (and remains) a verbal anarchist who has never made his peace with society, or himself. He had suffered so much from the divisions of caste, rank and class in the three societies he had lived in – India, the Army, and Britain – that even then he was living a marginal existence. Not exactly a down-and-out, more an intellectual dosser. He inhabited an upstairs room in a Victorian pub called The Grafton Arms where a picture of Franz Kafka presided over his dreams, or more probably his nightmares, as he lay in a sleeping-bag below it. As Philip Oakes later said memorably: 'His spiritual home is a condemned garret.' He seemed already to have found it.

The pub was run by Major Jimmy Grafton, a desert war hero and part-time writer for BBC comedy shows. Nostalgia for service life was as thick in the place as the sawdust that used to strew its floor. And the quartet's regular drinking sessions gradually turned into a vague, matey association dubbed 'a Goon club'. Spike found the name in the Popeye comic strip – it was applied to a mutant-like creature who talked in meaningless scribbles. He recognized a soul mate. The Milligan concept of the Goons seems to have had a blood-tie with Sellers's Toffelmen. 'What is a Goon?' asked James Thomas, then the *News Chronicle*'s radio critic, and answered it with: 'A Goon is someone with a one-cell brain. Anything that is not basically simple puzzles a Goon. His language is inarticulate; he thinks in the fourth dimension.' (Milligan used to describe Goon humour as 'dimensionalism'.) As much for their own entertainment as for the pub's regulars, the Grafton Arms Goons began giving impromptu concerts in an upstairs room. The radio connections of some of the customers pulled in the BBC's junior hierarchy for an evening's drinking and goonery. Who got the idea of making a recording of just such a night's entertainment it is now impossible to discover. But it is typical of the gadget-fixated Sellers that the acetate record should have been cut on a machine which he bought second-hand from a music publisher. They were helped in scripting the demo disc, entitled *Sellers' Castle* since Peter was marginally the best of them, by Larry Stephens, a radio thriller-writer who was to turn comedy-show scripter and share some of the Goon writing with Milligan. It was all done in a totally un-serious mood. 'For us three,' Secombe wrote, 'the Goon Show was like being let out of school – a chance to get together on a Sunday and indulge in our private fantasies. It was a time for hysteria and brandy, for soaring upwards on the thermal currents of Milligan's imagination, a time for wishing every day of the week to be Sunday.'

The disc was entrusted to the BBC's light entertainment moguls, and it succeeded in fascinating some of them and repelling others for well over two years as it made the rounds of offices. It had a reckless speed which seemed excessive to producers dealing with radio audiences of middle-aged people – though it was precisely this pace which a younger generation were quick to praise and latch on to. Most puzzling of all to the BBC were the verbal *non sequiturs*, the absurdist logic (the sound effects of horrendous complexity and fiendish invention were at that time beyond the resources of the team). And then there was the vague but definitely disconcerting feeling that the show had a destructive, nihilistic thrust quite different in tone from the supportive social comedy of the mainstream radio shows. 'It was like gibbering in the face of authority,' Milligan said, acknowledging how much his own rebelliousness had directed the show. Its sketches might be 'nonsense' in an English literary tradition that took in Carroll and Lear, but they released a pent-up hostility directed at sacred cows, ivory towers and society pillars. All of this the BBC sensed without being quite able to locate the objectionable epicentre of their apprehensive tremors.

It was a younger producer, Pat Dixon, who pushed the idea through to the point of a try-out. 'This is the BBC Home Service,' were the introductory words which listeners heard in the very first broadcast on Monday, 28 May 1951. There followed a cacophany of off-key musical instruments – Milligan's 'razzberry' blown at an organization which he was always to consider more tormentor than mentor. When the sound died down the announcer asked, 'What is the zaniest comedy show on the air today?' Sounding as if his voice had been buried in a graveyard crypt along with his corpse, Milligan ventured a guess. 'Er, *Today in Parliament*?'

'No,' cried the announcer, his voice throbbing with a confidence shared by very few at the time, 'it's those crazy people, the Goons.'

All this cautious build-up testified to the BBC's anxiety that audiences might not understand the radical new form of comedy that followed. They had originally attempted to have the show named 'The Junior Crazy Gang' – to give it a respectable provenance from the

Crazy Gang music-hall act. And for well over a year it continued to be called *Crazy People* – while BBC officials stumbled over the pronunciation of the mistrusted word and referred to 'the Go-ons' or even 'the Coons'.

The first of what became the Goon Shows – the title was officially adopted for the 22 June 1952 broadcast – was recorded in the lofty Aeolian Hall; later on the venue was the cosier Camden Theatre on Sunday evenings and it became fashionable for film and stage stars on their night off to drop in and sit among the ticket-holding audience. Eventually even Royalty was to come along. Those Sundays were Peter's happiest hours. As Dennis Selinger said, 'He'd have been content to climb into a time capsule and be sealed up in the Goon era.'

Harry Secombe's autobiographical sketches, published in 1975, *Goon for Lunch*, give a vivid impression of the way that anarchy was ingrained in the whole day's recording and behaviour of the performers at rehearsal, not just written into the script. The rehearsals already sound like the broadcast: 'As I enter the stage door ... I sing a burst of *Return to Sorrento*. There come cries of "It's Singo, the approaching tenor, folks," from Sellers, who is playing the bongos in a prone position, accompanying Milligan's frenzied piano playing. "Ah! The well-known danger to shipping has arrived. Ned of Wales is here." Milligan announces my arrival with a Naafi pianist's version of *We'll Keep a Welcome*. "They'll never take you back, Ned." I reply with a raspberry. "He's ad libbing again," says Spike. "Nurse, the screens at once." Bloodnok Sellers is now using the bongo drums as a pair of binoculars.'

Milligan later in the day insists that the sound of someone being hit in the face by a sockful of custard is not right and persuades one of the canteen ladies to cook him an egg custard, which he pours into his own sock and whacks against the wall for the sound effects men to record it. Some of the show's drollest moments could not be broadcast as they happened during the warm-up period, when the clowns would sit in with the band, horse around with instruments, debag each other and set the tone of hectic anything-can-happen-and-will expectation. No one could be in Milligan's company without catching his infectious zaniness. All the Goons had quick wits and the frenzied dashing around, from one microphone to another, encouraged the comic short-circuitry by which the jokes fused into a gigantic chain reaction.

Yet the differences between the clowns were as important as their congruities. Milligan and Sellers might behave like lunatic twins, but Spike realized early on that they were both essentially beings from different planets who shared the same orbit only by chance. 'Peter and I are like Gilbert and Sullivan. We love and hate each other at the same time. We have a completely opposite approach to what we want to do, but by hammering it out we come to some agreement. But it's hellish going. When we talk to each other over the phone there's always at the back of our minds the thought, "You're wrong and you bloody well know you're wrong." I'm deeper than he is. He takes things seriously, but in quite a different way. I think he's perfectly aware, too, of the hopeless state of *homo sapiens*, but he thinks – "What's the use?" He doesn't think deeper than that. I think humanity's a failure, but he doesn't care to think about that.' But these words were spoken well after the Goons had been launched. At the start of their relationship, they felt their way cautiously towards each other despite their spontaneous wisecracking. Sellers invited Spike to move in with his family at their East Finchley flat. He lodged there for six months, sleeping on the floor. Peg did not know what to make of the wild-eyed insomniac who babbled in tongues with a dementia that convulsed her son.

None of the characters later made immortal by the Goons was in that initial try-out. In fact the series of sketches comprising it was almost too well rounded and lacked the free-floating fantasy of later editions. There were skits, parodies and satires – send-ups of British institutions like the new BRM racing car (which collapsed upon being doused with champagne), or a BBC radio thriller like *Dick Barton – Special Agent* in which 'our heroes' get blown up by the atom bomb ('Quick, put your fingers in your ears') and a loony 'Quest' like the Tutankhamoun expedition which brought home conclusive evidence that 'The Pharaoh is dead.' But in the course of the Goon series, when each show was a Kafka-esque adventure like laying a telephone line to 14a Africa or sabotaging a haddock-stretching factory behind the Iron Curtain, Sellers began developing a range of voices to fill in Milligan's characters, the way he himself used mimicry to colour his personality. He based them on boyhood memories, war-time encounters and radio favourites.

Thus his Major Bloodnok, ex-Rajputana Rifles, decorated with the Military Cross for emptying dustbins during battle, was the voice of the Raj he had heard all round him in India infused by Milligan's hatred for the hang-over of Empire. Bluebottle was a reedy-voiced school swot from St Aloysius days. Grytpype Thynne, the arch-cad, was Sellers's take-off of suede-voiced George Sanders; Willum 'Mate' Cobblers, the timber merchant as thick as the furniture he sold, was the owner of a near-by store. Other Goon voices, as the critic Richard Mayne was to point out later, had origins in the pre-war radio shows: Milligan's ingenuous Eccles was reminiscent of ventriloquist Edgar Bergen's country yokel dummy Mortimer Snerd; Sellers's Henry Crun fluted like the inventor-cum-magician, in the Children's Hour serial *Toytown*. But all of them were distorted through the mouthpieces of their animators till they appeared as totally independent beings.

The public were quicker on the uptake than the conservative programme planners at the BBC imagined. The voices brought out the mynah-bird instinct in listeners that caused thousands of people – even, eventually, the heir to the throne – to imitate the Goons. They also recognized that at the heart of the characters, however eccentric their outlines, was a life-like truth. Hardly a single character Sellers developed then or later on the screen was without its roots in observable reality. This had a paradoxical effect on the Goons themselves. 'I wonder,' Secombe wrote later, 'how many people realize how near we have become in real life to the characters we played.'

But this was yet to come; Sellers is on record as declaring that he never knew how much his life would be changed when he took part in the broadcast on that Sunday in May 1951. As it happened, he had already taken what he considered a far more decisive step. He had got engaged to be married.

FOUR

He's Stolen The Film

Dennis Selinger was having trouble disposing of two spare tickets he had bought for the dinner-and-dance of the Water Rats, a show-business charitable organization, at the Dorchester Hotel in the winter of 1949. He decided to mix business with pleasure. 'Pete, it's time you got about socially and met people. You can make plenty of contacts at this kind of event. I'll introduce you around.'

Peter Sellers assented quickly, then said – surprisingly in view of his amorist ways – that he had no ready date. 'I'll see if I can fix you up,' said Selinger, and telephoned his own date, a nineteen-year-old Australian-born blonde called Anne Howe, whom he had known since she was fourteen. Anne Howe had been some years in England studying acting at the Royal Academy of Dramatic Art. She had changed her professional name to Anne Hayes, so as to avoid confusion with the already established actress Sally Ann Howes. Selinger, though not her agent, had been keeping a friendly eye on her. 'She had good looks and a shrewd mind and was very poised for her age.' He asked: 'Could you suggest a companion for Peter Sellers to take to the ball?' She suggested her friend June Marlowe.

'We all met for drinks before going on to Park Lane,' Selinger recalled. 'The minute Peter set eyes on Anne, I saw he was smitten – as quick as that! They never stopped looking at each other all evening. Poor June Marlowe had to make do with me. Never mind – she soon became Mrs Spike Milligan.'

Selinger noted a nervousness in Sellers whenever he met him during the next few weeks, and without too much trouble connected it with what Anne Hayes was confiding in him. Sellers was dating her regularly, but fearing that Selinger's heart would be broken if he got wind of their liaison. 'Finally, I couldn't stand Peter's evasiveness any longer. "Pete, she's never been my girlfriend," I said, "and she tells me she likes you very much. I'm delighted. Now stop all this acting – for once you don't do it very well – and let's all have a reunion dinner." '

Peg didn't take the news well at all. When Peter told his mother that he wanted to marry the girl, Peg said fiercely that she wasn't Jewish. Peter replied patly that this hadn't stopped *her* marrying Bill Sellers. She shifted tack. A wife would hold back his career. 'Give it a few months, Pete,' she pleaded, 'a year more won't hurt you both, if you really love each other.' In fact it was to be eighteen months between their engagement on 9 April 1950, and 15 September 1951, when Anne Hayes, aged twenty-one, became the wife of Peter Sellers, twenty-five, 'The Man of Many Voices,' as the papers inevitably called him, at Caxton Hall, Westminster. Peg's disapproval was overcome by apprehension for Peter rather than affection for Anne, for her son had begun to develop severe nervous depression as his emotions were caught in the two-way stretch between his mother and his fiancée. Matters came to a head one day when he telephoned home.

'Peg, I'm at Bedford – at the railway station. I'm feeling so low, I'm going to end it all. I'm going to jump in front of a train, Peg.'

Once again the Sellers family threw down whatever they were doing and dashed by car to Bedford railway station to find Peter sitting on the platform in a moody trance as the trains came and went around him.

'It might have made a difference had Anne been Jewish,' Dennis Selinger said. 'But frankly, I don't think so. It wasn't that Peg didn't think she was good enough for her son. She was relieved Peter had picked on a girl with a head on her shoulders, and a pretty one at that. She was simply afraid of losing him to a woman – any woman.'

The broadcasts of *The Goon Show* were now bringing the newly-married comedian such plentiful offers of work on the variety stage that he and his wife had the cash as well as the confidence to buy a £3,500 house on Muswell Hill, near where Peter had once lived with his parents. But Sellers's hatred of music-hall and its audiences hadn't abated. The cosy ease of weekly Goonery, playing to his fellow clowns without the chores of crowd-pleasing, now pushed him into some extreme demonstrations of his resentment. One of his appearances with Milligan and Secombe proved traumatic.

It was at Coventry Hippodrome, where the three Goons – not billed as such, for BBC copyright reasons, but well-known in such roles from the radio – were appearing as an acrobats' act called 'Les Trois Charleys', wearing white tights, red cloaks, leopard-skin drawers and gold headbands. Each of them, in addition, did an individual turn and Milligan's, in which he played some sour trumpet solos, drew catcalls from an audience that had no Christmas charity in their hearts for a man who they somehow sensed was hostile to them. 'They weren't yet educated in Goon humour,' Sellers said later. 'They couldn't always tell when we were gagging and when we were serious.' Milligan, who was feeling the stress of writing radio scripts for a bunch of variegated comics as well as the *Goon Shows*, seeking a new house for himself and his wife and not getting enough sleep on tour, stomped down to the footlights and yelled, 'You hate me, don't you?' The audience returned a storm-blast of 'Yes!'

Whereupon Spike, cut in two by this rejection as if it were a hail of bullets, fled down to his dressing-room, locked himself in and, when his fellow Goons broke open the door, was about to slip his head in a makeshift noose. It was a piteous cry for help. Sellers was badly shaken. The public humiliation of a friend, a man whose talents were underwriting his own growing reputation, demanded vengeance.

The next day he went on stage, scrapped his prepared act, to the consternation of the band, and staged a colossal show of contempt for that shabby beast called an audience which could be put through the ring at any fool's crack of the whip. Clad in his leopard-skin pants and wearing the thick horn-rims that had become a modest trademark of the outwardly conventional-looking Goon, he carried on stage a phonograph and set it on the small table already there. He bowed. Then in the tones of a BBC announcer, he said, 'Good afternoon . . . I'd like today to play you some *lovely* melodies. I myself have enjoyed them very much. I hope you will, too.' He started the phonograph, sat down and stared intently at the revolving disc . . . The bewildered audience first heard the strains of Wally Stott's orchestra playing *White Christmas*. When the last seasonable note had faded, Sellers applauded the disc. The audience, mystified, but docile, followed suit. Said Sellers later: 'I played the idiots three more of the tracks and each time the clapping got louder. Then I rose, bowed, and left the stage – to more applause. The manager was furious. "Why hadn't I been appearing 'as known'?" "Because," I said, "I've been entertaining them. They like it much better than my normal act. It's about their level. I'm bloody well not going to drive myself into a nervous breakdown for a bunch of morons. For all they care, I might have been appearing as 'unknown'."' All contractual hell broke loose – and Dennis Selinger was summoned by the next train to make the peace and salvage the booking.

'Peter told me, "Den, after what's happened to Spike, I'm through with this insanity. If I'm going to survive, it'll have to be as an actor on stage – or in films."'

70

Of course his resolution in this, as in so much else, did not hold. For one thing, there was too much money at stake. As well as the expenses of running a household, Peter had now developed expensive tastes in material things which a few nights' variety work helped pay for, in spite of the 'humiliation' involved.

'He'd occasionally telephone me in the early 1950s,' David Lodge recalled, 'and say, "Dave, how'd you like to do front man for us?" "Us" meant himself, Milligan, Bentine and sometimes Secombe. We'd take over a theatre, guarantee the "nut" [the break-even point at which, the house costs being met, the rest is box-office profit] and take sixty percent of the receipts for ourselves. Very lucrative, if the folks come. All this talk about Peter going through hard times is balls. Compared to most entertainers at the time, he was well off. The *Goon Shows* with repeats and other radio work and the occasional variety act would be bringing him £400 to £500 a week.' One would have to multiply that by five to allow for the inflation of later decades. Yet this was the time Sellers developed uncharacteristic worries about his financial future. Maybe it was the arrival in April 1954 of a baby son, christened Michael, which made him ask himself, superstitiously, what if it all stopped. It was in this baleful mood that he did an extraordinary thing – he wrote a begging letter. He had met a millionaire living in the tax haven of Jersey during his holiday-camp stint there. Now he pleaded with this man about the high cost of living, even telling him plaintively about the ruinous cost of running his car. (He concealed from this hoped-for benefactor the fact that he was well along the road to automotive extravagance, since he had begun buying a new car almost monthly.) The rich acquaintance was touched, but was no philanthropist. He wrote back: 'My advice to you is sell your car if it's costing you so much to put petrol in the tank.'

David Lodge said to him, 'You didn't really think he was going to send you money, did you?' But he had.

'When he was rolling in it, he'd be sure to overspend – and then balance the bank account by a kind of wishful thinking. He used to say that when he read Dickens, he wept – you can bet he never read about Micawber.'

His close friends also began to notice how the combative side of his nature was more frequently aroused by trivial incidents. Sometimes it wasn't obvious, unless one was used to reading the danger signals. David Lodge remembered doing a variety act with him in which Sellers started off as Sweeney Todd (impersonating Robert Newton's voice), suddenly and without explanation switched to mimicking Laurence

Olivier, who had just made his *Richard III* film and then, in the middle of that, veered into a 'private eye' routine based on television's *Dragnet*. 'The audience didn't know what the hell was happening. But it was Peter's way of demonstrating his continuing resentment of "these bloody places".'

On another occasion a couple of young dancers remarked to him that the orchestra conductor didn't like their act and had deliberately confused them with his accompaniment. The change in Sellers was frightening. He immediately sent for the conductor. 'How dare you behave to my brother and sister artists in this way!' he roared in a voice that could be heard outside the stage door.

Harry Secombe was disturbed by the suddenness with which this transformation could occur, even when it was literally 'in character'. 'Standing next to him on *The Goon Show*,' he wrote, 'I could never get over the way he could shrink himself for Bluebottle and then, seconds later, puff himself out for Bloodnok. It was almost frightening to see it happening.' His moods occasionally took on a complete transformation which had nothing to do with any role except the one in his imagination. Then he acted like a man possessed. 'You had to stick around patiently till the mood fell off him like a trance,' Selinger remembered. 'Once we were on the way to a television rehearsal. Peter hadn't shaved and was wearing a roll-neck sweater. A car cut into us. I suddenly heard a strange voice snarling "get him," and realized it was Peter. "Get the bastard!" I'm an even-tempered chap – in this business, if I weren't, I'd go dotty – but Peter insisted so fiercely that I put my foot down and my old Hillman roared off in pursuit. As we drew alongside the driver, Peter turned into a punch-drunk pugilist, rolled down the window, and began mumbling menaces, muttering threats to do terrible, unspeakable things to the other driver, who paled visibly, made a sudden turn and roared off down a street I'm sure he'd never meant to enter, just to escape. For the next twenty-five minutes, Peter kept up the act ... It really was unnerving.'

His wife Anne was finding out about his restlessness. He was an obsessional worrier, she discovered. Home for him was not a place to retreat to and relax with his new family – he was better with gadgets and machinery, she said, than looking after baby. He tired too quickly with children. Fatherhood appeared to be one role he had difficulty getting into. It was to remain so till the end of his days, perhaps because he himself possessed so many of those irresponsible drives that often make for enjoyment in childhood but have to yield to adult responsibilities. Peter in many ways remained a child at heart and in behaviour – it was a large part of his charm where women were concerned. 'Sellers married out of need,' said Theo Cowan, his public relations counsellor and life-long friend despite their occasional ruptures, 'but the girls he married found such needs attractive, even charming. A lot of his reactions to beautiful women were adolescent in their spontaneity and total commitment. He was emotionally twenty years younger than his chronological age, so he could identify with the feelings of young girls attracted to him better than a man who was as emotionally as mature as his years suggested he should be.' But what made him an enjoyable escort didn't provide any foundation for being a dutiful family man.

In these early years almost anything that had to do with films brought him running at top speed. The humblest chore was never too small. He was Humphrey Bogart's voice for a few lines of dialogue in *Beat the Devil* which director John Huston had to change for legal reasons when the star was unavailable. He mimicked a parrot in *Our Girl Friday* and at least six of the cast of a potboiler called *Malaga*. He even impersonated Winston Churchill's slurred and rolling oratory in an off-screen narration in the film *The Man Who Never Was*.

Even in *The Goon Show* he contrived to excel himself and, when Milligan was off ill for a few weeks, Sellers and Secombe did the broadcasts without him. Sellers, playing Spike's characters as well as his own, was sometimes talking to himself three times over.

One day, in the early 1950s, a friend telephoned to say he had got hold of some non-copyright Laurel and Hardy films, shorts they had made in the pre-talkie days. They needed dialogue to go with them. 'Peter was over the moon,' Graham Stark recalled. 'This was his chance to play a film role in sound while his two favourite clowns performed it in vision. He said to me, "You'd make a wonderful Ollie. I'm going to do Stan."' The three days they spent in a basement cinema recording newly-written 'dialogue' to the silent cavorting of the great clowns were among the happiest of Sellers's working life. To his death, he kept a picture of Stan Laurel in one or other of his several homes. Stark always thought it was Laurel's child-like side which touched something responsive in Sellers. Laurel, he noted, never wept when hurt physically – only when hurt emotionally, the way a child does. Sellers, too, had a child's instantaneous reaction to every unpleasantness – he either lost his temper openly or cried inwardly.

Sellers never consciously set out to become a straight actor. 'Straight' acting to him meant 'star' acting; this entailed playing yourself – or a part of yourself – a part you then standardized and repeated to give it a uniqueness that the public could, without effort, recognize and enjoy. Sellers was well aware that he didn't, in fact, have this 'star quality' in his own personality – he was not nearly as colourful as those roles *not* recognizable as part of himself which he played in his service masquerades or his vocal impersonations. But it is important to observe the stages he passed through before he formulated his desire to be a *character* actor.

He had appeared in a short comedy film entitled *Let's Go Crazy*, which he claimed had been made 'for about fifty pounds' in a basement in Wardour Street, where the film companies all had their offices, some time in 1950. He played a waiter and several of the guests in a nightclub. The first noteworthy feature film in which he appeared, *Penny Points to Paradise*, in 1951, was merely a way of using *Goon Show* characters (or near enough) in a plot that made simple sense, totally unlike the absurd antics of the radio broadcasts. Harry Secombe, as a simpleminded winner of a fortune on the football pools, hides the money in a seaside guest-house, where it's at the mercy of a suave counterfeiter and his stooge, played by Alfred Marks and Bill Kerr – both Grafton Arms *habitués*. Sellers played a wool-gathering major who might have been a vague cousin of the Bloodnok line. Within a year he was back on screen *as* Major Bloodnok in *Down Among the Z Men*, a caper about stolen atom secrets involving all four Goons. John Redway, then casting director at Associated British Picture Corporation, recommended the studio, on the strength of this film, to put all its comics under contract. The studio did not; and thus, in typical British fashion, lost a chance to corral the whole *Goon Show* talent for what might have been a hit series of comedies.

It was clear to Redway, who now had frequent meetings with him, that Sellers was eager for film stardom. 'He was hungry,' was how he put it. When Redway turned independent agent in 1953, the effect of his guidance was immediately evident. Sellers appeared in *Orders Are Orders*; and though his name was below the title, it was preceded by the distinctive 'with' used to denote a talent turning the corner into recognition. (The same credits announced 'Introducing Tony Hancock'.)

In this comedy about an American film unit infiltrating a British Army barracks, with predictable confusion, Sellers shared a scene with Bill Fraser, both playing private soldiers, and was supported by established comics like Brian Reece and Sid James as well as actors like Raymond Huntley, Clive Morton and Donald Pleasence. Graham Stark, recalling the film's preview, said: 'The people who'd been in it [Stark wasn't] were standing in the cinema foyer, all chattering in groups about themselves, the way actors will, when I suddenly said loud and clear, "You know the bugger who's stolen the film from you lot?" No one said anything, but it was crystal clear they all did. Peter didn't do anything in particular, except act. The rest of them were mugging hard enough to have a hernia.' Redway, too, discerned Sellers as 'the actor in a structure of knockabout comedy' and sharpened his focus on him. His career began to pick up speed.

It was just as well, for Sellers was now developing all the symptoms of a maniacal need to refresh the day – and soon it would be the hour – with constant novelty, regardless of expense. He entered Selinger's office one day, radiating the pleasure of a child opening his Christmas stocking, and heaped up all manner of camera equipment on the agent's desk. He had taken up photography, with Graham Stark as his mentor, and had been on a buying spree which made Selinger pale. 'How much is all this worth?' he demanded.

'About £1,500.'

'Pete, you can't afford it – you just *can't* at the moment.'

'I gave them a cheque,' said Sellers, as if that settled all debts.

'Pete, are you out of your mind? A cheque for that amount will bounce, then where will you be? It'll harm your career. The publicity it'll bring!' ('I was trying to teach him a lesson,' he added as he recalled the incident. 'You had to speak to him like a child.')

'What shall I do, Den?' asked the chastened camera buff, looking like a Stan Laurel who'd just had his nose tweaked.

'I phoned up the shop,' Selinger continued, 'and said, "When Mr Sellers bought all that equipment, he didn't know he was going abroad for a long period and it's inconvenient to take it with him. As it's never been used, would you mind taking it back? Perhaps something new will take his eye when he returns." Luckily, they agreed.'

Luckily, too, Sellers acquiesced. But the days were not too far ahead when any such clamp-down on his pleasures would lead to a tantrum and, usually, an instant severance of business relations.

He had also embarked on his life-long car-swapping mania. Anne found her head swimming as each month brought a new car – pronounced to be 'the perfect one this time' – to their doorstep. The first post-war car Sellers owned was a Rover 14. He traded it in after four weeks. Over the next twenty years some ninety cars passed through his hands, including a 2.5-litre Jaguar, a 3.8-litre Jaguar, an Austin 20/25, which he sold to Milligan, two Rolls-Royces, a Bentley Continental, a Mercedes 300SL, a Ferrari GT2–2, an Aston Martin DB41, a Bristol 407, two Cadillacs, two Buicks, a Bristol Viotti and an XKE Jaguar. At one time, when film roles necessitated commuting between studio and location, he considered adding an ambulance to his stable. After pondering the matter, he rented one. A car showroom in north London eventually had a man working exclusively for Sellers, scouting for cars he wanted, offering him new models on try-out terms, and disposing of those with which his love affair had waned. Contrary to what one might expect, he did not lose much financially: he wrote it off as a business expense. And he explained it all by an actors search for perfection in all things.

Actually there was sometimes a baser explanation. 'Once when we'd been to see Jon Pertwee in a stage show,' said Selinger, 'he looked at me over supper and said in his plaintive little voice, "Den, Den, Jon's bought a Rolls."

' "Forget it, you can't afford one yet."

'The next day, the phone went. "Den, Den, can you come round?" He was recording the Goons at the Paris Theatre. Outside sat a Rolls-Royce, all black, as long as a hearse, the sort a champion jockey would use to take himself to the races. "Pete," I said "it'll cost you a fortune to run, about seven miles to the gallon. You can't afford it." The sales people had opened up their showroom on a Sunday and he'd given them a cheque there and then, on the strength of his *Goon Show* reputation: he could now get all sorts of things on credit. They'd left it in this narrow street and when he got in to give me a spin, he couldn't turn it. He'd just passed his Institute of Advanced Motorists test, but no good – the car got jammed, it was so huge. It was there when I left, with Peter wondering what to do and a crowd gathering.

'At six o'clock that evening, the phone goes. "Den ... Den, I've sold it."

' "How much did you drop on it?"

' "I'll tell you ... tomorrow." '

Dennis Selinger had seen the signs that the variety stage, which had accounted for a large part of his bookings, was on the wane as television took more and more leisure time and money from the public. 'Peter wanted to get into films – and so did I. I saw him as the means to do it.' Selinger and Redway soon formed a partnership and, until different ambitions took them their separate ways, saw some of the best (and worst) of a client who was now about to cut himself out of the pack of current entertainers.

After playing a policeman's role in *John and Julie*, a sentimental comedy about kids running away from home to see the Queen at her 1953 Coronation, he was sent along by Selinger to read for the role of a punch-drunk boxer in Ealing Studios' production of *The Ladykillers*, in

1955. 'Frankly, we can't see him with a broken nose and cauliflower ear,' said the director, Alexander Mackendrick; but his associate producer, Seth Holt, suggested Sellers would be right for Harry, the retarded Teddy Boy among the gang of eccentric payroll robbers whom Alec Guinness assembled in a dear little old lady's guest-house while they plotted the raid. This was Sellers's only Ealing comedy, his first film of distinction – and a crucial encounter with Guinness.

He was later on – but not much later – to be called 'the next Alec Guinness'. At that time, however, he was still the apprentice in awe of a sorcerer whose shoes he must have been enviously aware he could have filled had the accidents of birth and opportunity been different. For they were much alike, except that Guinness was already a finely tuned instrument for acting, not just comedy. Sellers understood and admired the way he could 'become' someone else, turning a mild-looking man into a cadaverous mastermind in *The Ladykillers* with the addition of red-rimmed eyes, *Caligari*-like hair and rodent teeth out of the vampire classic *Nosferatu*. Sellers later confessed himself 'emerald with envy' at the creepy, leering voice which Guinness adopted.

Guinness gave him this advice: 'Never play the same kind of role twice over.' (Within a year he was to push the rule to extremes and play five different parts in one film.) But he was aware of another aspect of Guinness, divorced from his virtuosity as a quick-change artist of the flesh – or perhaps central to it. Guinness was the original 'man with no face' in the English cinema. Kenneth Tynan had already written – a year before this meeting – that Guinness 'looks unmemorable. Were he to commit a murder, I have no doubt that the number of false arrests following the circulation of his description would break all records.' Some of Tynan's other phrases and judgments might have been detached from Guinness and tied on to Sellers – especially when he was not acting, but facing interviewers' questions. 'Guarded and evasive ... he will communicate intimacy, but always from a considerable distance ... tethered to his own epoch.' Tynan's study helped define a public view of a very private Guinness. Sellers had read it (and in fact gave his copy to the present author). And by some process of envious osmosis, he began to absorb the critic's acute insights into the peculiar situation of being a personality without a recognizable persona. A very short time afterwards, Sellers's interviews – always more jokey than Guinness's, but essentially 'guarded and evasive' – begin to hint, then to insist, and finally to reiterate without end that he, too, had his own identity crisis, his own 'facelessness'.

But before this stage was reached, the encounter with Alec Guinness hardened Sellers's resolve to be something more than a comedian – to be a character actor. He realized that inside him, latent but ready to germinate, given the right roles, were talents akin to Guinness's – only Sellers had missed the fertilizing cinema tradition which had made Guinness's talents flower so splendidly – the Ealing comedies. They had established Guinness as the screen's most popular 'multiple personality'. But Ealing's sun of glory was setting. In a few years the studios which had nurtured Sir Michael Balcon's kindergarten of talent would be sold to BBC Television; even now the head of comic steam which had driven the great Ealing films like *Passport to Pimlico*, *Kind Hearts and Coronets* and *Whisky Galore* was dying down as inspiration faltered and the amiable, conservative, sometimes critical but essentially kind view of British society had to give way to social change that focused a sharper, more satirical light on post-war Britain. *Barnacle Bill*, in 1957, was the last 'pure' Ealing comedy – and the last one starring Guinness. Sellers had missed one cinema tradition – but he would not have to wait too long to be adopted by its successor, the Boulting Brothers' social satires, in which the apprentice would become the new sorcerer.

Anne was seeing less and less of him at home. He was appearing intensively in all the media. The *Goon*-type humour was being transplanted, with some success, to television; he had made a hit record called *I'm Walking Backwards for Christmas* (which sold over 100,000); he had a radio programme called *Finkel's Cave*; he was even doing provincial variety. In 1956 he had an income of over £23,000 and he moved his family to a £10,300 house in a fashionable Tory stronghold, Totteridge, North London, a few minutes walk from Milligan's home. Out of gratitude to the television goonery, *A Show Called Fred*, which was directed by Dick Lester, later to become the Beatles' favourite filmmaker, he renamed the house, which had been called St Neot's. It became St Fred's. The name 'Fred' was evermore to hold superstitious connotations for Sellers.

He was now consulting a two-guinea-a-time clairvoyant called Maurice Woodruff, who was to play a preponderant part in one of Sellers's least happy decisions a few years later. Woodruff encouraged him to think his career in films was about to explode – and in this he was certainly right, though whether he read the signs in the crystal or in the several cinema trade papers, where they were more immediately available, and at less cost than two guineas, is not clear. But Sellers, as usual, was pessimistic.

The Ladykillers, to everyone's surprise, had *not* been followed by further offers of film parts. Perhaps people felt *one* Alec Guinness was enough. 'Do you know what the powers of show-business call me?' he asked in an interview, early in 1956. 'That man who does the funny voices. Even now . . .' From now on his interviews with the Press illustrate the compulsive desire he had to be taken for a 'serious actor' – for a *character* actor, that is – even if it meant denying his celebrity as a Goon. 'I'm not a funny man off stage,' he said, in August 1956, one of the earliest mentions of what became an insistent refrain. 'I'm a serious person . . . I don't crack jokes . . . Don't call me a comedian.' In October of the same year, he was declaring himself 'tired' of the Goons, saying he had only agreed to the Goon-like *A Show Called Fred* in the hope that experience on the small screen would assist his ambitions on the large one. In December 1956, he essayed a television double: two more-or-less 'straight' roles in back-to-back playlets, as an old factory hand and a young bird-watcher respectively. The material was poor. 'His real ability as an actor remains untapped,' was the verdict of more than one critic.

What satisfied him more was his appearance in the Frank Launder–Sidney Gilliat comedy *The Smallest Show on Earth*, in 1957. The role of a sixty-eight-year-old projectionist in a flea-pit cinema which a young married couple have inherited was one that the makers at first couldn't see him in – surely a thirty-year-old couldn't straddle that yawning age-gap? Then they chanced to see Sellers made up as William 'Mate' Cobblers (born 1900, according to Goon genealogy) in the television show *Idiot Weekly*. After make-up tests, he got the part. Sellers characteristically referred his inventiveness with the old-timer's role back to Robert Donat's playing of the aged Mr Chips in the pre-war film. Donat had once been pressed into service by the youthful impersonator to woo his girl-friends; now he was the model for a comedian bent on proving his resourcefulness as a character actor cast as an old-age pensioner.

The film proved he was able to hold his own with two of the strongest character actors in the business – Margaret Rutherford and Bernard Miles – but as he *shared* the movie with them (and, as he complained, his scenes were the ones to be trimmed first in the cutting) it didn't prove the greatest show of solo virtuosity. But it brought work – in a flood.

The next film he made was the one that finally opened people's eyes. They saw the amazing breadth of his talent as a character actor. One has to grant Maurice Woodruff his bullseye, too. His 'prophecy' of an offer from a man 'with the initial "Z"' came true, though Mario Zampi and Peter Sellers were so clearly made for each other, it was hardly necessary to seek a paranormal connection. 'Peter Sellers establishes himself as the finest film comedian since Chaplin,' wrote Philip Oakes, reviewing *The Naked Truth* in the *Evening Standard*. The story of the blackmailing editor of a scandal sheet whose victims combine to bump him off, the movie offered Sellers a multiple role, including a chance (which he took with relish) to satirize the then *doyen* of the quiz-and-cash shows, Wilfred Pickles, who was transmuted into a hypocritical Scottish quizmaster, Wee Sonny McKay, who cosies up to the old folk on his TV show (a speciality of Pickles's radio *Have a Go!*) while, in his *alter ego* as a slum landlord, he screws the last bawbee out of them. In addition, Sellers played an ageing bureaucrat, a tweedy sportsman and a genial copper. The film couldn't sustain its comedy, but Sellers could. While the fun was faltering, he alone gave the impression that he could keep his own brand of virtuosity going forever.

Seeing *The Naked Truth* and relishing Sellers's dexterous impersonation was what convinced the young theatre director Peter Hall that here was a first-rate actor, perfect for the role of the wily, duplicitous Sultan of Huwayat, a small, impoverished Persian Gulf state and the setting for George Tabori's satire on power politics entitled *Brouhaha*. Hall's offer to Sellers of his first stage role coincided with his craving to break away from his radio and television image as the arch-Goon. He accepted and thus precipitated one of the best publicized episodes of theatrical misbehaviour in recent times, an affair which demonstrated how Sellers put his own standards before the customary compromises, and an episode which should have thrown warning shadows across the threshold of the new movie career that was now opening up for him.

The Sultan's role might have been made for Sellers, though in fact it was written with Charles Laughton in mind. Sir Peter Hall, now Director of the National Theatre, recalled that the humour of the play, in spite of being set in an Arab sultanate, was very Middle-European and Jewish: 'Peter's character was a kind of *shike* figure, a child-like anarchist bent on sending up authority, standing back and enjoying the fun. He proved a very confident performer – at first. He was quick to take direction, good at imposing himself on the material, very eager to contribute some inspired touches. But there was a strange reversal of form as the rehearsals went on and we got nearer the Brighton opening night. He didn't show up at the run-through. He missed the dress rehearsal. He confessed he'd got cold feet. The first night of the try-out didn't go well at all.'

Although London critics turned in mixed notices, it was soon clear that Sellers had scored a personal triumph. He wended a surrealistic way through the plot of the petty potentate inventing a local crisis which seems to threaten the international oil supply – although the place is so dry that even the anchovies lack oil – which brings the Great Powers running with their cheque books, just in time to let the Sultan settle his Mayfair gambling debts. Sellers's sad clown's face in coffee-tinted make-up seemed to set him apart from the action, while making a comment on mankind's inanities. He devised some first-rate bits of 'business', like nibbling the ear of the American lady ambassador, or apologizing for handing round the cocktails himself because it is the eunuch's day off. As these were what the public had come to know from his television shows, the play borrowed good-will enough to make it a financial success – for a time. The danger signs began to show early, however.

Peter Hall began to notice his star varying his act when they were still in Brighton: 'When we opened in London he was importing his own notions wholesale into the show. He would switch costumes. One night he made his entrance in hunting pink, which he'd hired from Moss Bros. On another, it was a morning suit fit for a wedding. He'd make his entrances from every direction, often surprising the cast, who'd have their backs to him. He ad-libbed dialogue – quite inventive stuff, but it would throw his fellow players.'

Dennis Selinger recalled that he even stood in the wings, filming the others on stage with an 8 mm camera. Some of his co-stars like Leo McKern and Lionel Jeffries had a case-hardened comedy approach to all this and could give as good as they got. But an imported American actor like Jules Munshin got very uptight. The truth was that Sellers was causing the play to fall to pieces by dissociating himself from what to him had plainly become a bore.

'What it proved was that he didn't want to be a stage actor,' said Peter Hall. 'He was such a quick, instinctive performer that, unlike most actors, he didn't want to master, standardize and refine his performance – he wanted to change it, give himself problems to solve. The result was a daily nightmare for the rest of the cast. No one knew for sure what any particular night would bring. The Press got wind of what was happening and began reporting Peter's "indulgences". Such publicity can only pay off for a short time. A play that was always in the news because of Peter's conduct (or misconduct) soon became a different kind of joke from the one the author had written and what started off as a commercial success began to turn into an artistic and then into a financial disappointment. In short, he had turned the play into a one-man *Goon Show*.'

One night he returned, as he put it, 'sloshed' from Alec Guinness's cocktail party at the Carlton Tower Hotel, given to celebrate his knighthood, and as soon as he got on stage and began, as he said, 'talking the audience into the play, I realized what a lot of impedimenta I had in my mouth. So I put it to them fair and square. "I'm sloshed," I said, "but I know my lines. I may not be able to say them all. But do you want me to carry on – or will I get the understudy in?"' This was unrehearsed Goonery all right. The audience roared its appreciation – and he stayed and played. The performance wasn't noticeably affected, but the management was furious. Indiscipline in an actor is the cardinal sin of any stage company.

Sellers's maverick behaviour continued. One night, while dancing the tango in the play, he overshot the footlights and fell in among the orchestra. 'Is that a new scene they're working into the show?' asked David Lodge, who was present. Anne Sellers had to drive her stunned husband home. From Australia, where he was working, Spike Milligan cabled: 'YOU DON'T THINK THAT ORCHESTRA PIT GOT THERE BY ACCIDENT, DO YOU?'

The showdown came in early December. 'The truth is,' Sellers was quoted as saying, 'I'm giving perhaps only two good performances a week now.'

Privately, Peter Hall sympathized: he was an advocate of plays-in-repertory and knew how performances, repeated for as long as the commercial run ordained, could get ragged and threadbare. But that wasn't how the management saw it. Pulling their forces together, they fired a broadside on 4 December 1958, said to be unprecedented in the English theatre. Four terse, public paragraphs rammed it home to Sellers that he had undertaken to 'appear at all performances and perform ... in a diligent and painstaking manner and ... play the part as directed by the manager'.

Any attempt to impose authority on him brought Sellers out in fighting mood. Significantly, one of his most celebrated creations, William 'Mate' Cobblers, was a figure he used for target practice, since this commissionaire-type had a set of catch-phrases which had at one time or another put his impersonator's teeth on edge: 'You can't park here,' or 'I spent four years fighting for this country,' or 'Two years in the Army would do 'em good.' When *Brouhaha*'s publicity manager, commenting on the statement, injudiciously referred to Sellers's 'conduct', the star exploded in wrath. 'Conduct! What does he mean – *conduct*? He was warrant officer in my RAF lot when I was A.C. plonk. Well, mate, we're all civilians now.'

A week later *The Stage* issued an edict of excommunication. 'Mr Sellers, in all fairness to the theatre, the management, and public,' it pontificated, 'should refrain from appearing in stage plays in future.'

Seldom has advice been so swiftly taken – so tenaciously adhered to. Sellers left *Brouhaha* at the first contractual opportunity, in February 1959, and never again was he to appear in a role behind the footlights.

Peter Hall said, 'He was a creature of the modern media. Theatre was all wrong for him. He always said he wanted to do something else in the theatre, but I never believed he really did. If he had, however, I'd have gone to see it – though I'd have gone on the first night.'

Another separation, however, had occurred slightly earlier, which testified to Sellers's mercurial temper and ruthless, self-centred protectiveness, as well as to the massive injections of confidence he required from others.

John Redway, present at the play's try-out in Brighton, went round to his dressing-room afterwards. 'There were all his mates, saying how terrific he'd been, how wonderful it was. Peter said to me in a low voice, "Johnny, I trust you. Come away from this mob. Tell me what you really think." ' Redway told him. The show was all over the place and he himself had gone over the top. 'He said quietly, "I knew it wasn't right – thank you." ' They went on to a party in the half-furnished house which Sellers had rented for the Brighton run and sat drinking until the early hours. Later that day Redway took a call from London. It was one of Sellers's friends. 'Johnny,' said the man. There was an embarrassed pause, and then, 'Peter's asked me to get in touch with you. He wants you to know he's decided to leave the agency. From now on, you won't be representing him.'

CHAPTER FIVE

Who Am I?

John Redway took the news of Sellers's defection philosophically. He already knew a lot about his client and suspected he had never really emerged from a childhood where a loving mother had decreed he must have every attention. The first chill breath of criticism – however well intentioned – withered his confidence in himself and brought the candid critic a counterblast of resentment. Others, too, would soon have to learn the lesson that the best way of fighting such childishness was not by opposition, but dissimulation. Redway bided his time. Actors were prodigal sons, anyhow, and liked nothing better than returning to the fatherly fold.

As it happened, Sellers had severed himself from Redway just when the agent had done him one of the best turns of his career. He had already got Sellers roles in a couple of minor comedies – in *tom thumb* he was a slapstick Oliver Hardy-type to Terry-Thomas's Stan Laurel; in *Up the Creek*, an Ulster-accented crew member almost too realistic for a nautical romp. These films kept his name in the credits without stretching his talents in the parts. Then came the day when Redway telephoned director-producer John Boulting and begged this half of the Boulting twins, John and Roy, to look at a sketch in which Peter was appearing that night on television.

'John,' he promised, 'this man's acting material, not a comic with the gift of voices.'

Now the Boultings had good reason to respect Redway's judgment. Some years earlier, when he was their casting director, he had urged them to look at a girl he had 'found'.

'We did so,' John Boulting recalled ruefully, 'and found something wrong for the camera in every angle and feature of her face – eyes too big, mouth too wide, nose too small. As we described her to a very disappointed Redway, she sounded a proper freak. She was, of course, Audrey Hepburn. This time we decided to pay more attention.'

John saw Sellers do a six-minute sketch as a sarcastic schoolmaster, wearing mortar-board and gown, no other make-up, and, incidentally, unaware that the Boultings had been told of his act. 'We could see what we were getting, and he looked ordinary enough. But the way he played – acid-tongued, very incisive. Brilliant! No need of a funny voice, either. As I recall, his voice sounded rather like Alec Guinness's.' John Boulting telephoned Roy, who had put his faith in a good dinner in Soho rather than a playlet on the box.

'Roy, this fellow Sellers is a marvellous actor. Redway was right.'

There and then they put Sellers under a five-year, non-exclusive contract, which meant he was free to accept roles in other people's productions, provided the time so used was added on to his contract with them. 'It's worth £100,000,' Sellers announced, duly awed. To the Boultings, it brought inimitable brilliance and endless trouble.

The pair of film-makers had a long, distinguished line of films behind them, including tough social criticism like *Fame is the Spur* and *The Guinea Pig*; the best adaptation till then (some would say to this day) of a Graham Greene novel, *Brighton Rock*; and a post-war run of relaxed, good-humoured but well-aimed satires on the legal profession, the Army, or red-brick campuses in such comedies as *Brothers in Law*, *Private's Progress* and *Lucky Jim*. They were a masterful pair, with a reputation for both guile and honesty, and they soon saw what they were taking on in Peter Sellers. Even so, the extent of his egocentricity was to appal them. 'A man,' said John, 'with an infinite capacity for sucking people dry.' 'A man,' said Roy, 'of immense dependence seeking ruthlessly, by any means, to establish his independence and pre-eminence.'

They were the earliest and shrewdest evaluators of the ambivalent role which Peg still played in Peter's professional life despite his marriage to Anne, a woman whom both brothers agreed had been prepared to sacrifice everything for her husband, including her own career, without gaining any proportionate gratitude. They quickly perceived that Sellers was more wilful than ever in resisting anyone whom he suspected of trying to dominate him. 'It is commonplace to say he loved his mother,' said John. 'He did, of course; he also resented her in small, not easily quantifiable ways. I remember we were all together one day and Peg said to her husband, "Bill, go and play Mr Boulting that piece we used to bring the house down with." Bill went and sat down at the piano with a great sense of doom and played a sub-Ivor Novello piece, of tremendously *ersatz* sentimentality, which he had composed himself. When he was through, Peg asked, "Isn't that just wonderful, Mr Boulting?" Her self-assertiveness prevented her seeing the expression on Peter's face at that moment. It was one of utter misery. He recognized only too well his mother's total lack of taste. Bill had been the lucky survivor of no talent. Peg was the driving ambition which fastened on her son. Peter was the boy who carried a load on his soul from childhood – and woe betide anyone who added to it. All the hostility he couldn't bring himself to work off on Peg would be directed at the outsider.'

But the Boultings soon learned to balance this private view of their new acquisition with unbounded admiration for his creative powers. In particular, they discovered how brilliant he was at starting a characterization from scratch and bringing it roaring to life within a few seconds.

They had just completed the script of their satire on Foreign Office diplomats, *Carlton Browne of the F.O.*, and it seemed the perfect chance to try Sellers out in a role, not unlike his *Brouhaha* success, as the double-dealing Premier of a cut-price British colony. Maybe it was because both brothers had mingled their genuine appreciation of his talent with cautionary advice that he still had to learn to be something more than a comedian, but Sellers at first proved surprisingly hesitant at 'getting' the character. It was as if he sensed the vaulting bar had been raised a couple of quality notches – and taking it in his Goonish stride wouldn't do any more. It was Roy Boulting who accidentally provided him with the solution that was to be the basis of all his finest comic performances – a basis in flesh-and-blood reality.

'This Levantine Prime Minister – I just don't understand the character, Roy,' Sellers said dismayingly – and, to Roy's impatient nature, irritatingly – when they met in King's Road, Chelsea, just as shooting was about to start.

Roy Boulting knew that Jeffrey Dell, the Boultings' favourite screenwriter, had based the character on Filippo del Guidice, the Machiavellian Italian entrepreneur who had promoted some of the finest British films of the period, including Olivier's *Henry V* and *Hamlet*, productions which required infinite persuasion rather than the prospect of instant profit to find backers with the ready cash. 'As well as I could, I gave Peter my impression of "Del" and, within two minutes, on the pavement, he proceeded to improvise dialogue and put on an act as a man he'd never seen which was more "Del" than "Del" himself.'

Terry-Thomas was the star turn in the movie, fluting out each asinine utterance as the Envoy Extraordinary with a sweetness that wouldn't make a candle flame gutter. But Sellers, as a politician of *fondant* duplicity, won his measure of praise and the Boultings lost no time in kindling his enthusiasm for the part they were writing especially for him in their next film. According to John, he was 'over the moon' at the prospect of playing Fred (that lucky name!) Kite, the trade union leader and factory floor's abominable 'No'-man, in a satire on British management and labour practices entitled *I'm All Right, Jack*. The Boultings sent him the script by special messenger. And with only the briefest of pauses, it came back as quickly – Sellers had turned it down.

The Boultings were incredulous – then furious. Didn't he trust their judgment? Or didn't he trust his own ability when it came to playing a role that merged with the social texture of the satire instead of having a comic frame put round it? They knew it was the latter when Sellers explained he'd read the script the whole way through and 'couldn't find the laughs ... the gags'. But this was only an excuse. 'He couldn't believe the script was funny,' said John Boulting, 'because he couldn't yet "see" the character. And whenever that happened, he got very insecure.'

John Boulting had him down to his country house one Sunday for 'a working supper'. 'I determined to be at my most insinuating, not to say insidious – subtly, patiently undermining all his objections.' But these grew as the night wore on and finally midnight came and went. Sellers desperately needed a marathon effort in confidence-building so that he would believe he could act the part. Sultans and Prime Ministers were simpler figures of fun; Fred Kite was outside his experience and, he feared, beyond his capacities. He kept on hedging, by saying it wasn't a big enough role. 'Peter, I grant you that,' John Boulting said, infinitely patient with him. 'It is not; but it is the one that will get most attention if you play it.' Eventually, at 1.30 a.m. on Monday morning, Sellers said, 'All right, let me do a test.'

'He said it with what we came to know all too well as one of his famous "resigned" expressions – a look of expectant martyrdom mingled with one of impending anger if he were proved right,' said John.

Roy added, 'When Sellers wore his "resigned" expression, then you had to watch out.'

After two dozen suits had been tried on at Berman's, the theatrical costumiers, the ideal one was found for Kite. It was constricting like the Marxism he espoused, yet baggy like the sloppy way he conducted his off-the-peg dialectic. The jacket didn't fit properly on his backside. Sellers already felt a little happier – he was glimpsing the externals of the character by putting them on his own back. In creating his film roles, he always worked from the outside in – the opposite of Guinness, who created an interior life before, as it were, drawing his skin round it. What Sellers didn't know at this time was that the Boultings had based the Kite character on a shop steward they knew well at the studios, sometimes to their cost. A diehard in the Electrical Trades Union, one of the most Leftward leaning in the business, this man looked sublimely innocent until he started going by the rule book – then he became a devil.

There was a great deal of industrial strife in Britain around that time. The petty bosses of the shop floor, with their sub-literate brand of 'union-speak', seemed never off the television screens; and Sellers had plenty of good visual 'copy' and verbal infelicities to record on tape, blend together and come up with a proletarian accent so coincidentally like the real Kite that, said John Boulting, 'had you shut your eyes, you would have imagined him standing at your elbow'. Sellers had his hair cut short, back and sides, the way he had seen his hated warrant officers in the services wear it: he gave himself a Hitler moustache. That was all the make-up he wore; but somehow his face seemed to change shape physically, becoming thinner-lipped, bug-eyed, and thick-skulled. Something, though, still eluded him. The characterization didn't snap completely into place till he found the walk – a wooden waddle, slightly robot-like as if Kite had been wound up with a key in his back to continue along the lines of his ideology regardless of what obstacles lay in his path.

'We looked in the dressing-room and hardly recognized him,' said Roy Boulting. 'It was another man entirely.'

The screen test was a two-minute scene in which Kite hectored the submissive workers and interrogated one of them, the boss's nephew, played by Ian Carmichael. As the Boultings were saving their pennies for the production, Carmichael wasn't used in the test. 'Peter played the scene with an assistant director filling in for the absentee, and towards the end I saw him begin to wilt,' John Boulting said. 'The trouble was, no laughter from the floor – for of course everyone kept deathly quiet while we were shooting, and while we had been rehearsing, the union members in the crew had been going about their business without bothering to listen. Peter was losing his confidence. I shuddered inwardly. As he finished, he stood there lamely, looking anxiously at the camera.

'Suddenly there was a gale of laughter, a round of applause from the workers who *had* been listening this time round and were savouring something they'd never dreamed of hearing – their own shop stewards turned into recognizable figures of outrageous fun. Peter got his confidence back in a flash.'

Said Roy Boulting: 'And this is an extraordinary coincidence: it also happened that, as we were filming, a seven-man union delegation was waiting to take issue with us on some perfectly petty point or other, led by the very man Peter was brilliantly taking off. Of course they completely failed to recognize themselves – or their leader – in his performance. They even joined in the applause. That little incident confirmed Peter's wavering faith in our ability to judge what was funny – and what was best for him. It was an inestimable advantage for the time it lasted – worth all the trouble of the test.'

But the Boultings noticed a somewhat disconcerting feature of that day's 'discovery' of Fred Kite – and the way in which the character grew in the actual shooting. They noticed how eerily the transformation stuck to Sellers even when he was off the set. He would walk to the studio canteen for lunch exactly like Kite leading his yes-men across the factory floor, and eat his food the way he imagined Kite did, holding his knife and fork the way Kite might, making table-talk of wondrous pomposity and pathetic ignorance the way he 'heard' Kite doing so. He wasn't Peter Sellers any longer.

Sellers always attributed to this phase in his career his discovery of that weird feeling he had, while playing many subsequent roles, of being taken over by the part – of being 'possessed'. It was as if by realizing the latent powers of performance, he had released something – or someone – that was just waiting to be summoned to creative and sometimes combative life by such a spell. Sellers was frequenting several mediums at this time, in 1959, as his burgeoning career presented him with manifold decisions he would rather have resolved for him by fatalistic 'resignation' than make for himself by the customary show-business methods of self-interest. (Self-interest could come later, on the cynical principle that once the contract was signed, then was the time to start the negotiating.) Maurice Woodruff, whom he was seeing every few days, had been joined by Estelle Roberts, a medium he turned to in the hope of contacting the late Larry Stephens, his friend and ex-*Goon Show* writer. The attempt in this case was fruitless. But the experience it gave Sellers of contacting the deceased became very relevant indeed to his film-making and eventually central to his life. The uncanny feeling that the medium was 'possessed' by those wanting to make their presences felt from 'the other side' helped Sellers define his own curious and rather frightened reaction to the characters he created. He came to see himself as a form of medium – as if the film characters had entered his body, transfusing his personality so powerfully with their own that they took him over. From that it was to be just a short jump in credulity to the point where he convinced himself that these were not simply fictitious characters, the offspring of some screenwriter's imagination – they were 'lives' that he himself, whoever *he* might be, had lived at other times, in other places, under other names. Acting, in short, was a process of past-life recall.

From the time of *I'm All Right, Jack* dates Peter Sellers's tireless refrain, echoed in interview after interview, that he feels he is living two simultaneous but separate lives while he is acting in a movie. One is his own life: the other, the character's. He left interviewers in no doubt about which life had more kick to it, to the extent that the 'real Peter Sellers' scarcely existed. This was going one better than Alec Guinness. Tynan may have called Guinness 'faceless', but he never declared him to be a non-entity. Sellers held this conviction sincerely, tenaciously and aggressively for the rest of his life. It was perhaps the unrecognized cause of more than one otherwise inexplicable dispute with film-makers, who could not see that the star they had hired at a collossal fee had in him, unpaid but more than willing to do the work, a separate 'life' almost ready to take over the movie as well as the man.

Sellers used to discuss with sympathetic friends what he claimed was the involuntary possession of him by 'tenants' who couldn't be dispossessed until the film role ended. One of these friends was the Rev. John Hester, later Vicar of Brighton, and at that time Vicar of St Anne's, Soho, and counsellor to many theatrical people through the Actors' Church Union. 'He had a great wish to know where we were all headed,' said Canon Hester, as he now is – a quest that had obvious bearing on where we all came from – or where his 'past lives' had been all the time. 'His fascination with life after death had no morbid undertones to it. But it was central to his personality' – and increasingly to his work. Film producers, however, were not all as scrupulous as a man of the cloth – who was soon to attempt Sellers's conversion to Christianity – and there is little doubt that some of them, in the years ahead, made profitable use of their star's hankering for spiritual affinity with the characters he played, by submitting ideas or scripts that had been cleared with whichever clairvoyant had found Sellers's favour at the time. 'He began living his life by omens and auguries,' Dennis Selinger said. 'I'd get the trick of calling Maurice Woodruff early in the day and finding out if it was a "favourable" one or not to discuss business. If Woodruff wasn't in, I'd ask later, "If you're such a good fortune-teller, why weren't you there when I telephoned?" We all had to find the means of talking Peter round his superstitions – some did it more benevolently than others, some more profitably.'

Although much perplexed by the conviction that he was 'taken over' by the character, Sellers soon appreciated the considerable advantages, even protection, this could bring him. It was early in 1959 that he began claiming, as Thomas Wiseman reported in the *Evening Standard*, that 'there's no such person as Peter Sellers'. This is one of the earliest interviews on the theme that Sellers reiterated, literally hundreds of times, to the media in the years ahead. 'I have no personality as such of my own,' Sellers is quoted as saying. 'Max Bygraves is Max Bygraves. But who am I? I don't exist. With me as myself, I might be some third-rate thing Carroll Levis [the talent spotter] dug up. I can't move; I can't talk; I'm a very odd bod. I only exist as the various characters I create. They are more than me.' Wiseman added, 'The only problem is that in the process of these elaborate masquerades, his own personality got lost among the masks.'

One is astonished at the accommodating credulity of the media over the next twenty years as Sellers pitched them essentially the same metaphysical line. Yet the notion of the mask that sticks to the wearer has a liveliness which yields 'good copy' – copy, moreover, which a journalist could personalize, yet which, by its very nature, shielded Sellers from queries that might have been more embarrassingly personal if directed at his private life. To be accepted at faceless value was intensely comforting, even though the independent 'lives' led by the characters he played added to the disturbance already apparent in his personality.

The Boultings always believed that Sellers knew only too well who he was and disliked facing what that knowledge brought him. They began to detect a growing peculiarity that quickly became the touchstone of his personal relationships. This was his habit of intuitively reading an expression he had caught, perhaps only momentarily, on someone else's face and invariably interpreting it in a negative way as something inimical to himself. Sometimes the unfortunate individual didn't need to be present. 'He would keep you up half the night on the telephone', said Roy Boulting, 'then when you yawned out of sheer fatigue, it would be interpreted as an unfriendly attitude. It got to be a killer, his "intuition". Even to say "Good-bye" first might be read as a wish to sever the relationship, never mind end the phone call. Homage always had to be paid.'

John Boulting was dining one New Year's Eve with Bill Wills, an accountant who had become Sellers's business manager after his break with John Redway. 'Wills said to me, "Peter's a little unhappy at the moment."

' "About what?" I asked.

' "Well, at Christmas he received the most extravagant presents from everyone in the industry. He was a bit surprised he got nothing from you or Roy. Not that he'd want me to mention it, of course."

' "Of course, Bill," I said. "But it is not our custom to deliver goods to those who already seem so well endowed with them and with something more important than worldly items – with their own talent. We received nothing from Peter this Christmas, and we expected nothing. All we might have wished for, we had already got when we directed him in our film." '

The reviews of *I'm All Right, Jack* certainly warranted the Boultings' gratified delight. 'I saw a great British clown shed his comic mask and become an actor to be reckoned with,' Leonard Mosley wrote in the *Daily Express*. 'It is Peter Sellers who gives the film its touch of distinction. Where all the rest are just playing for laughs, he is playing for the harder and more rewarding kind of humour – the kind that comes from observation of the way people really behave.' Previous Boulting comedies had poked fun at timeless institutions. This was their first to deal with a red-hot issue – unions versus management – and Sellers was the hammer which smote that issue into the memorable shape of Fred Kite. His performance was so rich and independent that it could exist without the rest of the film around it. All robot self-importance, grinding up ill-digested union maxims, woozy with misplaced sentiment for the Soviet Union – 'all them cornfields and ballet in the evening' was a line which broke Sellers up into giggles so frequently that thirty-eight takes, or half-a-day's work, were needed to complete the scene – he stands ready to do his duty before God and history. Yet Sellers made him a pathetically fallible human being. He was a type so durable in British life that even in the run-up to the 1979 General Election, BBC Television prudently cancelled a screening of *I'm All Right, Jack* lest the truth of Sellers's performance imperil the bipartisanship enjoined on the network at election time. Like the title of the film, the character became a catch-phrase for all that was wrong with British industry. Sellers gave film-goers the means of ventilating their sense of grievance against the growing power of union despots in the most injurious yet healthy fashion – by laughing at them.

'The Boultings speeded up everything for Sellers,' was Dennis Selinger's verdict. 'He couldn't have been kept down. People now knew what a gifted comic he was. They showed him to be an extraordinary actor – and put international opportunity his way.'

When the film opened in New York in the spring of 1960 it was lauded by the American critics. Paul Beckley of the *Herald Tribune* saw Sellers as 'one of the most accomplished actors of our time [with] an unerring instinct for the subtlest nuance of character'. And *Time*, not always the quickest to play the annunciating angel where British talent was concerned, declared him to be 'suddenly revealed as the most brilliantly ironic actor ... since Alec Guinness, [whom] he emphatically transcends'.

Yet it would be wrong to consider *I'm All Right, Jack* as the film which introduced Sellers to the Americans and started the Hollywood production machine on its quest for this transcendent British talent to gobble up. Before he appeared in the Boultings' comedy, Sellers had already made a film aimed successfully at the American market. *The Mouse That Roared*, directed by Jack Arnold and produced by Walter Shenson (later to produce the Beatles films), was made under the aegis of Carl Foreman's independent company operating through the British end of Columbia Pictures. It was a cosy comedy of the Ealing pedigree in which the petty European duchy of Grand Fenwick unilaterally declares war on the United States with the object of surrendering and coming in for lots of post-war American aid – essentially the *Brouhaha* stratagem over again. And Sellers played three parts. In one he was the duchy's wily Prime Minister, 'in the beard of Mephistopheles and the accents of Macmillan', as Paul Dehn put it in the *News Chronicle*. In the second he was the Grand Duchess Gloriana, a *grande dame* 'majestically dead to contemporaneity' who sends her regards to the US President – 'and to dear Mrs Coolidge, too'. In the third he was the commander-in-chief of Grand Fenwick's army, a shy youth fumbling his love affair with Jean Seberg. Only here did he falter since, as Dehn shrewdly observed, 'a shy character cannot convincingly be played by an actor who is shy at revealing his shyness'.

The film was irritatingly smug in its conviction that small is loveable and big nations will lay down their arms if an appeal is made to their better natures. But it shrewdly gauged the extent to which Americans liked to have their better natures appealed to, and its marketing in America was, for once, responsive to its whimsical character. It was sold carefully, nursed along for seven months at a central New York cinema while word of mouth spread its merits into the middle-class suburbs. By the end of 1960 it had been seen in over 8,000 American cinemas – and until the *Pink Panthers* came along, it held the box-office record as the most profitable film in proportion to its cost that Peter Sellers ever made. He was paid under £5,000 for it – but it made him known in America. With *Mouse*, he delivered his calling card: with *Jack*, he made his presence felt.

The Boultings paid him £5,000 for *Carlton Browne of the F.O.*, and £7,500 for *I'm All Right, Jack*. 'Quite good money for those days,' they said later. 'Don't forget, we taught him a lot, too – about the discipline film acting required, as against the inventive camaraderie of the Goons. At this stage of his career it was still necessary to indicate to him, when he had devised some new foible for Kite, that what was funny in itself was not necessarily in character – and persuade him to moderate it or drop it.'

Success had its own moderating effect on one of Sellers's resentments. One day, soon after the word had got out about his performance, John Redway's switchboard girl announced that 'a Mr Sallis' was on the line. In later years such an error on the part of an associate's junior employee could (and did) lead to an instantaneous severance of business relations. But Sellers was there to heal the breach with the humility of a man of restored confidence.

But almost as if he were convinced it would never last, he was signing to do films at breathless speed. Into Redway's office suite, so as to be near this precious client, moved producer Monja Danichewsky, an ex-Ealing hand, who set up *The Battle of the Sexes*, a vehicle artfully designed to exploit the American fondness for 'little British comedies'. Based on a James Thurber story, *The Cat Bird Seat*, it cast Sellers and Constance Cummings as, respectively, the meek old Scottish accountant in an Edinburgh cloth firm and the bustling female efficiency expert out to beat the dust from the company. His attempt to murder her recalled *The Ladykillers* too closely for comfort. Directed by Charles Crichton, also ex-Ealing, the film made no splash of its fun, but doled it out in small, constant tots. Sellers was likewise notable for underplaying. He sank Fred Kite's armour-plated, pop-eyed *caudillo* of the shop floor untraceably into the *persona* of a sad man with a sadder moustache and a pancake-flat cap whose accents sounded as natively Scotch as the creak of a whisky cork. He got nearly £9,000 for the role – and a trip to America in April 1960 to spend two weeks promoting *The Battle of the Sexes* and *I'm All Right, Jack*, which were both playing on Broadway. He took with him Graham Stark for the companionable security he offered in a country he had visited only once before, and then briefly, and it was well he did so – or he might not have stayed the fortnight.

For Sellers found he disliked America with an intensity that surprised all who knew him and who had imagined he would be in his element. After all, it was quite a beachhead: two Broadway movies, a disc of comic monologues almost ready for release, the *Goon Shows* being broadcast on a New York radio station and quite the fashionable thing to listen to. What went wrong?

As Sellers entered Hampshire House, where one of the two film companies paying for the trip had a publicity representative waiting to greet him, he heard the remark which the man tossed to the receptionist not quite *sotto voce* enough – 'The property has arrived.' Sellers instantly bristled. He was a perfectionist, not a property; an artist, not an artifact! His insecurity in a strange land may have caused him to bridle quicker than usual, but the harm was done. The going was rough after that. His sense of offence was compounded by what he read in the papers of the purge then being conducted against another great British comedian, Charlie Chaplin, already in self-imposed exile in Europe, but now to be denied his place among those premature immortals whose names were to be set in brass in a 'Walk of Fame' along Hollywood Boulevard. The news that he would not be there to be literally walked over might have made Chaplin smile cynically – but it made Sellers fume.

'Chaplin is a very great artist,' he snapped, 'and to hell with politics!'

Somehow the indignity to Chaplin tied in with the slighting reference to himself. From such an accidental conjunction came a good deal of the pent-up resentment he manifested later against Hollywood and all he fancied the film capital stood for.

Perhaps it also explains why, on the rebound from this grating encounter, he performed so many old-fashioned Goon-about-town antics, posing for Stark's camera (incorporated eventually in a valuable publicity spread in *Esquire*) as a variety of absurdist characters. It was really very hick stuff, trading on clichés abandoned by Americans decades before, such as the coronet and ermine cloak he wore ('working clothes back in the Mother Country') while he knighted New York cab drivers, or his satire on the Hathaway shirt man, whom he impersonated with one black eye-patch 'because I felt two would be overdoing things'. His happiest notion, nearest in spirit to the Goons' logic, was standing on skis, goggled and toggle-capped, and preparing to launch himself down the 'slopes' of Grand Central Station's steps – 'because they're there,' as he explained, impudently borrowing the explanation of those who attempted Everest. He later became somewhat ashamed of a study of himself in Stetson, sun-glasses and a tangle of cameras, clenching a huge cigar in his teeth and a less explicable giant display carton of Colgate toothpaste behind his back – and confiding it was his idea of how a New Yorker merged with his background.

Not a happy visit. He was glad to regain the Old English background of the *Queen Elizabeth* where he and Stark, like entranced children, enjoyed the full gamut of nostalgic ocean pleasures, the beef tea, tartan rugs, *chaises longues* and deck quoits: a little like being in a floating time capsule. For five days he was relaxed and in such good spirits that he scarcely minded being co-opted on the spot to play along with the night-club band, where he tossed up the drum sticks with éclat, caught them with a flourish and cried, 'See how my hands never leave my wrists.'

He arrived back in England in good spirits. And why not? A week or two later, in mid-May, 1960, he was at Victoria Station meeting the cross-Channel boat-train and a woman he had never dared believe would ever inhabit the same cinema screen as himself – for goddesses didn't mix with mortals, did they? Yet there she was setting solid foot on the *Golden Arrow*'s platform as he advanced timidly to meet her. The star of his next film – Sophia Loren.

CHAPTER SIX

In Love with Sophia

Peter Sellers had returned home from his American trip in the spring of 1960 to more than a new film and a co-star of a kind he had never had before – a leading lady of international repute: he also came back to a new home and what would seem like an attempt to make a new beginning in his marriage to Anne. His wife had discovered how unsettling Peter's temperament could be to live with, even though in public she gave the loyal impression that his genius made it worth the occasional domestic strain and stress. 'My husband is a very serious man about the house,' one interviewer quoted her as saying. 'A sort of quiet worrier. The more successful he is, the more he worries.' This was understating it by a wide margin. Sellers was now very successful indeed. From work in films, radio and television, as well as his best-selling records, he was making between £25,000 and £30,000 a year. He had gone into real estate, notching up considerable – and in those days untaxed – capital gains. But instead of making him elated, success acted on him as a depressant.

Anne saw his despondency and restlessness closing him off from her for long stretches of the day. 'He has to have everything done immediately,' she said. 'He can't understand why it takes months for a plant to grow. A couple of days after he puts in the seed, it should all be *there*.' He was trying to lose weight and give up smoking at the same time. He occasionally showed his frayed temper in public. Startled BBC television viewers saw him physically assaulting the roll of paper carrying the credits at the end of his new series. 'It's all Tom Sloan's fault – him and his liniment?' he cried. It turned out that producer Tom Sloan had asked him to ad lib for a few minutes in order to take up the time which was to have been filled by a parody of the Prime Minister, which was thought to be in poor taste – it had mocked pacifism as well as the premiership. This was the petty authoritarianism Sellers hated. He vowed never again to appear on the BBC channel, unappeased by the apologetic explanation that the non-commercial corporation had been more offended at his mentioning a proprietary product – Sloan's Liniment – than at any verbal assault on one of its executives.

Nothing held his attention for long. He lavished money on his house, built a small cinema in it, filled it with expensive playthings which momentarily caught his interest before being abandoned. He tried archery, shot a few desultory arrows in the air, then locked the set away; he had a model railway laid out in the grounds for Michael and Sarah (his daughter born in 1958) and then left it lying out in the rain as his own enthusiasm for it waned. His chief satisfaction lay in work, work, work.... Anne dutifully read the scripts, had his 'voices' tried out on her, occasionally added an idea to the germinating character – but his very success in assuming a role cut him off from her more completely than if they had been living in separate domiciles, which might have been safer.

When the film character began 'possessing' Sellers, Anne was never quite sure who might be returning home that night. Sometimes it was a stranger, whose trance-like state she was powerless to break and not a little scared to behold. Perhaps it wasn't so alarming when only a convicted mastermind came through the front door – fresh from filming the comedy *Two-Way Stretch* about a convict enjoying a cell with all mod. cons, including early-morning tea, while using his alibi as an inmate to cover the planning of a perfect robbery outside. A reunion with the Goons temporarily relieved the domestic pressures. Television director Dick Lester put the team, supplemented by Graham Stark and others, through the absurdist gags of *The Running, Jumping and Standing Still Film*, shot in two days at a cost of £700 (including £5 for the hire of a field). It actually gained them an Oscar nomination. It was shot with a new movie camera Sellers had bought: some said his impatience to try it out was the film's real *raison d'être*. Later on, Sellers remarked it was the only one of his films he could bear to look at without the despondent feeling that he could have done better. But Anne was grateful that the team effort dispersed any *angst* he might have brought home to dinner. Not so the role he played next, his first totally straight part.

Dennis Selinger had said to him, 'Peter, I'd love to see you try a serious part.' But the role of the vicious, violent stolen-car dealer in *Never Let Go* appeared more than a conscious effort to extend his range and savour public reaction to Sellers-without-a-laugh. It seemed like a role chosen to match his black moods: perhaps to release his undirected inner pressures. Anne found the physical alteration in her husband quite alarming. With hair too thick, moustache too trim, jawbone seemingly extended physically by sheer willpower into jutting menace, he appeared on screen as a cone of suppressed fury always threatening eruption. In one scene he crushed a pet terrapin under his boot. Though the 'animal' was plastic, audiences at this 'X'-certificate movie felt themselves loathing the character more for his cruelty to dumb animals than for the thuggery he displayed with iron chains, broken bottles, hydraulic jacks and vats of acid.

Worse still, from Anne's point of view, was his nightly return from work during the shooting of the film. He continued 'in character' for hours, shouting at her and the children in the rasping voice developed for the role. It was an appreciable time before his menacing glare and crude manners, which disconcerted any dinner guests, had faded, leaving a drained, apologetic and apprehensive husband almost scared by himself. The film was badly received and did poor business, but it remains a vivid testament to an almost pathological streak in Sellers's character. Even he seems to have considered it a warning that his off-screen life was in need of re-direction.

The solution he found was to re-create himself in a different image. By now he was capable of grappling with reality only when he had imposed a satisfactory role on the portion of it he was then occupying. The image he chose to escape into this time was that of the English film star who lusts after the comforts and status of Beverly Hills, while despising its vulgarity, and who realizes this image by aping the pretensions of the English landed gentry.

Sellers sold St Fred's at the end of 1959 (comedian Alfred Marks bought it and re-christened it St Alfred's) and for £17,500 he made himself master of the manor house of Chipperfield, a Domesday Book village in the Hertfordshire countryside just twenty miles as the Rolls flies from London's West End.

Apparently he never gave much thought to what it would do to Anne or the children to be taken out of their compact North London suburb and, for her part, to be made chatelaine of a sixteenth-century house, Tudor in the rear, modernized (i.e. 1714) in the front, with six acres of land, twenty rooms (including six principal bedrooms), gardens, greenhouses to stock them, fruit and nut orchards, paddocks, two tithe barns, a swimming pool (refurbished at an extra £3,000) and a garage large enough for several cars including the master's fifty-fourth, a blue Cadillac with a black hood he had bought on impulse in New York. The house required six servants to run, and looked, 'when the light is right', as Kenneth Tynan wrote after one visit, 'like a miniature Buckingham

Palace slowly sinking into a swamp'. There he accumulated a toy-shop of mechanical devices, seeking in each some proof that perfection was attainable, or at least that his mini-universe was controllable. The sensation lasted until they were broken or started to bore him, whereupon he would have one of his great 'clean outs', which later became a feature of his affluent life-style whenever he felt overwhelmed by costly goods purchased on impulse and now given away to friends in bulk.

He soon added a children's menagerie to the house, including dovecotes, exotic aviaries, a trained goose, four dogs and five cats – and a five-foot-tall mechanical elephant. As Sellers disliked domestic pets – he could no more give them his sustained attention than he could his children – the elephant represented an *idée fixe* of his own. He had financed its seventy-seven-year-old inventor until he had finished the petrol-driven pachyderm and then bought it as 'something to fall back on' in case his career came to an end. It was a bizarre symbol of 'security' in the midst of fantasy and plenty – a reminder of the begging letter he had once written his rich Jersey friend. It could generate a cash flow in lean times. He actually took it to the seaside, to generate pennies from children. But as the inventor had omitted to adjust the legs for uneven surfaces, the beast went splay-footed while chugging along at 7 mph, and was retired to a London garage to rust in peace.

But Sellers took his pleasures sadly. To Herbert Kretzmer, one of the English journalists closest to him at this time, he confided: 'Dammit, if I'm ever going to be happy, surely the time is now. I've got everything, *everything*.... So what's wrong? Why can't I be happy now? What am I looking for?'

From the shyness he displayed when he met her at Victoria Station, and later in the penumbra of the flashlights illuminating his new co-star at the London reception, one would not have thought the answer was Sophia Loren.

The truth is, the Italian sex symbol completely overawed him. Though her own social origins were even humbler than his, the inheritance of her family's looks and the way that the Neapolitan sub-world had taught her to wear and even flaunt them, had left Sophia Loren considerably more poised a figure. She had a confidence in handling herself that the Jewish boy from East Finchley found competitive and daunting. He would be able to meet Sophia Loren on his own terms only when he had elaborated the protective shell of a character for himself. 'His feeling on first meeting her,' said Dimitri de Grunwald, the silver-tongued ex-Russian film-maker who was to produce *The Millionairess*, 'was the same as most people have if they ever meet the Queen of England.'

Sellers's self-esteem would hardly have been increased had he known the thoughts of Sophia's husband Carlo Ponti. 'It is not right for Sophia to play with this comic,' he told the film's screenwriter, the astute, acerbic Wolf Mankowitz. 'Sophia is a big star.' She was, with Hollywood figures like Gable, Grant, Peck and Sinatra as her leading men: very soon, she would be a bigger one. In 1962, her film *Two Women* would win her the first 'Best Actress' Oscar awarded for a non-English-speaking role.

But even Sophia's ego might have been dented had she known that she had not been the first choice for Shaw's hard-headed heiress who lets the marriage drive get fatally mixed with the profit motive when she goes husband-hunting, only to succumb to the little Indian doctor whose passion her pulse-beat has precipitated. Twentieth Century-Fox, financiers of the film, had wanted Ava Gardner. De Grunwald resisted them for three months: 'That would be terrible. All the chemistry would disappear. You need Sophia's buoyancy.' When shooting began on *The Millionairess*, he noted with ironic satisfaction, Fox immediately opened negotiations with Carlo Ponti for a multi-picture deal involving Sophia.

For Sellers to have this beautiful, appealing woman as his star was the decisive factor in making him an international name. In no previous film had he played a romantic role. In no previous film had he played opposite a first-magnitude star. Propinquity to Sophia, their ill-matched but oddly touching liaison in the movie, conferred a sex appeal on Sellers's image without which all his artistry might have remained a source of enjoyment and admiration, but would scarcely have awakened the curiosity and speculation which give a star his public profile.

Playing opposite Loren did wonders for the private Sellers, too. It gave him the confidence to see himself conquering beautiful and desirable women: she supplied an image of himself he had never believed possible. She turned the womanizer into a courtier.

Her own reasons for doing the film had nothing to do with Peter Sellers. She hadn't seen a film of his when she agreed to the deal. She was attracted much more by the distinguished director Anthony Asquith. She was also to be paid $200,000 plus a percentage of the net profit. (Sellers had no profit participation, though, oddly enough, Alastair Sim had.) Sellers was paid a £50,000 flat fee, of which £17,000 went to Wolf Mankowitz, who was then engaged in setting up a company for the two of them and also forming a consortium of players who, like Sellers, wished to produce their own films and thus preserve the profits for themselves. Sellers's fee on *Two-Way Stretch* had been £15,000 – 'Thus I had doubled his salary at a stroke,' Mankowitz said, feeling that the star's gratitude would facilitate the consortium deal he was putting together.

De Grunwald and Mankowitz were Sellers's closest confidants at this stage of his career. Their view of the alleged relationship that now developed between Sellers and his leading lady is therefore to be respected.

But an old friend like Graham Stark later confessed to having an apprehensive twinge at the pre-production party which Sellers threw for Loren at Chipperfield. 'Here, Gra, come over and meet this angelic vision,' he called.

Sophia sat there, 'with that great slash of a mouth, only the thinnest of scarves covering her bosom in the untypically hot English summer, and gave every appearance of being entranced by Peter's wit and flattery', Stark recalled. Anne Sellers gamely played hostess.

It soon became the common belief of those on the movie set that the romantic liaison in Shaw's play was being re-enacted in real life, just as the mythology of stardom decreed it should be. It is quite certain that Sellers was deeply, closely attached to Loren. 'To him, she was heaven brought down to earth,' said de Grunwald. 'But there is nothing that will convince me Sophia returned his passion with anything more than the mutually narcissistic feelings such stars go in for when the limelight is on them and the film may be helped.

'Peter would come and hold Sophia's hand like a boy finding his way into his first affair. The nice way of describing her attitude is to say she was kind to him. The other way is to say that her attitude gave him greater hope than was warranted. Puffin Asquith said to me one day, "He looks like a boy with a pin-up in his bedroom." '

Wolf Mankowitz was not often on the set – Asquith feared the writer's presence might disturb the stars, particularly Sophia: 'For the first time in her life she has got to speak literate and intellectual dialogue,' said a production executive. 'We must give her time to get adjusted.' But he had his own theory of how star actresses behave to enhance their image. 'I always felt Sophia needed to feel her leading men loved her – it helped the scene. But I am convinced there was no way she was going to risk a split with Carlo Ponti.'

De Grunwald agreed. Every time he talked to Sophia about Carlo

Ponti, the refrain was the same – and in a way very reminiscent of Sellers's self-denigratory assertion that he was no one. 'Without Carlo, I am nothing,' said Sophia, according to de Grunwald, doing herself perhaps less than justice. 'If Carlo were not here, what would I do? I couldn't earn a crust of bread. No one would want me, not even for a *Vogue* cover.'

'As far as Sophia Loren was concerned,' said Mankowitz, judiciously summing up, 'Sellers was just like Alberto Sordi, only nicer.' How *much* nicer he proved when a cat burglar robbed Sophia of £85,000 worth of jewellery during the production – a day that de Grunwald remembered well, since it was one of those occasions when Ponti visited the set, lamenting his loss to anyone who would listen, '... and they weren't insured, they weren't insured!' Sophia was almost in a state of collapse: she hadn't yet come to terms with worldly things as well as she did some years later, after a similar loss (though perhaps insured this time), when she declared that her child's arms around her neck were more valuable than any necklace. Sellers did not bring his family in to comfort her, but sent to Asprey's for a large and expensive single stone to start her new collection.

One day, when shooting was half-way through, Sellers had the Rolls-Royce in which he and Mankowitz were travelling pull in at the side of the road. He made sure the glass division between them and the driver was shut. Then he said, 'I am in love with Sophia. I'm going to tell Anne.'

Mankowitz dryly replied, 'I'm in love with Sophia, too – why not tell Anne that as well?'

'She finds me very funny. I make her laugh a lot.'

Mankowitz was amazed at the huge emotional upset that might ensue from one man's vanity at amusing a woman who wasn't his wife. ('He didn't want to play Hamlet,' he later said, 'he wanted to play Antony.')

'Peter,' he said, 'generally speaking it's not a good idea to tell your wife anything about such matters. But if you *are* set on telling her, make sure you know the difference between fantasy and reality. Are you having an actual physical affair with Sophia?'

'No,' said Sellers. 'But I'm going to tell Anne that I'm in love with her.'

'Peter, that doesn't mean a damn thing. All you've done is be nice to her and told a few jokes she's laughed at. It won't mean anything till someone calls your wife and tells her that her husband is having an affair.'

'No, no ... I must tell Anne myself. She'll understand.'

Mankowitz said, 'You're so *wrong*! A wife's anticipation that her husband will soon be making love to another woman is far, far more wounding than a husband's confession that he actually has had a physical affair with someone else.'

Sellers disregarded this advice. Actually, he hardly needed to break the hurtful news – an act which Mankowitz interpreted as seeking to precipitate a situation in which it would come true. Friends who saw Loren and Sellers dancing the night away during a lavish supper in one of Chipperfield's tithe barns noted how withdrawn and unhappy his wife was. On hearing about Peter's passion, she was as distressed as any woman would be, left Chipperfield and for a time stayed with Graham and Audrey Stark. 'Peter came round,' Stark recalled, 'looking less like a husband than the traditional gentleman caller.' Eventually an uneasy reconciliation was effected. Anne Sellers told her husband it was the loyalty of the Starks which had helped them patch things up – for a time, anyhow.

The episode contributed to the divorce which took place soon afterwards – but some curious sequels of a less well publicized sort took place in later years.

One was the total exclusion of Peter Sellers's name from the memoirs which Sophia Loren published in 1976. Sellers, though privately very hurt, put on a brave face and joked, 'Well, of course I'm disappointed. But I'm disappointed to have been left out of the Bible and the Life of Buddha, though I'm working on it.'

The likelihood that he had fantasized the whole affair, however, is strengthened by a story that came to the ears of Shirley MacLaine nearly twenty years later. She had been cast opposite Sellers in *Being There* – their only previous film together had been an episode, twelve years before, in de Sica's *Seven Times Women*. Some friends asked her, 'Won't you be embarrassed to be working with Peter again after the affair you had?' 'What affair?' she asked, in utter surprise. They then told her of their experience of hearing Sellers, while they had been in his dressing-room, apparently holding an intimate telephone conversation 'with Shirley', as he had put it. They couldn't hear the voice at the other end of the line, but imagined from the amorous and collusive nature of the scene that Sellers and MacLaine were very intimate. Yet such a conversation had never taken place. Shirley MacLaine completely denied it. She never taxed Sellers with it, however, for she believed that he was still fantasizing an affair with her during the shooting of *Being There*. She was concerned for his health and didn't want to push him to the point where he had to admit to disenchanting reality rather than continue to insulate himself in his imaginary love-life.

Sellers's long-term attachment to Loren took ironic twists, not always helpful to his career. Two years later, in 1963, Jules Dassin, in London to cast his jewel-robbery movie *Topkapi*, offered him the role of the naïve but larcenous Englishman. Sellers enquired who else Dassin was considering for the picture. His attitude stiffened when he heard Maximilian Schell's name. He had been told he was a 'difficult' actor, he said. Dassin, surprised, informed him he had heard exactly the contrary. 'Well,' said Sellers, 'it's not what they tell me. The choice is up to you. Him or me.' Dassin, with the unfailing politeness which accompanied an integrity maintained despite the pressures of Hollywood blacklisting, thanked him kindly and proceeded to cast Peter Ustinov in the role he had offered to Sellers. It later occurred to him that professional rivalry might have played less of a part in Sellers's hesitation than emotional jealousy. Schell and Loren had won both the acting Oscars two years previously and in 1962 had starred together in *The Condemned of Altona*. Someone as hypersensitive as Sellers would hardly have welcomed the associations, personal as well as prestigious, to which Schell's casting in *Topkapi* might have exposed him. As it happened, Ustinov went on to win the 1964 Oscar for the Best Supporting Actor.

Dimitri de Grunwald always grieved over being the innocent means of disrupting his friend's marriage by casting him opposite Sophia Loren: though 'Anne never saw me about it, never asked me about it, never brought me into it at all.' For that, at least, he was grateful. He still had an agreement to do another film with Sophia Loren if a suitable subject could be agreed on; and when he was setting up a light comedy, *That Lucky Touch*, in 1975, he approached her about co-starring with Sellers. 'She turned the idea down flat. As I recall it, the idea of playing love scenes with him no longer held any attraction for her.' She said she preferred Roger Moore; but by the time de Grunwald had made the deal with Moore, Sophia Loren's ardour for the film had cooled to the point of disengagement.

'I had to lie to Peter for the first time in my life,' de Grunwald said. 'He had been avidly looking forward to a new picture with Loren. I put it down to my own inadequacy and told him the only way of doing the film was for him to put up the money. He wasn't prepared to do that. Whenever we subsequently met, the talk turned to Loren and the time they had made *The Millionairess* together. For him it was a turning-point.'

In terms of box-office (in England, anyhow: in America the film didn't do so well) the film confirmed the presence of a new element in Sellers's pulling power: the romantic as well as the comic. His love-shy Indian doctor, voice switchbacking up and down the cadences of a catch-phrase, 'Goodness gracious me!' that entered the national vocabulary and helped sell over 200,000 copies of a song of the same title performed with Loren, is one of his best-sustained light-comedy creations. His new-found tenderness became him, too. 'When he was vulnerable, he was twice as funny,' said de Grunwald. Sellers had learned how to play the part very nearly straight. He conveyed the second-nature saintliness of the little Brahmin doctor without a note of caricature – the best test of its success were the encomia he drew from the Asian community, who virtually adopted the figure as a racial mascot. Like his other characterizations, this one had its disconcerting aspect for Sellers, who again felt the power of 'possession' as he 'became' the role 'from the first minute he stepped on the set,' said de Grunwald. 'I felt I had actually been an Indian in some past life,' Sellers later affirmed, very seriously. 'Once, during filming, an Indian supporting player came up to me and said, without joking, that I was the new Messiah and ought to go to India and lead her people into a happier future. I even began to feel I had developed the power to heal people along with the role. It was frightening.'

He also found a change in the way he was regarded by people who had their thoughts fixed less loftily than on messianic crusades in the Third World. His fan mail now required three secretaries to handle and an overwhelming majority of writers were women, to whom he had ceased to be a chameleon-like character actor and become a romantic figure with whom they wished to identify. A small but significant point illustrates how swiftly he himself absorbed this change of perspective. From this point on almost all his published interviews referring to his awareness of a lack of personal identity begin to drop the comparisons he once made to comedians such as Max Bygraves or Jerry Lewis. It is now a romantic leading man like Cary Grant whom he envies for being 'himself' in picture after picture and being known as such. Sellers still bemoaned his own facelessness, but now he thought of it inside a romantic context, not a comic one.

Photographs of Peter before and after *The Millionairess* reveal the extremes he went to in order to make himself more physically attractive to women. But his fantasy about Sophia was not the only reason. He was very susceptible to anything written about him and he reacted energetically the day he saw a newspaper headline: 'Mastroianni: Peter

Sellers with Sex Appeal'. Marcello Mastroianni, star of *La Dolce Vita*, was one of Loren's most intimate friends and co-stars. Sellers immediately went to work on every part of himself. He had his teeth capped and fixed, so that they were no longer straight, but sloped outwards slightly. This in turn changed the shape of his mouth, giving him a peculiarly wistful, lop-sided smile. It was, however, the rigorousness of his diet which alarmed his wife and friends. 'Peter never did anything by halves,' said Bryan Forbes, the film director, who witnessed the transformation with some trepidation for what he feared would be its debilitating effect. 'By virtually starving himself for weeks, I believe he changed the whole metabolism of his body.' When Peter had his coronary in Hollywood, Anne, who was by then his ex-wife, immediately blamed it on his dieting.

Although he was in love with the desirable Loren, Sellers was not blind to the importance of money. He and Wolf Mankowitz had made an agreement to produce their own pictures, the first of which was to be *The Memoirs of a Cross-Eyed Man*, with Sellers playing the 'little man' who, despite his disability, falls in love, Walter Mitty-like, with a famous film star. Shirley MacLaine had been the first choice. Mankowitz had formed Sellers–Mankowitz Productions, with a logo of Daniel Mendoza in pugilistic posture on the prospectus. They planned four pictures together and, as has been mentioned, were hoping to work inside a consortium which resembled United Artists, the stars' co-operative formed in 1919 by Pickford, Chaplin, Douglas Fairbanks Sr and D. W. Griffith, to preserve their status as independent producers, collecting the profits of their pictures rather than letting other film moguls who had them under contract divert these into their own pockets. Other members of the new consortium were to be Diane Cilento, Anthony Newley, Sean Connery, Albert Finney and Peter O'Toole. But the deal hinged on Sellers: at that time he was the only star amongst these names on whom collateral financing could be raised. None of the others had done the films that were soon to make them famous. Impresario Jack Hylton was on the board, along with financier Howard Samuel and opera administrator Sir David Webster. The lawyer setting up the consortium was Arnold (later Lord) Goodman, a power-broker with entrée to the City's financial houses. He had arranged for a sum of up to £400,000 to be matched by a leading bank.

Sellers announced, 'I have found in Wolf a person who really understands me.' But how little Wolf understood Sellers became appallingly apparent to him as time went by and the deal never formally took shape. At 9.45 a.m. on the morning of the very day he was due to go before the board of the proposed consortium, Mankowitz received a hand-delivered letter.

'It was from Peter. He was withdrawing from the entire deal. I was utterly crushed and incensed. The letter said, "I have been thinking all night about this company. I have decided that I have to be free of commitments to follow the direction my career takes."' Mankowitz read the letter at the directors' midday meeting. 'Jack Hylton said, "I don't quite understand this, Wolfie. Did you not make a contract with Sellers?" I said, "This was to be an association of artists. I'm not a businessman. But if you want my personal opinion, I've probably saved you a lot of money."'

A month later, the simmering row boiled over publicly, perhaps precipitated by Mankowitz's learning that Sellers was to be paid £75,000 to direct and star in a new comedy, *Mr Topaze*. The notion struck him as one that was indeed profitably unhindered by commitments to other business partners.

Sellers said bitingly, 'In my opinion – though I doubt whether Mr Mankowitz will value it – he had too much on his plate ... he should concentrate more on one thing – like screen writing – and leave the impresario business alone.'

Mankowitz, who had absolutely nothing on his plate at that moment, believed this dismissive tone signified his ex-partner's guilty grab at any plausible excuse for his own conduct. He replied bitterly, 'The truth is, he has taken over Sellers–Mankowitz Ltd completely, and I leave you to guess who got pushed. Its collapse leaves me free. I am unbusy. I can tell Mr Sellers – actor, director, script-writer and recording star – that I shall be glad of the rest.'

Sellers had been heavily influenced by Dimitri de Grunwald in settling on a play by Marcel Pagnol for his first film as actor-director. De Grunwald's European *savoir-faire* seemed to give Peter's career its continuing international thrust. But de Grunwald began to have his doubts. 'The public wanted to see Peter in love with a woman and chasing her with utter incompetence,' he said – a remark that was prescient in view of what *The Pink Panther* would shortly achieve in public-pleasing impact. But a play that was a sardonic sermon on how power corrupts, and then how pleasantly the corrupted might enjoy it, was hardly a way of exploiting Sellers's romantic vulnerability. Just the reverse. Topaze, the innocent, underpaid and honest pedagogue, ends up flourishing more profitably and crookedly than the gang he has usefully taken as a bad example: but he is not a romantic figure at all.

He is a man who is morally weak yet exerts great power over others – a role that might be judged a temptingly close analogy to the film world.

Using the slightly sad drawl which, consciously or not, gave the impression that Alec Guinness was dubbing in his lines, he succeeded in suggesting under the Toulouse-Lautrec-like insignificance of the early Mr Topaze the dormant soul of a criminal Napoleon. But this time there was no Loren feeding yeast into his performance. The characterization was clever but flat; his direction of the film was directionless. A good cast was allowed to meander through surprisingly slipshod comedy scenes. 'He was not directing so much as acting the role of a director,' said de Grunwald later. 'Acting now came into all his relationships, on the screen or off it.'

Public response was poor. People didn't want to see a 'new' Peter Sellers, however talented. They wanted the comic-romantic whom *The Millionairess* had introduced to them.

Sellers suddenly felt his insecurity return like an attack of ulcers, gnawing away the confidence which the last few years' tremendous success should have given him. He had professed dissatisfaction with his own work when he saw it on the screen and had hoped to compensate for this by drawing 'great' performances out of others. He clearly hadn't. The fear that, as he expressed it to Herbert Kretzmer, 'it only takes two pictures to put you back where you were, or even farther back' now consumed his restless hours, to the extent that he rang up Spike Milligan and proposed they bring back *The Goon Show* on radio as a life-saver.

He even began to fear he would never again be given any work. And if there were no pictures offered him, what then would he do with himself?

At this moment Sidney Gilliat and Frank Launder, partners in a British film-makers co-operative founded in 1960 under the name of Bryanston, offered him the leading role in *Only Two Can Play*, a comedy about a lecherous Welsh librarian, which Bryan Forbes had freely adapted from Kingsley Amis's novel *That Uncertain Feeling*. Sellers grasped it gratefully – and gave a marvellously nuanced performance.

The part allowed him a delirious renewal of the amorousness which the average sensual man can muster when presented with the opportunity. Sellers utilized a sleight-of-hand that could suddenly broaden into slapstick and contract again in a second to reveal a character through the tongue's hesitation or an eyebrow's elevation. This time he adopted a soft Welsh drawl that mesmerized book-borrowers in the library which the character ran in the film and a dangling kiss-curl that resembled a baited hook. Having reached a dangerous age in his own marriage – the age of disengagement – Sellers may have found companionable solace in the character's own sense of marital disenchantment.

The film gave a forecast of how well physical comedy became him. Not just in the broad scenes of objects 'fighting' him – as they were to 'fight' Inspector Clouseau – but in the way his own body refused to aid and abet his amorous designs so that, pausing in his pursuit of Mai Zetterling in order to try out her husband's rowing machine, he almost emasculates himself before his pleasure can be attained. His escape from her bedroom, on the return of her husband, switches from the high comedy of seduction to the choice farce of a fleeing lover and includes Sellers's inspired moment of physical timing when he pretends to be a poker-faced butler and then, in one quick-change movement, dons the camouflage of a jittery plumber. His genius too, in following a comic character through to the serious core of his being, showed in the skill with which he rose to the final moment of self-knowledge and consequent sadness.

Yet while he was giving this performance in the spring of 1961 his mood remained bleak and beset by self-doubt. Discontent had set in, according to John Boulting, on the first day of location shooting near Cardiff. That night Boulting took a telephone call in his London home from a very depressed Sellers.

It was already 11.30 p.m. and the call lasted till 2.15 a.m. 'John,' Sellers said, 'I'm in a terrible spot here. This girl Maskell [Virginia Maskell, who played his screen wife], I've had her in my caravan. We went through two or three scenes together and she hasn't the right Welsh accent and can't act for toffee.'

The Boultings had had one earlier experience of Sellers's discontentment vis-à-vis a fellow actor, when he was making Two-Way Stretch and had complained about Lionel Jeffries 'going over the top'. They had put this down to the feeling he might have had that Jeffries was giving just too good a performance.

'But why he should have conceived such an immediate dislike of Virginia Maskell is beyond me,' Boulting said. The complaint poured on and on, then Boulting interrupted. 'Look, Peter, keep cool for a moment. If she is incapable of playing the role Sidney Gilliat will surely see it.'

'If she does play the part, John, I'm walking out,' Sellers said bluntly.

Boulting took a deep breath. It was time to inject a little parental discipline into this sort of tantrum. Lowering his voice, like someone talking to a fractious child in a public place, he said, 'Virginia Maskell is a very respected actress, Peter, especially by newspaper people. If it got out that you had had her pushed off the film, a lot of Fleet Street people might take a poor view of your conduct. Can you afford such a hurtful blow to your career, especially as it seems to be flourishing at the moment?'

The ensuing pause appeared to last five minutes. Then Sellers, who seemed to have returned from another planet in the interval, said that, well, he would talk to Sidney Gilliat in the morning.

'He did not,' said Boulting, 'so presumably my remarks got through to him and Virginia was not replaced. But the calls kept coming through to me nightly. I realized I was being used as a surrogate Peg. With Peter, you had to be mother, dad and psychiatrist – and it would help if you could throw in a shared Virgo sign.'

When the film was completed and Sellers saw the final cut, he declared it to be a total and irremediable disaster.

'But Peter, you give one of your best performances,' said Boulting.

'I don't know what we can do,' he kept wailing, 'it'll set my career back ten years, back to the beginning again.'

Sellers had ten per cent of the film's net profits, so the Boultings devised a stratagem to convince him how utterly sincere they were in their high opinion of him and the film.

'If you really believe it will be a total failure,' they said, 'we are willing to buy out your interest here and now.'

Sellers went away to think this over, still protesting his worst hour had dawned, etc., etc. Early next morning his financial adviser, Bill Wills, telephoned the Boultings. 'Were you serious in what you told Peter last night?' 'Of course.' 'Very well, I'll be round in an hour to talk business.' He was as good as his word and immediately enquired what price they put on Peter Sellers's net percentage.

'We said to him we must refer the proposal to British Lion, the distribution company of which we were directors. "Either it will make you an offer, Bill, or we shall feel free to do so." The company eventually bought Sellers out for £17,500.'

Only Two Can Play turned into one of the biggest successes enjoyed by the renascent independent British cinema of the 1960s. The last figures available to John Boulting showed that the percentage which the company purchased from Sellers had earned over £120,000.

When the film was seen to be a proven success, the Boultings sportingly offered Sellers a chance to tear up the agreement and revert to the *status quo ante*. They never heard from him.

His domestic troubles were preoccupying him once again – and once again he decided that their resolution depended on recasting the image of himself. Squire of Chipperfield had not proved to be the part he had hoped for; so he precipitately scrapped it. He suddenly moved Anne and his family back to London into two adjacent suites at the Carlton Tower Hotel, trying to lull a suspicious Press into believing that his move was caused by the difficulties of finding staff prepared to live in the country. So swift was his flit that even Peg was taken unawares and declared the report of it to be extremely unlikely when a newspaper enquirer called. 'Peter rings me up almost every night for a talk and he hasn't said anything. So it can't be true.'

Early in November 1961, he sold for £40,000 the country house he had bought barely two years before and, from across town, fixed his eyes on the homelier slopes of his North London childhood, eventually buying for £31,000 a seven-year-lease on a penthouse apartment in a Hampstead tower block and commissioning a very successful young architect, Ted Levy, to complete the interior design.

It was a move that his astrology charts ought to have discouraged. For very shortly afterwards Anne Sellers was destined to become Mrs Ted Levy.

SEVEN

Swings and Roundabouts

The next two years, 1962 and 1963, were the worst, and the best, in Peter Sellers's whole experience. His personal life fell to bits; his career touched a point of high artistry he would not again attain for a decade.

He later protested he had known what was going on between his wife Anne and Ted Levy, the South African-born architect he had commissioned to design and decorate the Northwood Lodge penthouse, then little more than a thirteen-room concrete shell. 'Anne loved this place,' he mused bitterly. 'She was always enamoured of Levy's designs and colour schemes. They kind of over-ruled me, always around, the two of them buying wallpaper and wood and stuff. Gradually I caught on. I saw this whole thing growing. I'm not very articulate, but I'm quite perceptive.' Despite his suspicions, he found himself involuntarily adopting Levy's South African accent when he joined in the discussions – talent, once formed, was a hard habit to break. Eventually, at about the end of February 1962, the Sellers family moved out of their hotel into an apartment that had 'Movie Star' written all over it. One room was equipped as a recording studio. There were five bedrooms and three bathrooms, of which the master's was done in marble and mosaic with wall-to-wall carpeting. Huge sofas and chairs that could have accommodated two people struck the predominant colour note of dark brown. Rosewood panelling and sliding screens of embossed leather covering the picture windows in place of curtains increased the dark, masculine ambience. It was less Hampstead Heath than Beverly Hills, to some people it was less a family man's London residence than a bachelor playboy's pad.

Though they were together again, the relationship between Anne and Peter Sellers was strained, unpredictable and a misery to their mutual friends, one of whom was summoned by a frantic phone call from Sellers at 6.00 a.m. to come and help make the peace between them. 'I got into the car, tore round, found them having a terrible row in the bedroom, eventually effected what I hoped was a reconciliation. The next day it was back to square one.' Constant, all-involving work was the only thing that took Peter's mind off how his married life was breaking up before his eyes. Sometimes even work didn't help. David Lodge was suddenly called to the Thames valley location shooting of *The Waltz of the Toreadors*, in which Peter, by unwelcome coincidence, was playing Anouilh's middle-aged general who discovers that his wife is about to desert him just as he is taking French leave with his mistress. Art wasn't aping life so much as supplementing it.

'Peter was in his trailer while everyone cooled their heels outside, including the cavalry horses needed for the scene, and producer Julian Wintle went out of his mind as the costs climbed hourly. Peter had a great heap of old-fashioned pennies in front of him – this was before our coinage went decimal – and he said, very piteously, "Dave, luv, take the money and go down to the call-box and get through to Anne. Tell her I'm sorry." But Anne wasn't going to forgive him for whatever had just happened. I couldn't tell Peter that in his state of mind. So I reported back, "She says she'll talk to you tonight, so get on with your work now."'

News of the widening split had not yet been publicly reported, though the newspapers were naturally suspicious of the sudden change of residence; but it was common talk in show-business circles. Anne found herself resisting one American film-maker, very much attracted to her, who wished her to make the break and join him in the United States: he even provided a suitcase containing £5,000 as travelling expenses. But Anne Sellers patiently, painfully, held on to her marriage, for which she felt she had sacrificed so much and the children of which were close to her heart, until she passed the point of no return. Even then her husband refused to face the fact that it was all over. He took a lease on a detached house not far away in the hope that having Anne near him physically would promote a reconciliation. It was in vain. Sellers was granted a decree nisi in March 1963, in an undefended suit, the judge exercising his discretion in favour of his own admitted adultery. Anne and Ted Levy were married in October 1963. In interview after interview in subsequent months, Sellers gave out that he would 'never marry again': it was like a man tossing 'Help!' bottles into the passing current. His hopes were finally dashed one evening by Dennis Selinger. 'Peter,' he said quietly, 'Anne's expecting a baby.'

Work became the one and only antidote to what he saw as his wife's rejection of him. Though it was a situation which he realized, in calmer moments, he had himself precipitated, it was the first time he had been on the losing end of a relationship: he passed from remorse to resentment, from guilty acceptance of the blame to bitter assignment of it to others.

He plunged into film after film as a form of therapy, conscious of but barely grateful for the fact that 'the cure' brought him (instead of costing him) increasingly large sums of money. Each film he accepted possessed a Catch-22 for him. As his consciousness of his own artistry came into sharper focus, so did his dissatisfaction with the end result. To watch himself in the rushes, see his performance in the completed film, grew progressively more painful for him. 'It wasn't out of conceit,' said his friend Lord Snowdon later, 'it was out of an unremitting search for perfection.' 'I don't really want to do more than two pictures a year,' he told Robert Muller, the journalist, in 1962, a year in which he did six. 'That's the ideal. That's perfection. But when you get all this stuff to sift through, you don't know what to do. The thing is to take off to some little place and think, but I don't relax easily. And the moment you try to relax, they all descend on you, you get all these moguls with ideas, and they say, "Let's do it now, it's marvellous, it's wonderful," and they usually don't even have a script.'

His own nature built up the artistic tensions that already made him 'difficult' to work with and would soon inflate some budgets to profligate dimensions. Producers who caught his attention had to work tirelessly to keep him interested. 'Throughout my association with Peter, it had to be a constant courtship,' said Dimitri de Grunwald. 'He was a great enthusiast, but nearly always for the basic idea, the first treatment. The novelty was what fired his engines and they had to be continuously fuelled or else the project became a bore – and, as with a bored child, you were in for trouble.'

Sellers's second film for de Grunwald was *The Dock Brief*, a clever screen adaptation of John Mortimer's first radio play. Basically a dialogue for two characters – a scruffy, hen-pecked wife-killer awaiting trial and the mouldering, day-dreamy barrister assigned to the defence – it juggled visually with time and place to allow Richard Attenborough (the prisoner) and Sellers to portray their respective downtrodden backgrounds as well as letting the camera pop round the courtroom with Attenborough appearing on the judge's bench, in the jury box or the public gallery while Sellers put his lines of defence to the test. For a long time Sellers couldn't decide how to play the barrister. The very day before shooting began he ordered a shellfish dish in the studio canteen. The whiff of the seafront that accompanied it brought him a

Proustian memory of the holiday resort of Morecambe, where he had played with his father – which in turn suggested a North Country accent and a faded moustache. 'He had been thrown the lifeline of a voice,' said John Mortimer, 'and work could begin.' But two days into shooting, Sellers summoned his agent, John Redway, to vet the rushes. He declared that his client was surprisingly coarse-grained – and work had to begin again. His performance was, eventually, admirable: but it was not the one that *The Millionairess* public wanted to see him give.

Nor was *The Waltz of the Toreadors* the hoped-for success. Sellers played the general with an eye for the realistic heartbreak of a farcical lecher. It is not just the easy bits of business he gets so true to type – the eye rolling amorously off the Colours on parade and on to the pretty bosom in the crowd, or his horseback posture of a superannuated Lochinvar. Out of the character he teases pity, too: pity for the hollow old man who knows that every advance he makes on love's battlefield is really only a cowardly retreat from reality.

When Sellers viewed the film, however, it plunged him deeper into what he called 'the blacks'.

'The whole thing looks terrible,' he said to Muller, 'amateurish, bad. And you want to pack it all in and look round quickly for a means of employment. Suicide? No, not that. But who can you talk to, who'd understand your problem? You've got to carry on, try something else.'

What he tried was hardly guaranteed to cure his depression. After his first hostile brush with America, he went back in May 1962, to promote his new film, *Lolita*, and pushed on from Washington D.C., where he did a wickedly funny impersonation of Prime Minister Harold Macmillan (in the presence of President Kennedy), to make his first contact with Hollywood. He was so much the child still that he even brought his autograph book. Though he'd been warned he wouldn't like Hollywood, he said: 'I don't believe that for a minute.' It took two weeks to convince him that he hated it. He sensed exploitation hanging like smog in the balmy air. He felt sands shift beneath his feet every time a 'firm' offer was delivered to his hotel suite – and he got twenty-one scripts offered – by producers who now talked generically of 'A Peter Sellers Film'. The famous stars who now treated him as a 'hot' property were not exactly patronizing – but he felt the insubstantial nature of a welcome based on roles in movies which his own driving perfectionism perversely convinced him had been missed opportunities. His autograph book didn't collect many signatures: the glamour faded before the page was opened. A visit to the studio was an additional depressant. He saw his childhood screen memories mouldering away, untended and uncared about, on the back lot – Esther Williams's swimming pool, Mickey Rooney's hometown.... He hated Hollywood as if it had committed an almost personal assault on him by failing to care about his nostalgia. He was invited to parties day and night and was appalled to see the way some of the brand new, as yet publicly unseen new movies were treated when they were screened in the drawing rooms of the 'Bel Air circuit'. Those who earned their own affluent livings from the industry took a sadistic relish in accompanying the films with a sarcastic commentary – or else shutting them off before the end to get down to the poker game.

'Can you imagine that,' he said on returning to London, 'somebody's creation cut to pieces for an easy laugh.'

Above all else he sensed a lack of lasting substance behind the busy purposefulness of the company town. It brought back sore memories of public fickleness. When Lynn Tournabee interviewed the saddened ex-fan on his return through New York, he told her, 'On Sundays we'd go visiting outside London where all the old vaudeville entertainers live. My mother would say to me, "You remember George here – don't you, Pete?" "You remember" – those deadly words! And there sits a man who was the greatest singer of his day, or greatest actor. It happens to everybody in show-business. I want to be ready for that. I want things to go back where they were. I'm not a star, you see, and I don't know what's happened.'

But he *was* a star, even though his options for satisfaction were narrowing dismayingly in the aftermath of his broken marriage. Happiness came to reside more and more in the act of performing.

He touched what was, even for him, a new intensity when he appeared in Stanley Kubrick's *Lolita*. Kubrick had seen *The Battle of the Sexes*, listened to his LP disc, *The Best of Sellers*, and, enormously impressed by his range, offered him what Sellers characterized at the time as 'a small part, not much more than five minutes on the screen'. It soon grew. It was that of the malevolent and decadent playwright, Clare Quilty, who steals the nymphet Lolita away from Humbert Humbert. Sellers at first sensed it was outside his experience – as Fred Kite had been – and grew nervous. Kubrick dined at his home three or four times, noting that Sellers's depressive states now probably outnumbered his manic ones, and then engaged jazz impresario Norman Granz to record Quilty's dialogue on tape for Sellers to study. Once Peter found the voice, the character took shape round it – but this time it kept growing.

For the first time he tasted what it was like to work creatively *during* shooting, not just in the pre-production run-up. He and Kubrick had a shared liking for trying all the alternatives, enjoying the expensive indulgence of working through the options, until the 'critical rehearsal moment' produced an illumination of scene or character. Recent events had conspired to make him as cynical about life as Kubrick generally was held to be. They were made for each other, and drew mutual trust from the fact. Together they elaborated Quilty's disguised appearances – as the garrulous cop menacingly prying into Humbert's activities, or the German psychiatrist exemplifying prurient inquisitiveness – in a way that used the script to take off from the grotesque surroundings of a real world to the rarified regions of the surreal.

'When Peter was called to the set,' Kubrick recalled, 'he would usually arrive walking very slowly and staring morosely. I clear the crew from the stage and we would begin rehearsing. As the work progressed, he would begin to respond to something or other in the scene, his mood would visibly brighten and we would begin to have fun. Improvisational ideas began to click and the rehearsal started to feel good. On many of these occasions, I think, Peter reached what can only be described as a state of comic ecstasy.'

All the characters Peter played were groped for; it was an on-the-spot flash of inspiration that transformed him, not the blueprinted advance plan. He'd rehearse the scene, giving only the vaguest hint that he might be working on it imaginatively. Usually he did the Quilty monologue on the first run-through as Nabokov had written it. Then a chance remark of his own or someone else's would break him up. His inventiveness took over. He would ad lib, swerve spontaneously into disconcerting *non sequiturs*, drop in a snatch of impromptu parody. The enthusiasm his performance generated in himself and the crew was fuel to him and he'd incorporate these marvellous additions when he shot the scene. He didn't need to use 'idiot cards' containing the new dialogue and it is unlikely he ever needed to hear a play-back: if the ideas were memorable, he could repeat them with infinite finesse. Even so, Kubrick used two or three cameras on him, for the quality of his improvisations was magical on the first take. The second take would be fifty per cent down. By the third take, the charge had exhausted itself. It was the experience of *Brouhaha* all over again: only this time he was 'licensed' to break the rules, indulged in his liking for setting himself problems, encouraged by Kubrick to explore the outer limits of the *comédie noire* – and sometimes, he felt, go over them – in a way that appealed to the macabre imagination of himself and his director.

Dr Strangelove was still a year or so ahead: but on this film their collaboration was even more sensational. The subject matter, a night-marish comedy of an errant H-bomb which turned a situation so plausible that one could not contemplate it soberly into a fantasy so grotesque that laughter made it appallingly viewable, gave Sellers the opportunity to play a trio of characters which showed his genius at full stretch: the US President, an English RAF group-captain, and the eponymous nuclear scientist. One came out of contemporary politics, one out of his own Service life, one out of the Old High German cinema of Fritz Lang and Murnau. His genius lifted all these characters on to the same comic plane.

'He was harder to reach,' said Kubrick of the *Strangelove* period. On *Lolita*, he had been more 'together'. Kubrick hadn't glimpsed the 'madness' that he was now able to refer to inside his creative conscious-ness. But that was undoubtedly what was needed. Kubrick had origi-nally wanted him to play more than three parts. Sellers was earmarked for the role of the Texan commanding the aircraft bearing the H-bombs en route to Russia. Explanations differ about why he didn't play it – Slim Pickens did. One story has it that he couldn't get the Texan accent: this is very unlikely. Another was that he didn't want to continue the freakish side of his genius by 'doing a Guinness' and playing multiple roles in the same film, sometimes in the same scene or even shot. Anyhow, he had an accident, a cracked ankle, which ruled him out of the athletic activities of the character scrambling around in the bomb bays. Kubrick conceded that he might have subconsciously wished such an injury on himself. Whatever the reason, it left all his creative energies free to flow into and transform the other three roles.

'We never hesitated to jettison anything that wasn't working,' said Kubrick. He had begun playing the US President in a very effete way, with a nose-inhaler and limp-wristed gestures. Kubrick disliked this – the President should be an area of reasonable sanity amidst the accumulating chaos. So he re-shot the scenes and this time composed the character in a dimension of liberal-humanist apology for the coming apocalypse which some said was how Adlai Stevenson might have reacted had American electoral history been different. 'I don't think he made up a whole scene that didn't already exist,' said Kubrick, 'but he did a bit of embroidery. In the famous phone call to the Russian Premier, for instance, he may have added the rueful line, "Well, how do you think *I* feel, Dimitri?"'

His English group-captain was also much as written: but again an inspirational ad lib transformed a shot. When Sterling Hayden, as the berserk base commander who alone knows the H-bomb recall signal, calls on his captive RAF colleague to help with the submachine-gun he's using to hold off the Government troops, Group-Captain Mandrake's wincing reference to his gammy leg ('My string's gone, I'm afraid') was suddenly introduced by Sellers in the middle of the take and joyously retained.

The most extraordinary creation was Dr Strangelove, the White House's sinister adviser on nuclear warfare and post-nuclear survival. The wheelchair he sat in had nothing to do with Sellers's own injury – as has been sometimes alleged. It derived from Kubrick's obsession – shared by Sellers – with power figures who are themselves impotent in some way or other. Superficially, the character's tics were borrowed from the pre-war German cinema – including the arm that uncontrollably resisted democratic remedial training and was always trying to reassert its inbred Nazism. But Sellers transposed every such borrowing into blacker farce.

The characterization of Dr Strangelove was taken by many people to have been inspired by Dr Henry Kissinger.

'I think this is slightly unfair to Kissinger,' Kubrick said, 'but I suppose I can see what they mean. It was certainly unintentional. Neither Peter nor I had ever seen Kissinger before the film was shot. It was an amazing coincidence, similar to one which occurred in *2001: A Space Odyssey*, when Arthur C. Clarke and I called the computer HAL, which is an acronym based on the words "heuristic" and "algorithmic", the two forms of learning which HAL mastered. Several years later, a code-breaker friend pointed out that the letters of HAL's name were each one letter ahead of IBM, and he congratulated us on the hidden joke. Strangelove's accent was probably inspired by the physicist Edward Teller, who became known as the father of the H-bomb, though Teller's origins are Hungarian and his accent isn't really that close to what Peter did.'

By this time, Peter had apparently developed a grim, bleak sense of humour about the world. It was a good guide to the territory that *Lolita* and *Strangelove* took him into. When he turned back to straight comedy, it was evident he was having a good time. But he was seldom as interested as he was when Kubrick and he were collaborating.

Meanwhile, into Peter's erratic and melancholy off-screen life had come two people who attempted to bring order and relief to him.

One was Bert Mortimer, his chauffeur, valet and constant bodyguard-companion; the other, Hattie Stevenson, his secretary. Both stayed with him for years – Bert for over sixteen – taking knocks, giving some, but usually loyally trying to cushion him against his own self-destructive reflexes.

Bert, a tall, well-built, friendly man who looked as if he could handle himself (or others) if the need were there, had a sensitivity and knew when to stick around, or make himself scarce, or stand up for Peter, or tip others the wink that it was a bad moment. 'He saved people the embarrassment of what Peter could do to them – and Peter the hurtfulness of what he might do to himself,' was how the Boultings put it. He had driven Peg a few times before passing on to Peter, so he knew the mother-and-son attachment to be strong, but sensed that after the break-up of Peter's marriage, the only mature relationship he had attempted, the son's attitude to his mother was one of duty rather than of love. 'He was so isolated and lonely that I got scared for his safety. He would sit in the penthouse – "My bloody palace," he'd call it – and threaten to tear "Ted Levy's Teutonic look" apart. "Over-masculine – it's just not me," he'd say.' He looked so wild and suicidal at times that Bert was on edge in case he threw himself over the balcony. Some nights Bert stayed up with him till 2.00 a.m., then David Lodge or Bill Kerr would take over the 'suicide watch'. Bert asked him once if he'd ever thought of going to a psychiatrist. 'Oh, no,' said Sellers revealingly, out of the depths of his misery, 'psychiatrists only talk common sense to you.' In other words, they would have awakened him to his problems, not offered him a cure. He would have had to realize where he was at – and this, except at rare moments, he resolutely refused to know.

On the nights that Bert or his friends weren't available to share the vigil in his lonely penthouse, Peter would call Bryan Forbes and his actress wife Nanette Newman. Though the Forbes lived over an hour's drive from London, they would motor up without delay, sometimes in their nightwear, wondering if they would find he had already jumped off the roof. 'Sometimes I'd lie beside him on the floor,' Forbes recalled, 'holding his hand till he dropped off to sleep.'

Bert saw Peter's superstitions tighten their grip at this time, as he sought a purchase on the plane of daily life which his broken marriage had tilted alarmingly under him. If he put a sock on inside out, he'd leave it that way; if he went out of doors, he'd walk a few steps to the left first. Keys must never be left on the table: green was a colour to be avoided.

Occasionally he and Bert would drive down to the West End after nightfall, leave the limousine, and Bert followed while Peter mooched dejectedly around, sometimes stopping among the tramps preparing to sleep rough in the unpatrolled fringes of the Royal parks. Peter would impulsively go up to one of them and stuff a £5-note in his pocket. 'You'd see the man flinch, thinking he was going to be hit,' said Bert, 'then fish out the note and stare in utter disbelief at it.' This was superstition, too. Peter's father had always jokingly said his son would finish up as a road-sweeper. Peter was always sympathetic to the down-and-outs, as a way of deflecting any misfortune that might make him one, too.

Ordinarily now he travelled without any money in his pockets, using credit cards or cheque-books, famous enough for his signature alone to have the collateral of money in the bank – much as his ancestor Daniel Mendoza's privately-printed bank-notes had assumed a value and a glamour beyond ordinary money.

His earnings from films and other sources in these two years were an estimated £150,000 a year and were looked after by Bill Wills, his business adviser, who handled the money end of his contracts, allowed him a personal (frequently exceeded) income of £20,000 a year and salted the rest away in Switzerland under the fiscally advantageous 'slave contract' that permitted a high-earning artist to sell his services exclusively to a foreign-based holding company. But Bill Wills, a man uncomfortable in show-business idioms and nervous in the presence of other high-powered stars, had to reckon with Peter's increasingly costly 'impulse buys' – like his decision to have a £75,000 motor yacht built for him in Italy. It was part of his restlessness and part of his unwillingness to be pinned down by simply standing still. 'It will make me absolutely free. No ties: nothing. I can take it everywhere, to the Med, anywhere I choose. I've already joined the Motor Yacht Club of Cannes.'

He had gone on a crash diet and lost over 50 lbs, so that he now assumed the lithe and boyish line he would keep till the end, till it took on an uncomfortable gauntness. Douglas Hayward, who became *the* tailor for the Swinging Sixties people, was just starting up in business in the West End and already almost despairing of his show-business cronies ordering enough to pay the rent when in walked Sellers one day and ordered seventeen suits – 'at a go'. He liked Doug Hayward's tailoring because it flattered his new-found slimness – but the tailor-confidant noted an in-built obsessiveness in the fittings, a sort of sartorial anorexia nervosa.

' "I want you to get the suit slim, Doug, really slim," he'd say. "I'm dieting. I'm going to lose five pounds more. Take a bit more in. A bit more, Doug." I'd say, "But Peter, the jacket will hardly meet around you." "That's all right ... I never use buttons. It's the hang rather than the fit that's important." So I'd run him up another twelve suits and then he'd call me and say in his little plaintive voice, "Doug ... Doug, I can't get these suits buttoned," and I'd have to take them away and do them all over again, and that went on two or three times.' Hayward got to the point where he would pretend to make the alteration, bring the garment back and hear Peter say, 'Ah, Doug, got it right this time. That's better ... that's what it should have been like.'

Hattie Stevenson was hired to work for Peter in 1961/62. She was the daughter of Mr Justice Melford Stevenson, a judge noted for his controversial remarks. 'If I get into trouble,' Sellers had joked, 'you can always slip a word to the old man.' (Actually, when the police gave him a ticket for some minor traffic offence and he left it too late to have a collusive word with the station officer, he petulantly cancelled the police concert he had agreed to do.)

Bill Wills had warned Hattie when she arrived at Shepperton Studios, fresh from a BBC job, that 'Mr Sellers is in a bad temper and has a stinking headache.'

Mr Sellers's first words to her were, 'Hello, Miss Smith, and when would you like to start?'

'He made up his mind on first impressions, always,' said Hattie Stevenson.

Business he found tedious: though he insisted every fan letter get an answer, he left Hattie to compose the reply and use his signature.

Hattie noticed that Peg had now regained her place at the emotional centre of her son's life. But the sheer scale of his success had left her oddly disoriented. As she no longer needed to encourage him, she fed off his achievements. 'Peter occasionally felt his own immaturity was due to his mother and would show sudden resentments and bawl at her,' said Hattie. Then he would feel guilty and pack her off in the new Bentley he had bought her. 'Go and spend what you like, my darling. Have it all charged to me.' Bill Wills would go pale and Peg, with a cringing Hattie in tow, would storm into the West End stores as if capturing a Normandy beach-head and announce to the salesgirl, 'I'm Peter Sellers's mother, and I want the best, darling.' Hattie cringed even more.

She and Bert were helpless to deal with the endemic restlessness that gripped Peter Sellers between films. He would make up his mind to go somewhere, anywhere, just to get away from where he was. 'For the first few days,' said Bert Mortimer, 'he'd rape the place. He'd photograph everything that caught his eye. Once he felt he'd conquered it, all he wanted to do was get away from it. Sometimes he'd take the children with him to prove to himself he was having a good time by giving them one.' Bert would have the chore of photographing all of them in every 'fun' situation. But it was over and done with inside a few days, then Peter went off on his own devices and Hattie and Ber† were lumbered with Michael and Sarah. 'He wanted the photos to establish that he'd had children and was capable of playing the father to them the way fathers are supposed to do. The sad thing was, children really didn't interest him at all.'

But as 1963 passed, and his depression started to lift, other interests, and not exactly fatherly ones, reasserted themselves. Instead of going to the West End to see the down-and-outs, he began to go on the town. One of Hattie's duties – not her favourite – was renting flats for the girlfriends he started acquiring. He didn't like women as live-in companions: he feared they would start living *on* him.

Contrary to the image of the playboy suavely manipulating the opposite sex which some of his later films assiduously fostered, he showed a distinct lack of talent in setting up his assignations. Not only had Hattie to rent the amorous set-up: she had to lay in the toothpaste, soap and other creature comforts for the girls who occupied the apartment. Some stayed only a night or two, leaving a large unexpired portion of the lease. Eventually Hattie or Bert (or Bert and his wife, who became Sellers's housekeeper) used these *pieds-à-terre* for more ordinary domestic purposes of their own. Not surprisingly, Hattie Stevenson's view of her boss's sudden passions was tinged with cynicism. According to her, he was 'absolutely hopeless' with women and asked for trouble, never really understood them as individuals and mistrusted them as a sex. At the same time she often saw the humour of situations he got himself into and felt a sympathy for the persistence of Peter's romantic illusions.

One incident illustrated both.. In mid-1963, she and Bert accompanied Sellers to New York, where he was to make *The World of Henry Orient*, in which he played an *avant garde* pianist, resembling a Salvador Dali with cut-back moustache, who is over-rehearsed in the bedroom and out of practice on the concert platform.

One day he got a fan letter from a girl – a blonde, to judge by the head-and-shoulders snapshot she enclosed. Sellers impulsively invited her to come to New York – she was living in another part of America. On the day her plane was due, Sellers, Hattie and Bert motored to the airport. Prudently at this stage, Sellers lurked behind a pillar, saying he would signify his joy or disapproval as Hattie and Bert greeted the

The famous boxer Daniel Mendoza, who was Sellers's great-great-grandfather.

Peg and Bill Sellers.

Brother Conelius's class in 1938 at St Aloysius College; Peter Sellers is standing behind his teacher.

Above: Spike
Milligan, Peter
Sellers and Harry
Secombe
rehearsing a *Goon
Show* in 1952.

Right: Peter Sellers
as a television quiz
master (right) and
Wally Patch in *The
Naked Truth* (1958).

Above: Peter Sellers as the union foreman negotiating with Dennis Price in *I'm all Right, Jack* (1959).

Left: Anne and Peter Sellers with their children, Michael and Sarah, in the Carlton Tower Hotel, London, in October 1961. Despite appearances, the marriage was coming apart.

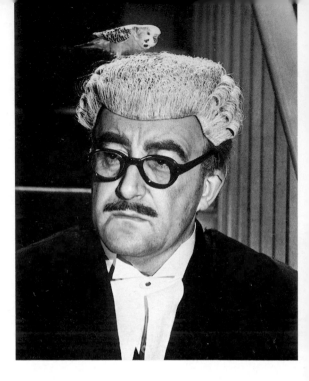

As a barrister in *The Dock Brief* (1962).

Inspector Clouseau makes his entrance.

Peter Sellers as the
US President with
George C. Scott as a
Pentagon hawk in *Dr
Strangelove* (1964).

Peter Cook observes
Peter Sellers holding
the 'blotting paper'
kitten in *The Wrong
Box* (1966).

Above: Miranda Quarry and Peter Sellers, who had only been married a month, ran into Britt Ekland at London's Round House in 1970.

Left: With Princess Margaret and Yul Brynner, Sellers talks to Lord Snowdon.

Above: Dancing with Lynne
Frederick in *The Prisoner of
Zenda.*

Right: A rejuvenated Fu
Manchu imitates Elvis
Presley – the final shot of Peter
Sellers in his last film.

Lynne Frederick's favourite shot of Peter Sellers, at peace with himself in the Swiss Alps.

visitor. Off the aircraft she walked, or, rather, waddled, for she must have weighed 200 lbs. From his hiding-place, Sellers wildly signalled 'Negative'. The girl was taken to a hotel near the Plaza, where Sellers was staying in state, and kept there for a few days before he got word to her that he expected her to slim down before they met. The poor girl went on a crash diet, weighing herself on the bathroom scales in the morning and calling Hattie or Bert in the afternoon to ask plaintively if she'd lost enough and could she now see Mr Sellers. This went on for three weeks. By day, Peter would be putting on his cowardly Casanova act and romancing Angela Lansbury, who was cast as a matronly meringue of indiscretion; by night, he would be chatting up the girl on the other end of the phone, telling her to get down below a certain weight and then, oh *then* they could meet! She lost a good 30 lbs, was rewarded with a huge 'engagement' ring with a large stone in an expensive setting, and even received a marriage proposal from the star. It all sounded as if the character had once more 'possessed' the player. Eventually the 'affair' grew tedious and the girl was returned home, single, but richer and infinitely more svelte. Said Hattie: 'It was a better story than *Henry Orient* turned out to be.'

From the flesh, he turned to the spirit in the hope that he'd find there the elusive contentment that his post-marital misery denied him. The Rev. John Hester was then Vicar of St Anne's, Soho, just round the corner from Sellers's Panton Street offices, and found the actor frequently climbing the stairs to his study and engaging in long discussions to try to reconcile the world of plenty he inhabited with the emptiness of soul that oppressed him. Riches were a penalty, he said, and took the vicar out to lunch to prove his point.

They went to the *Jardin des Gourmets* restaurant in Soho. 'Instead of having a punchbag in life,' said Peter, as they opened their menus, 'you feel you're lamming away at a bag of feathers.'

To show what he meant, the Rev. John Hester recalled, he summoned the waiter and ordered some nonsense drink whose recipe he made up as he went along. The barman solemnly went through the pantomime of mixing the horrible ingredients. Peter sent for some real orange juice, which was brought in a little jug and poured, like a *coup de grace*, over the revolting concoction.

'Peter contemplated the hideous mixture sadly and said to me, 'You see what I mean – now that's terrifying." I took the point. Money could buy you people to do your bidding: it couldn't buy you certainty of spirit.'

The priest found his friend deeply perturbed, plying him with queries about baptism and eventually undertaking to pursue a course of instruction with a view to being received into the Christian religion. He didn't belong to any church, Peter said, because he 'hated joining things'. His own religion, he added rather ambiguously, was doing unto others what they would do unto you.

He had plunged into a part that, coincidentally but usefully, reflected the spiritual certainties which life wasn't catering for. The Boulting Brothers' *Heavens Above* ought to have approached the Church of England in the spirit of a vivisectionist, but too often simply used the satire to milk it for laughs. But Sellers's vicar, whose simple faith is as unpretentiously anchored to him as his bicycle clips, brought to lovable life the one believable being in the film. As has been mentioned, he resembled a younger version of his old Roman Catholic schoolmaster, Brother Cornelius; but the Rev. John Hester was later to say that the character of the simple-witted but transparently honest 'holy fool' whom Sellers played in *Being There* was the *Heavens Above* character twenty years on.

An event occurred in October 1962, which smote Peter to the core. His father died, aged sixty-two, of a heart attack while undergoing surgery in the Middlesex Hospital, London.

His own success had paradoxically brought the son closer than he had ever been to the man with the failed career who had settled in the background of his son's life. Peter now looked in his mirror and saw the face of someone who had achieved all his father had missed – money, celebrity, adulation. Yet inwardly he felt himself to be just as much a failure as Sellers Sr.

The death had another depressing feature. It recalled the history of heart trouble on his mother's side of the family. Peter made a mental note to have a check-up, then found no time between pictures. He settled for the customary examination which precedes every picture for insurance purposes, rather than undergo a more investigative probe. If anything, the death quickened his desire to 'get away from it all'. He decided to leave Britain for good.

He put his Hampstead 'torture-chamber' up for sale and grasped at a film called *The Pink Panther* which would take him out of England – and thus, he hoped, out of himself. It wasn't the star role: but anything was better than sitting around moping. He hadn't even been the first choice for the part. But he had resolved that after *Heavens Above* and a comedy romp called *The Wrong Arm of the Law*, which was a return to his multiple-role period as Monsieur Jules, suave Bond Street salon owner, also known as 'Pearly' Gates, Cockney crook of the London underworld, he would do no more 'little English pictures', only *international* movies from now on. *The Pink Panther* was that all right.

Its American writer-producer-director, Blake Edwards, was a proven hand at comedies like *Operation Mad Ball* or *Breakfast at Tiffany's*, combining the zany raciness of the comic strip with the high-gloss finish of the Hollywood article. It had a multinational cast: David Niven, Robert Wagner, Capucine, Claudia Cardinale – and would have had Peter Ustinov as well, except that he had withdrawn, reportedly out of disappointment that Ava Gardner was not cast opposite him. 'The excuses Ustinov offered made little sense,' Blake Edwards recalled, adding, 'which I have since learnt is simply par for the course with a lot of actors.'

In the emergency following Ustinov's departure, Edwards was 'desperately unhappy and ready to kill, but, as fate would have it, I got Mr Sellers instead of Mr Ustinov – thank God!' The price was high: £90,000 to be precise, for five weeks' work. Sellers and Graham Stark got out pen and paper – 'this was before pocket calculators,' said Stark – and reduced it to a breathtaking daily rate of £2,555. 'We were like schoolboys. Peter had never seen so much money.'

Pausing only long enough to take a quick lesson in the steps of the bossa nova from none other than Anna Neagle – it was needed for a dance sequence in the film – he jetted off to the Cinecitta Studios in Rome at the end of 1962. As he flew south, his mind was assembling those bits and pieces of comic invention which, unknown to him or anyone else at the time, were going to create one of the most universally popular characters of the contemporary cinema – Inspector Clouseau.

EIGHT

Enter The Panther

Peter Sellers got the idea of Inspector Clouseau from a box of matches – a very old-established British brand of safety matches: 'Captain Webb' matches, to be precise. The colophon on the label showed a man in a long, old-fashioned, striped swimsuit, the kind with short legs and half-sleeves. On his face was a look of virility and a big moustache. This practitioner of the strenuous life couldn't have been more Anglo-Saxon-looking; yet Sellers immediately associated him with the ostentatious virility he'd noticed some Frenchmen affecting. There and then, at 35,000 feet up, he decided the big moustache was going on to Clouseau; round his own fined-down form – he had been taking slimming pills for over a year – he'd wrap the same Burberry trenchcoat he was taking to Rome against the winter's nip.

'I'll play Clouseau with great dignity, because he thinks of himself as one of the world's best detectives,' Peter decided. 'Even when he comes a cropper, he must pick himself up with that notion intact. The original script makes him out to be a complete idiot. I think a forgivable vanity would humanize him and make him kind of touching. It's as if filmgoers are kept one fall ahead of him.'

It was one of the very rare occasions when 'finding the character' gave him no trouble at all. Clouseau stepped off the plane in Rome.

Blake Edwards was waiting for him – the first time the two had met – and he and Sellers passed that all-important matriculation test for a comedy director and his star on the drive to the Excelsior Hotel. 'We discovered we both possessed a similar sense of humour, that had its origins in Laurel and Hardy and Keaton and Harold Lloyd,' said Edwards. Edwards claimed that no great change in Clouseau's character was necessary. 'Clouseau was there in the original script: we just added things that made him funnier.' Sellers sent to London for the Robin Hood hat that always looked like the character's self-conscious dip into the prop hamper for a sleuthing disguise. His extraordinary French accent, which sounded as if the vowels were being given the third degree, was Sellers's invention: the physical clumsiness, Blake Edwards's contribution. Clouseau's dignity would be all the funnier, he reckoned, if he were appallingly accident-prone.

Thus began Sellers's first exploration of the physical world of slapstick – or, in his case, slipstick. He skidded into pure acrobatic brilliance. The world was not his oyster, but his banana peel. Clouseau's imperturbability came in direct line of descent from Keaton, who survived earthquakes straight-faced, and from Chaplin, who picked himself up and dusted down his glad rags as carefully as if they were bespoke tailoring. But the real influence which Sellers claimed to feel at work on him was his own preferred comic maestro, Jacques Tati. Tati, too, inhabited a world where things were against him. Clouseau is the victim of inanimate objects like shifty door-knobs, bathrobe cords that fight back, globes of the world that revolve the instant he leans his hand on them and send him spinning. Edwards's trick was to devise more physical ways than one would think humanly possible for a person to lose his balance but never his dignity. And to dignity, Sellers added a gift of immaculate timing that can be seen at its smoothest in the first two *Panther* films – the second, *A Shot in the Dark*, was put into production in London at the end of 1963, before the first had even opened. By then the creators knew what they had got – an annuity for life in the humour that attracted identification in every country in the world. The *Panther* series is second only to the *Bond* series at the global box-office.

Sellers's inherent grace and subtlety permitted him to use physical comedy to explore character – particularly in *The Pink Panther*, where the mishaps become a hilarious, ultimately pathetic runr ug-and-tripping-up commentary on the married life of a Little Man in .ove with his disdainful wife (played by Capucine).

Eager to be in bed with her, he tangles the tassle of his robe and has to step shame-facedly out of it; gallantly trying to whirl an extra blanket over her, he muffs his cast and has to crawl humiliatingly into bed with it draped over him like a collapsed tent; bending over her like Don Juan poised for conquest, he kisses the pillow at the exact second his impatience lets her slide off the slippery quilt and between his knees; and even when their lips safely meet, his hat is left pendant on her hair-pins. When he pops from bedroom to bathroom in search of a sedative, Blake Edwards switches from a sight gag to a sound one – we see nothing, but we hear a hail-shower of sleeping pills, then the resigned crunch-crunch of slippers walking over them. In later films, the element of comic surprise was replaced by the public's warm welcome extended to predictable situations and familiar characters, especially Clouseau's karate battles fought with his Oriental henchman, Cato (played by Burt Kwouk). Sellers in these first two films retains a gravity which suggests the rest of the world is leaning at an angle to him – he keeps us continuously guessing wrong when we try to forecast the next accident that will befall him.

The gags were usually worked out to the tiniest detail, but a lot of improvisation went on during shooting. Sellers had some of his old mates in the pictures, like Graham Stark, and their clowning generated a euphoria on the set as their comedy reactions answered each other, flash by intuitive flash. 'In one of the *Panther*s,' said Stark, 'Blake Edwards said to me, "Now, Graham, you turn to Peter and both of you synchronize your watches." Then he added, "By the way, how exactly *do* you synchronize watches?" The ensuing sequence wasn't even rehearsed: it was totally ad-libbed, Peter and I knew each other so well. Blake supplied the inspiration; Sellers, the performance.'

Inevitably, neither man saw the division of labour quite as equitably as that. 'In happy times, Peter would be enormously inventive,' Edwards said. 'When times were bad, we differed often. Then it was imperative that I, as director, prevailed.'

A friend of both men said, 'With Blake and Peter, it was a love-hate relationship. They were either in happy collusion or embittered conflict. At one time, each said of the other, "I'll never work again with that son of a bitch." For days on end, they would communicate by written messages. Both were arrogant men, each convinced of his own rightness. Peter was a perfectionist. Blake is not. He can be slap-happy. "If there's a short way round, let's take it ... cut corners ... patch it up." That sort of thing. Their difference in attitudes was what led at times to violent scenes of recrimination, and one suspected each of going out of his way to annoy the other. Blake needled Peter by his emphasis on "A Blake Edwards Production", and Peter persuaded himself it should be 'A Peter Sellers Film". Peter even hated a moment in the cartoon credits showing the Pink Panther preparing to crush the little Clouseau type with dumb-bells: he thought Blake had had it put in intentionally. It really was rather funny at times. All the *Panther* films were elaborated without regard to cutting costs – but spending money never deterred either Blake or Peter and maybe they had more in common than either would have admitted. They had tunnel vision – and at the end of the tunnel they saw only themselves. Each was a law unto himself, in a different way – yet it gave them a bond of shared experience. It was all good for the films in the end.'

Edwards commented: 'Peter was a mercurial clown who could get you laughing one minute and cut your heart out with a bloody axe the next.'

Peter's escalating fees helped him nurse any injury to his ego inflicted in these wars of attrition. 'He began by taking a very little salary and a larger percentage,' said his director. 'He ended taking a large salary and an even larger percentage.'

Sometimes, though, money was no good at all. It couldn't reach to the place where Peter really lived: his pride as a creator. A struggle for supremacy between him and his producers over the third *Panther* films led to Sellers withdrawing and the role going to Alan Arkin. 'There's not a bloody thing I can do about it,' Sellers told this writer, grinding his teeth at what he saw as his unique inventiveness being hijacked for someone else. 'In all the years I knew Peter,' Edwards commented when this question was put to him, 'in spite of all the times when he swore he was never going to do another *Panther*, he never stopped complaining about the fact that the Mirisch Company [the producers] had chosen Arkin. Peter was a collector of grievances. But he seemed to bear more of a grudge concerning the Arkin thing than just about anything else. For the sake of my own sanity, I have long since stopped trying to figure it out, but it is interesting to note that the Arkin role [in *Inspector Clouseau*, made in 1968] was first offered to Peter – and he refused it. Also, it was the only unsuccessful *Panther*, yet Peter seemed to take little consolation in that.'

Between the first and second of the *Panther*s, an extraordinary prophecy had been made to Peter by his clairvoyant, Maurice Woodruff. He was told he was going to take a new wife. The news was like a reactive agent and Sellers's depressed post-marital spirits gradually rose as he talked himself into playing a new role – that of a remarried man.

He had moved into the Dorchester Hotel's Oliver Messel suite. This rather over-decorated £410-a-week apartment gave him the round-the-clock service his restlessness required. Doug Hayward used to say, 'All Peter's apartments looked like hotel suites, tenanted but not lived in.' But he had also acquired a country house on the advice of Bill Wills, who saw its investment value. It was a sixteenth-century manor called Brookfield, at Elstead, Surrey, with a seven-acre pasture and garden: his fourth home in seven years.

He was staying at the Dorchester when he met Britt Ekland (or 'Ecklund', as she still called herself).

It has often been assumed that it was she whom Maurice Woodruff had in his psychic vision when, in about the autumn of 1963, he informed Sellers that a person with the initials 'B.E.' would make him very happy. Peter himself had assumed that happiness of the kind he had in mind could only be supplied by someone of feminine gender. But the initials 'B.E.' could have applied equally to Blake Edwards – and Maurice Woodruff's prophecy would have made his subsequent life less fraught if he had seen this possibility earlier.

Sellers collected the London evening newspapers as he and Bert Mortimer returned to the Dorchester from the *Shot in the Dark* set in early February 1964, and to avoid the eyes of others in the lift, he flicked through the pages. His eye lighted on a picture of a blonde Scandinavian starlet who had come to England to play a role in a heavily masculine movie about a regiment in India, *Guns of Batasi*, being made by Twentieth Century-Fox.

'She looks a bit of all right,' he said to Bert. 'Find out where she is.' Nothing was simpler. She was staying in the same hotel: as if she'd been planted there by fate.

'See if she'll come in for a drink,' said Sellers.

Bert knocked on her door. 'It was as if she'd been waiting for us. "I'm with Peter Sellers," I said, "would you like to come up for a drink?" Half-an-hour later, she rang our bell and I said, "Mr Sellers, this is Miss Ekland."'

According to Britt Ekland herself, she chose something 'thick and tweedy' and lechery-resistant to wear at that fatal meeting. Sellers took photos of her, which was the way he proceeded with most of his short-term romances, then took her out to see *The Pink Panther* and wound up the evening with caviar, champagne and a marijuana joint – he'd been buying pot, the use of which was relatively restricted in London then, for some months, after picking up the habit while filming *Henry Orient* in New York. So far the encounter was the film star's par for the romantic course. But it must have been impressive, at that stage in her career, to Britt-Marie Ecklund, only daughter in a Swedish family of four children, who could have been mistaken at the age of twenty-one for a young Brigitte Bardot. A year earlier she had caught Darryl Zanuck's eye, passed a screen test and landed a contract for parts in fourteen movies to be made over seven years – if she stayed the course.

There the interlude with Sellers might have ended, reasonably satisfactorily, the sort of thing that happens to movie folk. Ekland certainly didn't recognize how serious Sellers was.

Nor, perhaps, did he till he began reading the interviews which his infatuation now impelled him to grant to an ever-ready Press. Peter tended to be easily persuaded into believing what he read about himself, if it were favourable enough. His words became detached from the inverted commas of quotation, almost the way his film roles assumed independent power of possession over him. Words out of his mouth put thoughts into his head that had never been there before. It is no exaggeration to say that he probably talked himself into marriage with Britt Ekland. On 9 February 1964, a headline in the *Sunday Express* told him: 'Britt? She Really Is Sensational, Sighs Sellers.' Underneath, he found himself to be telling columnist Roderick Mann: 'I really believe this may prove more than just a casual relationship ... I certainly hope so ... Funny, isn't it? I keep saying to you I'll never get hooked again; that I'm tired of having my heart bleed; but here I am, waiting to be hooked.' He spoke of the fears that went with falling in love with glamorous girls when one was not glamorous oneself. Such girls met other men – 'and that's courting disaster from the start. Especially if you tend to be jealous like me.'

Then he added an illuminating comment on the way he viewed the woman who was soon to become his second wife.

'My trouble, I think, is that as a child I was influenced by too many Mrs Miniver pictures. You know the sort of thing: ideal wife, loyal, devoted, mother enough to make sure you take your pills each day, yet sexy enough to be waiting breathlessly for you to come home every night.'

Looking for a sex symbol who was also a mother figure might have seemed an incompatible quest and a clear warning of what troubles were to come. But as Sellers read and re-read the column in Bert Mortimer's presence, the words convinced him that his feelings were true and sound and his fears less important than his pleasurable anticipation. 'Peter's needs were very much on the surface in those days,' said Theo Cowan. 'He felt what he felt he needed to feel.' At that moment what he needed to feel was in love. The article made a decisive contribution to his self-hypnosis. The very next day he called Britt Ekland long-distance in New York – she had gone there for a week's pre-production preparation – and asked her to be his wife.

They were married barely ten days later at the registrar's office in Guildford, Surrey, on 19 February 1964. 'Our daughter seems to have chosen well,' said Britt's young-looking father at the reception at

Brookfield, where the tiers of the wedding cake were dressed in instant Polaroids of the wedding – a celebration of the groom's love of gimmicks – and the two children of his previous marriage went out in the snow to sell slices of cake through the wrought-iron gates to some of the three thousand spectators who had scraped and dented the couple's fawn Bentley. Peg hadn't attended the ceremony, where David Lodge and Graham Stark had been joint best men. She gave her blessing to her son: but Aunties Ve and Do and she had not been all that enthused when Peter summoned them to Elstead at short notice to meet his fiancée. The tea she had served them – probably with hands inexpertly versed in English customs – was deemed colourless and nearly cold; and after loyally hanging about for a while as Britt in a pretty chef's cap busied herself cooking a little chicken in an even tinier frying pan, Peg and her relatives grimly departed for a good tuck-in of pub sandwiches on the road back to London. Britt, however, maintained that later she got on with her mother-in-law very well.

There was no time for a honeymoon. Both bride and groom had films to start. While Britt began work on *Guns of Batasi*, playing a Swedish UN worker who falls in love with a British private (played by John Leyton), Peter flew off to begin his Hollywood comedy, *Kiss Me, Stupid*, which Billy Wilder was directing. He was looking forward to working with the man who had made *The Apartment, Some Like It Hot*, and other comedies he inordinately admired: but anticipation quickly became disenchantment once the shooting got under way.

Wilder loved to keep an 'open' set and filled it with cronies, visitors and random onlookers, believing the 'happy' atmosphere contributed to his players' relaxedness and receptiveness to his instructions. For some, it worked. To Peter, it was agony. He felt required to give two performances, one in character as the insanely jealous husband in the small-town farce about an amateur songwriter seeking favours from a famous recording star by using his wife as a lure, and the other for 'Billy's Bystanders', as he dubbed the hangers-on come to kibbitz on 'Peter Sellers, famous funnyman'. His concentration was being continually shattered by 'people licking ice creams in the corner of my eye'. Bert Mortimer noticed his employer's anxiety increase as he discovered that Wilder's methods were exactly the opposite of the relaxed and collaborative exploration of scene and character he had found so fruitful when working with Kubrick. 'You take three paces to this point, Peter, hit your mark, turn slightly, look at him, speak your line....' Peter couldn't tolerate such cut-and-dried instructions. He asked Wilder's favourite actor, Jack Lemmon, how *he* coped. 'When the scene's set up,' said Lemmon, 'all I do is close my eyes and say to myself, "It's magic time." It always works.' *It's magic time.*' Peter repeated it like a mantra – and it didn't work once.

He'd already realized that the script by Wilder and I. A. L. Diamond would need all his comic inventiveness and pathos to purge the plot of its pimpish implications of unpleasantness. For the first time he was learning, in unpropitious circumstances, the make-or-break burden that stardom carried. It was 'up to him' – yet he wasn't in control. He was passing restless hours off the set, too, fretting over what Britt might be doing. His first wife, Anne, had voluntarily abandoned her own acting career upon marriage. But he knew only too well that his own stardom put an aura around his new wife and he knew the forces in the film industry that might well be tempted to exploit it. He was also more fearful than he cared to admit at the time as to whether, in fact, she really missed him.

Perhaps it was the irresistible carry-over effect of the film role he was then engaged in playing – but jealousy over her film role, playing opposite handsome John Leyton, kept him constantly calling her until she took advantage of the short Easter break to fly to California. She wasn't to be found when work resumed on *Guns of Batasi* after the holiday. She was still with Sellers, in the palatial marble-floored mansion rented from Spyros Skouras (ironically, he was president of the company that was making her film), where she found her husband's dogged wiles had already furnished a bedroom closet with a complete wardrobe to replace the one she had left behind in her hasty and secretive flight. After fruitlessly trying to pressure her into returning, Fox substituted Mia Farrow in her role, reshot Britt Ekland's three weeks of scenes and hit her and Sellers with a £500,000 suit alleging breach of contract on her part and inducement to breach it on his. This was a shock. Bill Wills notified Peter that he didn't have that kind of money. But the impenitent husband laid plans for a £1,500,000 counter-suit.

It was a haggard, fatigued man, worried by all these legal problems, who made anxious and none too satisfactory love to Britt on the night of Sunday, 5 April 1964, stimulating his efforts with isobutyl nitrite, which he had been using for almost a year to enhance his sexual satisfactions by prolonging the period of orgasm. Soon afterwards the pains began in his chest: he was on fire. Hattie and Bert were out. There were no servants. They had given notice because – they said – the marble floors were too hard on their feet. Actually, according to Bert, they left because the boss was too hard on their leisure time. Bert got back to find Britt's note on his bed, saying that Peter was ill and that Dr Rex Kennamer, a noted cardiologist and Elizabeth Taylor's physician, had been to the house and Sellers was going to the Cedars of Lebanon hospital for a thorough check next day. When Hattie heard the news she immediately thought, 'To what lengths will he go this time to get out of a film he hates?'

As soon as Dr Kennamer returned to their North Hillcrest home early on 6 April, he advised Britt to take her ailing husband directly to the Cedars. Bert followed and it was he who actually signed the document to say he would pay the medical bills for his millionaire employer. Britt was too distressed to read or sign anything. Still, Peter's condition was diagnosed as mild. A few weeks rest would see him on his feet....

Sellers admitted the use of isobutyl nitrite. But he kept to himself what he had been doing immediately prior to Britt's arrival in Hollywood. And this was probably a far more likely reason for the mild coronary that was then suspected.

For he had been slaving away at building up his muscles for one of the most macho roles of the screen – James Bond. Producers Harry Saltzman and 'Cubby' Broccoli owned the rights to almost all the Ian Fleming thrillers and had already seen the extent of the goldfield they were sitting on. But Charles Feldman, a rival American producer, had rights in the one book they did not own, *Casino Royale*, and had approached Peter about playing 007. Ridiculous! Preposterous! And yet ... Sellers as Bond? This was problem-setting on a scale to seize Sellers's fantasies as his initial pooh-poohing was superseded by a challenging 'What if?....'

To play a super-hero, as dexterous in pulling the birds as he was at aiming the bullets, had a certain appropriateness for a man well aware that while his new bride was just twenty-one he himself would soon be into his forties.

Sellers hired a work-out expert and set himself a rigorous course of body-building exercises which he began each evening on returning from the studios, when he was already fatigued from a disagreeable eight-to-ten hour stint on a film he now detested. 'He would run round the pool,' said Bert, 'do hectic half-hour bouts of exercise, practise his "panther" walk' – for with Peter, how the character walked was vital, and he associated Bond with big cats – and, after all this, submit to a punishing massage.

It all took its near-fatal toll on a heart which, as Peter later recollected in the enforced tranquillity of convalescence, had already suffered more than half-a-dozen largely unrecognized attacks, put down to indigestion, in the preceding ten years.

At 4.32 a.m. on 7 April 1964, his heart suddenly stopped beating. It stopped for one-and-a-half minutes. Dr Kennamer insisted on manually re-starting it, there and then – which probably saved Sellers's life – then rushing him to the Cedars's intensive care unit, installed just two years before, where a pacemaker fed such powerful electric shocks into him that 'it almost knocked me out of bed,' as he later recollected.

Seven more times that day, Sellers's heart stopped from acute myocardial infarction – a complete block. Technically, he was in the condition known as 'dead'.

When he could look back on it all, he realized just how tranquillizing 'death' was, almost like dozing off to sleep, then being returned with a jolt and finding 'all you cats', as he called the doctors, gathered around him. 'I'll never fear it again,' he said. But other sensations of a more profound kind which he claimed to have undergone while 'dead' had a more disconcerting and a more enduring effect. The repeated act of 'dying' became for Peter Sellers the most important experience of his life.

To Shirley MacLaine he confided a description of it that lost none of its graphicness in the fourteen years between his undergoing it and his entrusting its secret to her when they filmed *Being There* together in 1979.

'The first time Peter's heart stopped,' said MacLaine, 'he said he felt his soul leave his body. Suddenly he was looking at himself lying there, with Rex Kennamer desperately pressing his chest cavity. He saw the other attendants frantically pressing his heart. He saw Rex open his chest and described the rough, restorative treatment he gave his heart muscle. All the time there was white light enveloping Peter. He saw a circle – with a welcoming hand come through it. He didn't want to die, but he felt a strong, friendly attraction to the other side. Then he felt his consciousness dissolving back into his body and he knew Rex had succeeded in re-starting his heart and that he would have to stay alive.'

But what bothered Peter Sellers from that moment till the end of his days was – why had his life been spared? 'He couldn't figure out why he was alive, when all the medical evidence told him he had died.'

Sellers had already persuaded himself that his art in impersonating characters was a psychic bonus he enjoyed from the lives he had lived in earlier incarnations. But if so, he thought, who was the person called Peter Sellers who had been so miraculously recalled to life after eight 'deaths'? And for what purpose had he been spared?

The Rev. John Hester had flown to Los Angeles at his own expense on hearing the bad news. He arrived with holy oil to anoint a dying man and was staggered to see him sitting up in bed. The experience of resurrection intensified Sellers's spiritual concern and friends discerned the start of a new introspection, a sense of his not 'being there' in spirit, though present in body. Britt Ekland found it especially unnerving that a man whose restlessness had once perturbed her was now sitting still for lengthy periods, saying nothing, but staring at her with his thoughts turned inwards. MacLaine is convinced that the experience shuffled Sellers's psychic identities and was the cause of confusion in some of his relationships in the years ahead. 'All those people he had been in other lives were now slopping over into his own lifetime, confusing him, activating bad vibrations between himself and people who were inimical to them. Peter used to say to me, "I know my conduct sometimes makes people deeply unhappy. But I don't understand it myself."'

To the outside world, however, the revivified Sellers spoke in plainer terms. He anticipated doing 'no work for a year', starting with a six-months' convalescence in England, where he had bought a red setter to bound beside him on the recommended walks, a pair of matched palomino ponies for more vigorous exercise and, inevitably, an £11,500 blue Ferrari (his eighty-fourth car) as a token of his recovery and restored youthfulness. 'I suffer from a prolonged mechanical adolescence,' he joked.

Before he left America in June, after settling a £26,100 medical bill, he signed his name in the wet concrete outside Grauman's Chinese Theater, adding a heart beneath it. But there were few valentines for Hollywood in the first words he spoke to this writer back in London. 'America I would go back to tomorrow, but as far as Hollywood is concerned, I've taken the round trip for good ... they give you every creature comfort except the satisfaction of getting the best work out of yourself.' When this was sent over the wires, Hollywood blew him a collective raspberry. 'Talk About Unprofessional Rat Finks,' chided a well-publicized cable despatched a few days later signed by Wilder, Dean Martin and Kim Novak among others. (He had been replaced by Ray Walston in *Kiss Me, Stupid* and his illness brought him respite from Fox's law-suit, which was eventually settled with the promise of his giving favourable consideration to making a film for them.) Sellers riposted to his peers' rebuke with a £750 full-page advertisement in *Variety* – a firm, courteously worded defence. 'I did not go to Hollywood to be ill. I went there to work and found, regrettably, that the creative side in me couldn't accept the conditions under which work had to be carried out.'

Theo Cowan and Dennis Selinger noticed that, the spiritual confusion of his coronary experience apart, Sellers's sense of self-interest had been remarkably clarified by his aborted film experience. The ensuing spell of enforced inactivity gave him what he had previously lacked or deliberately avoided – the time to brood on his career. When Theo Cowan said, 'He now had the conviction that he was the best judge of what was right for himself,' he did not mean that Peter had ever been timid about it in earlier days. But a director of equal tenacity of opinion – a Kubrick, Blake Edwards or, in their early days, the Boultings – opposed him with a creative sense of challenge which he found fruitful, even if he resisted them at times, because he recognized their own truly creative energies. But it is noteworthy that following his Hollywood experience he tended to choose directors either compliant enough to go along with his ideas or else not sufficiently experienced to have the clout to make things difficult for him.

At first he worried that he might have lost his touch – mightn't even be able to remember his lines. But a chance to prove himself and make a charitable gesture came with a small part in *Carol for Another Christmas*, a TV film directed by Joseph L. Mankiewicz in New York in aid of the United Nations. His fee was a token 350 dollars.

A week after his three-day stint ended, and for considerably more money, £125,000 to be precise, plus a percentage, he stepped into a clinging black velvet suit, put on a Richard III wig, and started work in *What's New, Pussycat?* as Peter O'Toole's nutty psychiatrist. Sellers's doctors believed it was better to put him to work than let him fret in enforced idleness. The problem of insurance coverage was boldly sidestepped by producer Charles Feldman, who earmarked £200,000 of his own money to cover the morbid possibility of having to shoot Sellers's scenes again with someone else if illness or death intervened.

What's New, Pussycat?, directed by Clive Donner, mustered the largest group of kooks hitherto seen on the screen and rushed them through a series of barely linked situations that resembled *La Ronde* with the brakes off. It was a good-omened entertainment for what was then being perceived – though not yet officially dubbed – as the 'Swinging Sixties', with their erratic, way-out, do-your-own-thing sense of accelerating anarchy. The mood of the times suited Sellers perfectly. It was as if *The Goon Show* had 'gone international' and its characters got 'high' on the hallucinatory drugs then coming into fashion. The film's huge box-office success – which overcame notices of extreme hostility from the New York critics, who called it 'salacious', 'leering', 'over-sexed', and, at its mildest, 'distasteful' – was largely credited to Sellers's artfulness. After all, it was his kind of humour, wasn't it? What was overlooked, by those who either praised or blamed, was a hyper-thyroid character in the film who was also the screenplay's author and almost a Sellers look-alike. Comedian Woody Allen even walked into Britt Ekland's bedroom one day to say hello and, 'for a moment', was mistaken for her husband. As for rivalry between the two, there was 'no problem', Allen recalled. 'I had never done a film. I was a complete nobody. Sellers was an absolute giant and I was delighted he'd consented to do my script and I was going to share the movie with him. To me, nothing else mattered. I'd have been happy to hold his coat.'

Though outwardly restored to his exuberant working self, an inwardly moody Sellers interspersed the filming with deep, serious discussions on religious topics with the Rev. John Hester. Hester sometimes went over to Paris. Sellers's hatred of petty officialdom – or not getting his own way – hadn't lessened. 'Once I arrived at his hotel around midnight and he demanded a room for me. The hotel said it hadn't any. "Of course you have," Peter exploded. "Find my guest a room – or else." They were stubborn, so there and then he upped and packed and decamped and we all spent the night in a different hotel.'

Hester started preparing Peter for conversion to Christianity. He took one lesson a week, usually half- to three-quarters of an hour, designed to stretch over a three-month period. 'Peter didn't take *any-thing* on trust: he was continually asking me questions. Ursula Andress [his co-star in *Pussycat*] sometimes sat with us in his Plaza-Athenée suite, dressed in leopard skin or cheetah, while Peter and I discussed God's relationship with man, the Testaments, the sacraments and prayer. One thing he frequently mentioned was Jesus walking on the Sea of Galilee. It fascinated him. He'd visited Israel two years earlier and told me how he'd followed Christ's footsteps, on the shore, anyhow, and had been moved to demonstrate his Christian sincerity. One of the last postcards I received from him before his death came from the South of France. "All there is here is water," he wrote. "You know what J.C. did with that."' Sellers's fascination with this particular miracle was to lead to behind-the-scenes controversy over the ending of *Being There* – where the character he plays walks out of the film on the placid surface of a lake.

He didn't stay the course of conversion. 'He eventually felt that if he were baptized and received into the Christian faith, he would be cutting himself off from all ties with other faiths – above all, his Jewishness.'

Sellers had always an ambivalent attitude to his Semitic origins. After his illness he had been desperately anxious to play the Fagin role in the film of Lionel Bart's *Oliver*. The character must have inevitably displayed less than flattering Jewish characteristics. But it was a legal decision, not a conscientious one, which dissuaded him. The judge who forbade Bart to dispose of his rights until a trial determined which of two competing companies was entitled to buy them showed that there was at least one person in the kingdom who was unimpressed by Sellers's uniqueness. 'There is ample evidence,' he said, 'that there are other eminent actors who could play this part with great and, not to be invidious, equal distinction.'

Sellers always felt he had let the Rev. John Hester down and tried making it up in other ways. One plan was to donate all his fee for one of his films to rebuilding the Church of St Anne, Soho; but Bill Wills found some financial obstacle to that. For Christmas, Sellers presented the priest with a set of LPs of Olivier reading the Bible. And he invited him to be godfather to his daughter, Victoria, born to him and Britt Ekland in January 1965. The cleric was touched. 'He did for his child what he could not do for himself.'

In May 1965, a villa, concealed among the cypresses of a private estate on the Via Appia Antica outside Rome, echoed throughout its marble interiors with what sounded like Laurence Olivier reciting, in his Richard III voice, cold as an executioner's axe, the words, not of Shakespeare, but of the Beatles hit, *A Hard Day's Night*, whose yeah-yeah-yeah beat had been mischievously transposed into the lilt of a madrigal. 'Olivier' chopped off the words of the lyric so that every one seemed a head falling off the block.

People took several seconds to realize that this was one of Sellers's most ingenious impersonations.

It was typical of his good mood and his restored capacity for over-loading his day, lest any free time in it give him a headache over how to fill it, that Sellers had cut this inspired disc while setting up the first film for his own company, Brookfield Productions, which he had formed with designer-turned-producer John Bryan to make six pictures. After the *Pussycat* triumph, finance was no trouble.

After the Fox had all the appearance of a hand-crafted work. Every constituent looked a winner: screenplay by Neil Simon, direction by

Vittorio De Sica, starring Sellers and Britt Ekland. 'A milestone for me,' said Sellers, 'not as a return to active life, but in my ambitions for Britt.' These were nothing less than to make her as great an actress as Sophia Loren.

To visiting journalists, Sellers oozed confidence. The well-concealed reality was somewhat different. No sooner had De Sica been signed than Sellers became disenchanted. It was the old story: anticipation is nine-tenths of the pleasure of possession. He had always held De Sica in awe. After all, he hadn't just made pictures – he had made history with his neo-realistic comedy *Bicycle Thieves*, which still appeared on many of the 'World's Ten Best' film lists. But Sellers now found De Sica's English too poor to convey his ideas and he resented the director's fall-back resourcefulness in miming how he wanted Peter to play the part of a small-time Italian crook masquerading as a famous film-maker to facilitate a bullion robbery. Britt, in a black wig, played his sixteen-year-old sister. Neil Simon's script, which had looked like an Ealing-style comedy set in Italy, played like a Broadway sitcom filled with Jewish jokes given a Latin complexion. De Sica privately said he despised it: his lack of interest became evident. Sellers, aware that his own performance was falling below his hoped-for perfection, tried to have De Sica fired: but Bryan, aware that another director might add much to the budget but little to the movie, resisted him. The air was cool in Rome and Ischia that summer.

'This was the first time I noticed Peter thinking about his long-term career instead of just his current performance,' said Theo Cowan. 'The production troubles – his own company, remember – made him aware how vulnerable he was. If the movie were good, he took the credit: if bad, he copped all the blame. It was one of the earliest times that he had a view of himself wider than that of a working actor. He told himself, "If I have to interfere in future, I shall interfere – to protect myself as much as the picture."'

The film was poorly received and did correspondingly poor business. It had 'the sort of jocularity you find in Jerry Lewis films', wrote Bosley Crowther. Kathleen Carroll made her displeasure plainer: 'It has a near-fatal disease diagnosed as acselleration, or, in layman's language, too much Peter Sellers.'

It was a relief to see Sellers back with quality, and strictly rationed quantity, when he did a cameo role as Dr Pratt in Bryan Forbes's *The Wrong Box*. This was an unrecognizable Sellers – a drooping, haunted face, shoulder-length locks, a paunch, spindly legs, plush carpet slippers, a frock coat distempered with breakfast droppings and a stethoscope that coiled eerily into his waistcoat in a way which suggested it might – just *might* – be directly connected to his intestines. Surrounded by clowns, he confirmed that he still knew the difference between a comedy act and comedy acting.

'We couldn't really afford Peter's asking price for a cameo role,' said Bryan Forbes, 'so a compromise was reached. We didn't pay him anything at all for being in the film, but we donated £25,000 to charity.'

Though the part was brief, shooting it over five days involved Forbes in what had become a constant problem on every Peter Sellers film – convincing the star that he wasn't giving a terrible performance. 'After a day's shooting, Peter saw the rushes, decreed he was dreadful and wanted it all re-shot – failing that, he would quit the picture. "Look, you're my oldest friend," I said, "you have *my word* you are excellent. I've never lied to you; I'm not lying now." When he saw I was telling the truth, then he came to love and indeed possess Dr Pratt. He'd go into the voice on every occasion. When he was filming, he kept dropping things on the suit at every meal. When he went home, he slept in it. And to the end of his days every letter he sent me was signed "Pratt M.D."'

Forbes also witnessed what he believes was Sellers's most inspired piece of improvisation.

'He was doing this scene with Peter Cook in the doctor's cat-infested surgery. He had to open a desk drawer, draw out a kitten and say, "You wouldn't like a moggy instead of a death certificate?" Cook had to reply, with considerable patience, "No, doctor, I collect eggs." At that point in the filming, Sellers said vaguely, "Eggs? Ah, yes. Ah like an egg meself. But they don't make good pets. Too quiet. You can't call 'em in at night." We just got three frames past this glorious *ad lib* when Peter Sellers broke up, Peter Cook broke up, the entire crew – myself included – broke up. It was brilliant. The thing about Peter was that if someone gave him the clues across, he would work at the part like a crossword puzzle and come up with some staggering solutions to the down words.'

Charles Feldman, producer of his next movie, *Casino Royale*, had to pay rather more than £25,000 – one million dollars, to be precise and not to charity, either.

Casino Royale was no longer seen as a serious rival to Sean Connery's Bond movies. Feldman was convinced there was a timely fortune to be made in a Sellers send-up of the genre. His gratitude to Peter for pumping Goonish life into *What's New, Pussycat?* had been lavishly expressed. 'I came out of my Elstead house one morning,' Sellers said, 'and waiting for me at the end of the drive was Charlie's thank-you present – a new Rolls-Royce. I mean things like that don't happen in real life, do they? Only in films.'

But gratitude was now tempered by his going-rate. An event had occurred which was designed to force Sellers's price up to heights he had never dreamed possible. Two hard bargainers called David Begelman and Freddie Fields were now representing Sellers in his American deals – Dennis Selinger and John Redway still looked after his British interests, so the companies overlapped to some extent. Selinger and Redway were in the middle of pressing the American company hard for the privilege of taking on Sellers when Begelman – who now heads production at Metro-Goldwyn-Mayer – reminded Sellers that they had brought new life to the traumatic career of Judy Garland. Had Peter heard how they had staged the big come-back concert for her? He hadn't even heard the record of the event? Well, that was easily fixed. There and then, by phone, he arranged to have six copies express-airmailed the next morning. Awed by the name of Garland, impressed by these men's decisiveness, flattered by their attentions, Sellers agreed to go with them without more ado. 'It was masterly timing,' said Dennis Selinger ungrudgingly, 'I'm sure the record swung the deal.'

One man who remained unimpressed by Charles Feldman's coup in getting Sellers was Wolf Mankowitz. When Feldman asked him to write the *Casino Royale* screenplay with Sellers in mind, the man whose business venture with the star had come mortifyingly unstuck five years before urged him: 'Charlie, do not have Sellers in this film. The man will delay everything, destroy the schedule – and you.'

Feldman said, 'Columbia are bananas about him after *Pussycat*. It'll cost four or five million dollars but take only four or five weeks.'

'Charlie,' Mankowitz said, 'it'll take so much longer than four or five weeks. It will be catastrophic.'

'Wolf,' Feldman replied, suddenly looking as if he had been talking up his own confidence, 'stay with me.'

In the event, it *was* catastrophic. Peter now had considerable say-so in the production: not of a contractual nature, but of the kind a star needs to keep him happy. At his urging, Joe McGrath was signed to direct. Sellers had first met McGrath, a genial Scotsman with a pawky sense of the ridiculous, ten years before. McGrath had been to see *The Naked Truth* in a suburban London cinema. As he came out, he spotted Sellers standing at the side of the foyer listening to people's remarks. McGrath boldly accosted him and said, like a newspaper reader out to win a recognition contest in a seaside holiday resort, 'You are the *real*

Peter Sellers and I claim the £10 prize.' Sellers broke up and led him off to a new-fangled *espresso* coffee bar and a heart-to-heart talk. When next they met, McGrath was Dick Lester's assistant director on a Sellers series on television. This time Sellers's jocular greeting was, 'So you got to the top without my help, Joe?' But their mutual bonhomie soon ran out on *Casino Royale*, for between them fell the enormous shadow of Orson Welles.

NINE

Royale and The Royals

The stunt man noticed that the star's trailer parked on the set of *Casino Royale* was rocking on its axles. He could hear voices inside rising in argumentative intensity. There was a sudden bang, like a fist hitting the thin metal sides of the vehicle. 'My god, they're fighting,' he thought, and, running over, yanked open the door. Inside, director Joe McGrath and Peter Sellers were tussling with each other after a fisticuff exchange that had mercifully deteriorated into schoolboy side-swiping and then, as each recognized the childishness of their anger, into helpless giggling.

This explosion of tempers in which Peter, suddenly stepping into Inspector Clouseau's shoes, had flung a karate chop at his director, was symptomatic of the gradual disintegration of Charles Feldman's production since shooting had begun at Shepperton Studios in February 1966. The huge unexpected success of *What's New, Pussycat?* had tempted Feldman to start the picture before he was confident of his script. A script, somehow, no longer seemed to matter so much when the style of visual anarchy, narrative *non sequiturs* and every star being allowed to do his own thing appeared to be the recipe for box-office success. 'When they'd been shooting four weeks,' said Graham Stark, 'I got a phone call out of the blue asking me to report the next day for a role that was being written that night. I found Peter being fed a steady supply of gags on flimsy paper by a relay of writers working away in a caravan just beyond camera range. We shot for six days and it was sheer lunacy.'

'That was the fashionable way to make a film then,' Wolf Mankowitz confirmed. 'It was also a very, very expensive way.' About a month into filming, Feldman realized how high the bill was going to be, and even then he had to keep adding to it. Mankowitz saw his tightly plotted scenario reduced to ruins.

Peter Sellers, too, realized that nothing was going right, and it was at this point that he lost confidence in 'the Prince of Darkness', as he had begun calling Feldman. Then things started to go very badly wrong indeed.

In retrospect, Sellers has been blamed for almost all that ensued. This is unfair. In taking on *Casino Royale*, Peter had stepped into a bigger and rougher league of film-making than he had ever known. His new team of personal managers had created an enviable position for him, in terms of rewards and prestige, by getting him a million-dollar fee. But Sellers knew the film business well enough by now to appreciate that a star in this kind of international project gets his way only during the shooting of it. Once it is over, once he has recorded his image 'as directed', he is left with little muscle to flex. He can do only a limited amount to protect himself in the cutting rooms, or influence the way that the film is released, advertised and promoted. Law suits were possible, but such procedures took years to come to trial (if they ever did), drained away a star's energies as well as his bank balance, and in any case united the Hollywood companies, on whom he now depended exclusively for six-figure fees, against stars who were 'difficult' enough to insist on their contractual rights. Accordingly, Sellers insisted on his artistic rights while shooting was in progress and, unfortunately, it was like building foundations on shifting sands.

Casino Royale was based on the conceit that everyone and no one was James Bond. A handful of international stars played various relatives of the Bond family: David Niven was Sir James Bond, Woody Allen was his nephew Jimmy Bond, and Joanna Pettet was the glamorous spy Mata Bond. Sellers played Evelyn Tremble, author of a book on baccarat, who is recruited by the Secret Service to ruin the SMERSH villain, Le Chiffre, at the casino gaming tables. Le Chiffre was played by Orson Welles.

'Joe,' said Sellers to McGrath, before shooting began, 'we have got to watch Welles. This man has a reputation for taking over the films he appears in. We must not let him do it with ours.'

'I don't see Orson as a one-man fifth column,' McGrath protested.

But Peter viewed the corpulent co-star with the deepest suspicion. Peter at the time was almost painfully thin. Like many fatties reformed by masochistic dieting, he tended to treat the unrepentant gourmands of the world with a mixture of condescension and contempt. 'I felt Welles's physique had something to do with Peter's coolness when the three of us first met,' said Mankowitz, himself no flyweight in those days. When Peter started hinting that it only required self-discipline to shed excess weight and clearly Welles hadn't got what it took, the glowering American growled that acting was more than standing still on a set of bathroom scales. It was an inauspicious beginning, but there was more to Peter's apprehension than the dislike engendered by Welles's weight. Peter, as has already been remarked, always stood in awe of stars who had claimed their niche in film history. As *Citizen Kane*'s principal begetter, Welles had carved his impressive features on the cinema's Mount Rushmore: Peter was aware that his own comedy talents were still written in sand. And there was an aspect to Welles that made him intuitively shy away from close contact. As he expressed it to this writer, 'Welles is a bad witch.' Welles had a reputation as a very skilful conjuror and illusionist, talents that in olden days were associated with 'dark powers'. To a superstitious person like Peter, who regularly frequented his clairvoyant and consulted his astrologer almost daily, the Cagliostro side of Welles was a constant source of unease. He feared that Welles would penetrate his psyche, and he simply didn't want to be 'hexed'.

As for Welles, he could be as obstinate as Peter. Between mopping his mighty brow under the arc lights with a damp chamois leather, he made it clear he did not intend to deviate from his conception of Le Chiffre to reconcile it with Sellers's performance in a comic key. The scene was set for a confrontation, and it merely added to the troubles that the confrontation literally never occurred. For although the big scene between the two characters consisted of a duel of wits and cards at the baccarat tables, Peter decreed that the scene would 'play better' if McGrath shot him and Welles separately, while the other wasn't present. They could be brought together in the editing.

'This was my first film in Panavision, the letter-box-shaped screen,' said McGrath. 'You could hold a hundred yards of the set in the lens. We had seven hundred extras for the gaming tables sequence – but we had no way of bringing our two stars together in the same shot!'

Peter said, 'Shoot Orson with the background action going on, Joe. Then come round towards his view-point of me. Cut to a single close-up of me and I'll think of something funny to do.'

McGrath had not found Welles to be the stealthy saboteur that Peter had feared. 'After a day or two of this, he raised one big eyebrow and said to me, "Joe, this may take some time." Orson was shooting a film of his own in Madrid, off and on, and looked on his fee from *Casino Royale* as production coin to resume work on his own pet project. He certainly didn't want to linger longer than necessary with us. Moreover, he was eating his head off in the apartment he'd taken near the best restaurant in Mayfair. As the delay got longer, he got fatter.'

To get the illusion of togetherness between Sellers and Welles, the harassed McGrath was obliged to open on Welles in tight close-up, then pan upwards to the casino's mirrored ceiling and catch Peter's reflection in the glass.

Peter was, meanwhile, being nagged by other worries than a Wellesian *coup d'état*. It seemed to McGrath that he had begun the film without succeeding in 'getting' the character. 'I think I'll play Evelyn Tremble in a Birmingham accent,' he told Feldman pensively. 'A what?' Feldman exploded privately, appalled at the prospect of his multi-million-dollar movie having a star who spoke in one of the most impenetrable provincial accents in England. But he told McGrath, 'If he wants to play it that way, let the guy do what he wants. We can cut what we need out of it later.'

Personally, McGrath had begun to doubt that there would be that much to cut. In the event, Peter played the character straight – all too straight. 'He was walking through the role giving a vocally featureless performance. It was like he was trying to play it *à la* Cary Grant.' Peter was attempting to solve the character problem as he shot the part. 'Acting is like walking a tight-rope,' he told his director. 'You may fail miserably. You may succeed brilliantly. That's what taking a risk means in this business.' But Charles Feldman was paying for certainties, not risks. His despondency infected everyone, including Peter. 'Charlie had lost faith in everything and everyone,' said McGrath, 'and Peter realized it. He and I had production conferences in which it was obvious to me that Peter was hundreds of miles away. "Look, Peter," I'd say, "it's not working. Nothing's coming through." It was then he threw his karate chop at me.'

Joe McGrath parted company with the production soon after this episode, reflecting realistically that as he owed his job largely to Sellers's support, he couldn't complain too bitterly if he had forfeited that support by his frankness. But he bore no grudge. 'Not long afterwards, Peter wrote me a letter saying how sad and sorry he was. That must have cost him an effort. Years later he asked for it back, "You might publish it, Joe," he said. Even when he knew he had been in the wrong, admitting it was anathema to him.'

Peter himself quit *Casino Royale* before his role was completed. He claimed, correctly, that the time allocated to it had expired and he had production plans of his own to be getting on with. For a time they thought of using a double for the un-shot scenes which Robert Parrish was now directing, but no one could be found who looked like him; presumably Woody Allen wasn't asked.

Casino Royale consumed three more directors – John Huston, Ken Hughes and Val Guest – and uncredited hands galore worked on bits and pieces of its script. All sank without trace in the production bedlam. Despite patches of extravagant fun, and enough stars to constitute a population explosion, its plethora of talents amounted to no more than decorative confetti on an elephant. However, a scapegoat was needed for Columbia Pictures' corporate wrath – not long afterwards, Charles Feldman died – and Peter Sellers fitted the role to perfection. Though his contribution to the chaos had been in proportion to his limited role in the production, the publicity he had engendered over his stubbornness had been disproportionately glaring and unwelcome. A high-ranking company executive vowed that Sellers would never again work on one of their films.

Off screen, too, Peter's life was disagreeably unsettled. He realized that he had married a woman who was still determined to pursue her career. Even the trivial matter of her having her initials B.E. put on her travelling cases seemed to him to be a defiant brandishing of her professional independence – perhaps it also recalled Woodruff's prophecy. Britt's family, in particular her two brothers Bo and Bengt, had become an irritant to him. The Swedish contingent used to descend on the Elstead home, and it didn't take long for Peter to feel that they had outstayed their welcome. Actually, he never liked having many people around him, in anyone's house, never mind his own. His dislike of having to share space with others is fairly commonplace among film stars: in Peter's case, it developed into a phobia which cost him a small fortune in exorbitantly purchased privacy.

The *Casino Royale* débâcle had sharpened his self-interest; now it had an edge on it like a razor blade. Too often, he succeeded in wounding himself as well as some of those most devoted to his interests. He had become totally unable to relax and seemed to resent others who had that facility. Bert discovered that no sooner had the boss left, as he sometimes did, alone for a weekend abroad than the calls would start coming in from Peter's destination, which gave the faithful Bert no peace of mind or leisure time. Hattie Stevenson finally parted from Sellers over her ski plans. 'Impossible,' he snapped, when she mentioned she was taking February off to be on the slopes. 'You'll have to wait till May.' In May there'd be no snow, she pointed out, feeling that he knew this only too well. Deadlock. So Hattie left. Theo Cowan also found himself more than once summarily dismissed – on one occasion because his office switchboard girl didn't catch the name of the caller and said, 'Peter who?' But Cowan cannily stayed in friendly contact, corresponded with Peter when he knew his temporary secretary would be out of town and he'd have to read the letters sent him, and found his services still being utilized. 'One got re-engaged almost by default,' he said.

All these people liked Sellers despite his faults of this nature: if examples of his misbehaviour are still painful for them to recall, their understanding of his vulnerable character, which they tried to protect while working for him, demonstrates the hold he still has posthumously on their affections.

One of his later assistants, Sue Evans, said of him: 'If anyone he respected was unimpressed by his outbursts or took a decisive opposite view, he tended to calm down and see reason. If he felt someone was an idiot or unprepared to discuss and challenge his ideas, he could be the must stubborn man alive. He was genuinely annoyed when his instructions were not carried out, and often had good reason. He never settled for second best, though sometimes his definition of second best was a little egocentric. Somebody whom someone else had thought of and he had not, for example – that was second best. But he simply had to protect himself. Plenty of people were ready to exploit him. The task *we* had was to protect him *from himself*. Another trait of his that made for a lot of unintentional unpopularity was that he found it impossible to say "No" to people's faces. He either changed his mind when they weren't around, or delegated someone else to do the dirty work.'

Peter was now leading a private existence at an increasingly high level of extravagance. He found he needed the million-dollar fee, or even more, to sustain it. As he'd never counted the pennies, he certainly wasn't going to pause to count the hundred-thousands. That's what he employed Bill Wills for. But this helps explain why the films he made during the next few years are in general so lack-lustre. Many were put together simply for the money that Hollywood companies were prepared to pay in order to acquire Peter Sellers. He was the essential ingredient, not the movie, which might never have been made at all if he hadn't indicated interest. In short, 'the deal' was taking him over. When he had been making 'little British comedies', his fees had been infinitely smaller and his satisfaction correspondingly greater; but once he became an international movie star, everything had to be in proportion to his artistic status and financial expectations. He had a team of personal managers, who were at that time second to none in escalating their client's fee; for they had all previously been agents. They knew the Hollywood deal-making game – which Pauline Kael would later characterize as the film colony's 'only art form' – on every square of the board. Peter was one of the most valuable pieces of it. He made it possible. Too late, he found he had then been left to make the picture work.

If he didn't get a fee for *The Bobo*, which he made in Rome at the end of 1966, to touch *Casino Royale*'s million mark, this was because there was no Charles Feldman; he was making it for his own production company and deferred instant gratification for the prospect of satisfaction to come.

'For most people happiness is the lips of a woman; for me, it is the ears of a bull,' was one of the happier lines in this comedy about a small-time Spanish matador who wants to become a big-time opera singer, but first has to seduce a bitchy beauty from Barcelona in order to avenge a jealous impresario. The sloppiness of the comedy and soppiness of the sentiment were only partially redeemed by some of Sellers's sure-footed miming. He revived one of his early television sketches about the suburban commuter treating his bus like a bull and performing *veronicas* and other corrida-like passes at it with umbrella and newspaper, only this time it was a Maserati he stopped in its proud tracks with his cape and sword. In it was Britt Ekland. Her appearance in the film had been preceded by one of those stormy on-again, off-again patches that marked the couple's periods of domestic disaffection and forgiveness. It was a bad time for their marriage as well as their movie. He regarded her dogged pursuit of her own career as a form of desertion, yet he genuinely didn't wish to jeopardize his own production by casting her in a part before he was satisfied she could play it.

When her agent tried to protect his client, it was the marriage that took the strain, and it was in a poor state to do so.

Bert Mortimer's wife, who was looking after the house in Elstead, lost count of the times a phone call from Rome, usually in the early hours of the morning, brought an agitated command from Peter: 'Pack the bitch's things.' She concluded this meant Britt Ekland's belongings. Into the expensive cases they would go, only to be taken out again and laid back in drawer or closet, when the countermand came in an hour or a day. Eventually she kept them packed, relying on the driving time from airport to home to be able to restore them to their customary places before the lady of the manor arrived.

The Bobo's production pressures increased Peter's emotional insecurity. Britt Ekland's own ambitions – she was going into a Yul Brynner film and there was talk of one with Frank Sinatra – led her to adopt an attitude that seemed to him, at least, unsympathetic. Work on the film was no refuge this time. He believed he had earned the right to share director's credit on the film with Robert Parrish. This became a matter of bitter dispute with his producer Elliott Kastner, who at one moment appeared in Sellers's house, where the reluctant star had closeted himself after a difference of opinion, and blows were exchanged. Kastner honestly believed Peter had not earned the credit he sought. His gesture in withholding it is commemorated in a framed telegram from Sellers on his office wall: 'Have received your message and am not surprised. It is typical of you. I have given all there is that any artist can possibly give to you. *The Bobo* is the last time we will work together.' Such flare-ups are part of the bush fires that threaten many a troubled production, but Peter's search for perfection, his misery when he didn't find it, was the match that lit the production timber. His resentment fanned the contagious sparks.

In the middle of the film he suffered the worst calamity of his life – Peg's death.

She died on 30 January 1967, at the age of seventy-two. To some sons, who resented as much as they indulged such a maternal attachment, it might have meant a guiltless release. For Peter it was an occasion to blame himself, because he did not return from Rome in time to see her before she died.

Peg's health seemed to have been robust enough, but her drinking had increased to the point where Peter had privately decided to put his mother in a nursing home. This had been kept secret from her. Only Ve and Do, his aunts, had been told and he had sworn them to silence. Much of Peg's matriarchal energy had seeped out of her as she saw her son pursuing his sometimes embattled life and career in parts of the world where she couldn't follow with the same managerial tenacity that had once led her to rent trailers and live near his RAF camps. The cleaning woman would sometimes smuggle her in a half-bottle of brandy, which she secreted in flower vases that Peter used to sniff at suspiciously on his visits. But in death she showed a characteristic flash of the old East End pugnacity. A heart attack led to her admission to the Royal Northern Hospital. Aunties Ve and Do were with her as a nurse kept coming in and out of the room, saying, 'Mrs Sellers, you really will have to try and eat something.'

'Peg was only interested in drinking something,' Aunty Ve recalled. After this had happened a few times, she found it getting on her nerves. The nurse came in yet again and said, 'Mrs Sellers, haven't you eaten your supper yet?' Peg turned to gaze at the woman, then she said very clearly, 'Oh, piss off.' After which, she put her head down and died.

'When we told Peter this,' said Aunty Ve, 'he sighed and said, "Oh, Ve, if only I could do the same."'

Peg's casket was carried in at the brief memorial service to Ivor Novello's melody 'We'll gather lilacs in the spring again', and the old lady went off to meet her Maker to the strains of 'I'll see you again/ Whenever spring breaks through again.' Her son's choice of music for his own memorial service thirteen years later was just as personal and rather more bizarre.

Why had Peter not dashed back home from Rome immediately on hearing Peg was ill? 'He thought he knew what a heart attack was all about,' said a friend who was with him at the time. 'After all, he'd survived his own.' But other people felt that he wished to avoid the inevitable anguish of visiting her on her deathbed; it was easier to accept a *fait accompli*. He asked one of his closest companions, the Earl of Snowdon, then the husband of Princess Margaret, to visit Peg for him; but Peter didn't return until he had steeled himself for what he knew he had to face. Aunty Ve went round Peg's apartment with him as he supervised Bert Mortimer packing his mother's belongings. 'Peter picked up the little tray on her dressing-table and tipped the contents into his pocket. "Bert," he said, "I want this place stripped. Everything, even the blankets off the bed."' Peg had a favourite handbag which had a watch set into its leather side. Slightly timorously, for Peter seemed in a trance she didn't like to break, Aunty Ve indicated she would like it as a keepsake. 'Peter just stared straight through me and said nothing, as if he was saying to himself, "How *dare* she ask for anything of Peg's." I said, "Peg always promised Do her eternity ring, Pete." But he didn't speak. He just said to Bertie, "When you've finished here, bring it all out to Elstead." Almost everything Peg had owned in the world was burnt by Peter on the back lawn of his country house.'

Weeks went by. Then, one day, Aunty Ve got a phone call from Peter, who said in his old, normal way, 'Ve, dearest, I've got Do's ring. I've had it cleaned. And look, I've been to Estelle Roberts and she says it's all right for Do to have it.' He had visited his spiritualist to determine the rightful inheritor of his mother's jewel. Thereafter Peter treated the two aunts with a generosity that took their breath away; nothing was too good, too lavish, for a couple who, as he said, 'never asked a thing from me'.

It was for the same reason, perhaps, that he had turned to Lord Snowdon when Peg was stricken. The friendship each felt for the other transcended and outlasted any relationship that show-business fostered. The banker Evelyn de Rothschild was another intimate friend who returned Peter's affection and respect. These were people outside the industry, who did not impose on him for professional favours or seek to gain his confidence in order to exploit him to their own advantage. 'We were outsiders, if you like,' said Snowdon, 'but more trusted for that reason. When someone like Peter was working all out, or was very unhappy, or both, you sensed these times. You learned to offer help. The important thing with Peter was to know when he wanted to be quiet and when he needed to perform.' Sometimes Snowdon would save him the embarrassment of refusing when thoughtless hostesses suggested that Peter do 'something funny', by dropping a conversational hint in advance that would remind Sellers of something that was indeed funny, and so cue him into an inspired piece of anecdote-acting. Sellers valued this companionable diplomacy.

What brought the two of them together on intimate terms was more than their mutual love of gadgets, though this played its part. Both were highly skilled photographers – Sellers liked nothing better than toting his camera across the globe to do a photo assignment for Beatrix Miller, editor of British *Vogue*, in which Snowdon's own brilliant photo assignments appeared frequently. From one such trip to America to photograph President Ford's daughter, Sellers brought the Snowdons a transistorized microphone, originally designed for bugging executive suites. Princess Margaret put it to use monitoring the night nursery in Kensington Palace. Both buffs would exchange cameras or together try out some new model. Snowdon recalled fondly 'that lovely enthusiasm Peter would have for anything new. He'd have Bert read out the instructions to him very carefully, and then his impatience would run ahead of him.' 'Peter,' Bert confirmed, 'never let anything or anyone dictate to him, not even the maker's instructions.' Snowdon bought Peter's Aston Martin, a bargain at £3,000. 'He was thrilled when I presented it to Lord Montagu's car museum at Beaulieu – his car a part of automotive history!'

But another bond between the two men was Snowdon's own considerable but little publicized skill in impersonation. He and Sellers would hold long, uproarious telephone conversations in the voices of some of their famous acquaintances. 'Talking in *the mood*, not just the voice of a particular person – that was Peter's great art,' Snowdon recalled.

One of their favourites was the Poet Laureate, Sir John Betjeman, with whom they once intended making a film. But when they arrived at the Royal Automobile Club to discuss it with Betjeman, the budding film-makers were initially refused entry, because neither of them was wearing a tie. This kind of rule made by bureaucrats was anathema to Sellers, who once drove in and out of BBC Television Centre to show his annoyance at a one-armed gatekeeper whose single limb had been enough to bar the way to him in the days before his celebrity.

Snowdon sometimes suffered from Peter's extreme touchiness over imagined slights. 'I was brought up to believe that using the telephone was an expensive means of communication,' said Snowdon. 'Much better to drop a note in the post. And anyhow, calls should be kept as brief as possible. But with Peter, time was no object. On one occasion, after we'd been talking for three-quarters of an hour, I found myself thinking what this long-distance call must be costing him and found some excuse for saying goodbye. The next day his telegram arrived. "Why did you hang up?"'

Through their friendship with Princess Margaret and Lord Snowdon, Sellers and Britt Ekland moved into the circle of the Royal Family and their friends. It was a time when Buckingham Palace, infected by the quickening tempo of youthfulness in the swinging London scene, was judiciously adopting a populist image of accessibility to the media. Television features, like Richard Cawston's astonishingly candid, even Goonishly-flavoured film *The Royal Family*, televised at the end of 1964, admitted the nation into the centre of the apparently relaxed, informal, ad-libbing household of the Queen of England, her children and relatives. The presence of some of the Goons at dinner parties at the Palace and on other Royal occasions was part of this policy of associating Majesty with the people's pleasures, no longer confined to a single exhaustingly dull Royal Command Variety Show each year.

Monarchy felt secure enough to weather one potentially embarrassing incident that occurred on the Queen's thirty-ninth birthday outing to see Spike Milligan's adaptation of the play *Oblomov*. In the Royal party were Prince Philip, Prince Charles, Princess Anne, the Snowdons and the Sellers. Suddenly from the stage Milligan yelled, 'Is there a Sellers in the house?'

'Yes,' shouted Sellers from a seat almost beside the Queen.

A cross-talk act ensued, generally of hoary old wisecracks: 'Why does Prince Philip wear red, white and blue braces?'

'I don't know. Why does Prince Philip wear red, white and blue braces?'

'To keep his trousers up!'

Whether the Queen was amused at the attention her party was getting is unknown.

Hattie Stevenson always felt Sellers carried *lèse-majesté* to risky lengths, taking a managerial attitude towards Princess Margaret and assigning Hattie to telephone Her Royal Highness and pass on some message or other that his secretary thought he should have had the courtesy to deliver himself. But she found the Princess charming on every occasion. The Snowdons ran into their own marriage problems a few years' later, but at this period they enjoyed the relaxed atmosphere that Sellers and Britt Ekland, carefully patching up their domestic strife for the occasion, created around them. Bert Mortimer once even had to suffer embarrassing evidence of just how relaxed Royalty could be. When accompanying Sellers and Snowdon on a duck shoot, he had waded into the water to retrieve a bird one of them had winged and was standing trouserless, drying his garments at a stove in the tithe barn, when in walked Princess Margaret in search of the men. 'Don't worry,' she said, turning smartly on her heels, 'I've seen it all before.'

With Snowdon as cameraman, the Princess and Sellers appeared in a fifteen-minute movie made in 1964 at Testbourne, the Hampshire home of Jocelyn Stevens, owner and editor of *Queen*, an influential magazine of the Swinging Sixties. Stevens said later, 'Knowing how he hated his miserable music-hall days, I think it's significant that Peter first comes on as a hammy artiste muffing every impersonation he attempts – Queen Victoria, Lord Kitchener – and drawing boos from the rest of us, who included my wife and Britt.' Then Sellers announces his famous impersonation of Her Royal Highness. He goes behind a screen. Clothes are flung over the top, then out steps a fully-clad Princess, curtseying and blowing kisses. She retires and Sellers re-appears, boasting of his talent. The film ends with everyone – including Princess Margaret – exiting in a high-kicking chorus line to the *Gang Show* signature tune, 'Rolling along on the crest of a wave'.

Inevitably there were rumours that Sellers's relations with the Princess overstepped the bounds of friendship, but there is not the slightest truth in this, though envious people may have wished to think otherwise. Sellers himself might have been tempted to fantasize a romance, as he did with Shirley MacLaine, but the fact is he didn't. 'Bert and I asked him once,' said Hattie Stevenson, 'and his reply was a firm "No". Knowing Peter, he just wouldn't have been able to stop himself telling us if the truth had been otherwise.'

Snowdon did Sellers a favour without realizing how the comedian would turn it to comic advantage, just before he died, in his film *The Fiendish Plot of Dr Fu Manchu*.

'When Peter and I were both in Italy, I took him to see Harold

Acton,' said Snowdon. Sir Harold, sometimes regarded as a model for one of the Oxford aesthetes whom Evelyn Waugh satirized in his novel *Brideshead Revisited*, was then living in a beautiful Florentine villa. He greeted the actor with the avowal, 'A great honour to meet you, Mr Sellers. Admired you on the celluloid.' Sellers was enchanted: he couldn't have thought of a better parody phrase. Acton had lived in China at one period and Sellers detected in his courtly voice a peculiar sing-song rhythm which overlaid his cultured Eton and Oxford tones. Though Sellers's schoolmate, Bryan Connon believed he heard the prototype of Fu Manchu's voice issuing from Sellers in the 1930s, Snowdon detected more than a touch of Sir Harold Acton in the movie – and Sellers specifically stated that he hadn't adopted a strong Chinese accent since it was his belief that the fiendish Doctor had learned all he knew about torture while at Eton!

Sellers was never obsequious in the presence of Royalty. Nor is it likely that he plied his Palace friends with hospitality or gifts in return for favours of a kind that are only within the monarch's gift, such as a title. (He cried when he read Britt Ekland's cruel insinuation to this effect in her ghosted memoirs.) He was created a Commander of the British Empire in 1966, but this distinction had been well earned. Indeed, many felt that a knighthood wouldn't have been a premature recognition of all he had achieved in art and entertainment.

However, he never quite lost his giggly sense of amazement that he a little Jewish backstreet lad, should be Royalty's table companion and house guest. 'I always find myself wondering if my underwear is clean,' he cracked to Dougie Hayward; and to Joe McGrath, when they met at some film première graced by Royalty, he would quip, with a reference to Marks & Spencer's brand-label on their best-selling men's underpants, 'Checked the "St Michaels" tonight, have you, Joe?'

Peter's fondness for bestowing expensive gifts on people – not always his friends in any true sense of the word – had its neurotic side and sometimes it could be breathtaking. In a telephone conversation with Bryan Forbes, when the split finally came with Britt Ekland, he began 'Bryan, I want you to have Elstead.' He was proposing that, there and then and without more ado, Forbes should accept his country house as a gift. 'It's got bad memories for me.'

'Come off it, Peter,' said Forbes, 'I've got one country house as it is. And how can it have bad memories? You haven't ever spent more than a week at a time in it.'

Almost regularly, Peter would call his friends to come over to when ever he was staying and have impromptu 'shower parties' of the costly, impersonal possessions he had collected. Now that there seemed no end to the money coming in, the playthings got bigger and more expensive; but the time it took for him to fall out of love with them seemed to decrease.

After Stirling Moss had played the role of a get-away driver as a casting gimmick in *Casino Royale*, Sellers signed up two other professional racing drivers to drive a couple of Lotus 35 Formula Three cars on the circuits for him. Between March and April 1967, his own garage was swollen by the addition of an E-type Jaguar and a Lamborghini Mura. He made room for them by moving out the Ferrari Super-Fast roadster, an £11,500 two-seater with barely 10,000 miles on the clock, which he had bought little more than a year before. Although the number of days he could legally stay in Britain were limited by tax regulations, he acquired the lease on a £35,000 Mayfair apartment and had it decorated in modern Italian style with ultramarine stained wall fabrics, concealed spotlights and an acreage of 'distressed' mirror glass which, despite the ravages of time that had been artfully fabricated on its sullied surface, did not lessen the impression that the apartment was a particularly grand but unlived-in hotel suite.

In 1967 he ordered an eighteen metre, fifty-ton motor yacht, costing over £100,000, from the best boat-builder on the Mediterranean, Cantieri Baglietto of Verazze. He wanted it to be the fastest yacht in those waters and specified that it be fitted with twin V12 Caterpillar engines. He called it *The Bobo*, after his recently completed film, and proudly took possession on the day it was commissioned and declared seaworthy. What then happened shows the strength of Peter's determination once he had invested his enthusiasm, as well as his money, in any project or possession.

As the boat was beating through the Mediterranean en route to St Tropez, another Baglietto motor yacht was observed coming up behind. Soon it became clear that the stranger was gaining on them. Peter began to fret. 'Come on, Captain, more speed. Let's go. Let's really go.'

The captain warned, 'We're doing nicely, Mr Sellers. We've got new engines. They're not run in, we can't go faster.'

'I say we're to go faster.'

'But, Mr Sellers, we're already racing the engines more than is good for them.'

The other boat was by this time drawing level and looked as though it would soon leave *The Bobo* bobbing in its wake. 'I was promised this would be the fastest boat in the Mediterranean,' said Peter stubbornly. 'More speed. That's an order.'

'But, Mr Sellers, you can't. . . .' That was the red-rag phrase. Peter's answer was to grab the throttle and throw it wide open. *The Bobo* leaped ahead, the engines screaming. He was determined to beat the other boat, even if it meant tearing the heart out of his own.

Eventually reason returned and *The Bobo* made port intact. 'But if you told Peter something would happen,' said Bert Mortimer, 'then look out – it *had* to happen.'

After the failure of *The Bobo* film, the boat was renamed *Victoria* after the daughter to whom Britt had given birth in 1965. It was eventually sold in 1969 to a South American property dealer for £80,000. Its owner had hardly used it.

When Peter travelled by air at this time, he would frequently charter a plane if the scheduled flights didn't suit his own appointments or destinations. Once he sent a chartered jet all the way back from Nice to Zurich just to pick up some forgotten suitcases. He talked of buying a helicopter to commute the fifteen-minute air journey between his Elstead home and Battersea heliport in the centre of London.

All these extravagances severely tested the investment plans of Bill Wills, now resident in Switzerland and trying to insure his employer's financial future, while making allowances for his fantasy life-style. But it seemed that the money would always be rolling in.

In fact, precious little of it had been coming in to the Hollywood companies which had backed some recent Sellers films. Columbia were particularly embittered by the inflationary heights to which his conduct had helped take *Casino Royale*'s budget, without any compensating prospect of box-office profit.

Their reluctance to back any film starring Peter Sellers helped lose him the chance of working with the great Indian director, Satyajit Ray. Ray had written a script called *The Alien* about a celestial spaceship which lands in a lotus pond near an Indian village. Out of what was described as 'a poetic interior that is almost a living organism' emerges a benign Being, who confounds the mortals and ends up spiriting one of the local children away to another plane of divine existence. The producer was to be Michael Wilson, a New Zealand-born writer and friend of the science-fiction author Arthur C. Clarke. Wilson and Ray cabled Sellers in February 1967, offering him the serious role of a Bengali businessman who believes that money can buy anything or anyone. Sellers showed immediate interest.

In a two-part article entitled 'Ordeals of The Alien', published in

The New Statesman of Calcutta in 1980, Ray wrote: 'If, as I suspected, [Sellers] knew only one kind of Indian accent – a vaguely South Indian one – I was sure that if he agreed to play in *The Alien* he wouldn't mind making an effort to add a new and authentic one to his repertoire.... The two LPs of his that I possessed held proof that he could do things with his voice and tongue which bordered on the miraculous.'

Sellers hadn't seen any of Ray's films at this time; but when the director visited Hollywood in 1967 to secure the finance from Columbia, which had rupees blocked in India, Sellers viewed *Charulata* and, when the lights went up, was sufficiently impressed to declare himself redundant, 'I'm not better than any of your actors, you know.'

But Peter appears to have fallen, little by little, out of love with the project. Michael Wilson believes he mistrusted Ray's sense of humour; he thought that the poem which Peter sent Ray, written in the uniquely bathetic style of his favourite Bad Versifier, the Great McGonagall, was designed to elicit a response he could compare with his own sense of humour. It was about Ray's film *Pather Panchali*: 'In which there is a scene of two children in a field of barley / Watching a train go by / Under an azure sky / So beautiful you want to die.' Ray's response is unrecorded: but he visited the set of *The Party*, which Peter was then engaged in making, and noted sadly how the comedian seemed to aid and abet the coarsening of his style. Not at all like the absorbed being he had witnessed sitting at the feet of Ravi Shankar, while the great musician taught him how to finger the sitar.

Whatever might have resulted from the co-operation must remain a matter for conjecture. For when the project was transferred from Columbia in Hollywood to the company's British set-up, Peter's diminishing confidence was further undermined by Columbia-British's persistent reluctance to trust him again in one of its movies. (There were also differences with Michael Wilson, who subsequently departed the film scene and became Swami Shiva Kalki.) Peter eventually rejected the role on the rather curious ground that it was incompletely developed. The director interpreted this to mean that it was not big enough and now it was his turn to reply, somewhat smartingly, in McGonagall style, blaming Sellers for 'Causing a great deal of dismay / To Satyajit Ray.'

As if he sensed that *The Alien* disappointment could be an omen, Sellers contemplated returning to the familiar fold of his former agent, Dennis Selinger – there had been yet another of those hiatuses in their relationship.

The two men met for a dinner of reconciliation. The next day

Selinger received a letter delivered by hand from Peter's Clarges Street apartment.

It read: 'Dear Den, It was good seeing you last night. This note will be short and straight to the point. I would prefer to keep you as an old and valued friend than ever have you working for me as my agent. When, the other day, it occurred to me that it might be good for us to be together again, I was unprepared for the surprise I got last night when I sat back and listened to us both talking. Clearly you have become dotty with power, and I am a hard cynical article. Let's not make it nasty and uneasy for each other. I remain, as ever, your friend Pete.'

To this day, Selinger has no idea how he came to give the impression of being 'dotty with power'.

One man, however, with whom Peter had effected a reconciliation was Blake Edwards. 'To be honest,' he said, 'I thought I'd never work with him again. During *Shot in the Dark* we were quite incompatible. But I'm the last person to condemn temperament in this business. What matters is, can you produce the goods?' Blake Edwards proved he could, up to a point, with *The Party*, the first film Sellers made in Hollywood, in 1967. He skilfully blended the gentle Indian in *The Millionairess* and the accident-prone Clouseau into the character of an unflappable Hollywood small-part player from India who is invited in error to a splashy Beverly Hills party in a producer's home and innocently causes havoc from incidents as natural as an inability to find the loo or as surreal as washing an elephant in a lily pond. Sellers with his air of good will to all men, even those whose homes he was wrecking, and his stiff-legged gait which gave the impression of thin ice under him, proved yet again that he did not need to do anything to be funny. Andrew Sarris considered this role to be 'his masterpiece of mimicry' and spoke warmly of the way he 'breaks through to the likeability and sense of honour lurking under the surface of the character'.

However, the film's distributors had to be content with its cult status. Its box-office results were disappointing. Nor did *I Love You, Alice B. Toklas,* which he did immediately afterwards, revive his bankability. A late-blooming satire of the hippy-flower-child-acid-head era, with Sellers as an up-tight Jewish lawyer who switches life-styles, its jokes about long hair, bead necklaces, psychedelically decorated station-wagons and one's own personal *guru* had all become very *passé* when it appeared in 1968.

Sellers had to fight on two fronts. From one direction, a snipers' nest of Hollywood gossip columnists, remembering his incautious remarks four years earlier, accused him of eccentric and wasteful behaviour on the set. To Peter, this was only the necessary defence against a front office that was more concerned with profits than performance. 'Warners hacked the picture around with nail scissors,' he later alleged.

He even went to the extent of bribing a night-watchman to let him into the studios to splice back into his movie some interviews with Timothy Leary and Allen Ginsberg. 'People are gonna know about Leary and Ginsberg in Orange County?' asked the irate front office. Sellers protested, 'They're *not* for Orange County. They're for the world.' In vain. They were for the cutting room floor again.

Peter himself was sampling the pleasures of mildly hallucinatory drugs at this time, which had one ironic consequence. He had gathered together a party of friends, plus a newly-baked batch of cookies containing hash, for an evening screening in a private projection theatre of a new Fellini movie, but at the last minute Warners refused them the print. To save the evening, the projectionist screened 'an odd little movie' he happened to have in the box. 'It's called *Springtime for Hitler*. Something Mel Brooks has shot. Nobody knows what to do with it.' Sellers and company soon found themselves laughing uncontrollably at Brooks's satire on Broadway show-business and its opportunism in a movie later re-titled *The Producers*. 'I laughed so helplessly, I had to crawl to the loo on my hands and knees,' Peter said. 'When I got back, the others were sitting howling with laughter at an entirely blank screen. It was a minute or two before someone's head cleared enough for them to yell to the projectionist, "Change the reel." ' The next day, sobriety restored, he saw the movie again and found it still so funny that he underwrote an advertising crusade the next few months to endorse 'one of the greatest comedies' he'd ever seen; but his good deed was interpreted by the columnists as just one more effort to curry favour with the Hollywood colony.

He returned to England in the spring of 1968, tired, depressed and facing a wife who was unable to help him get to grips with his collapsing career.

Rows were, according to Britt, frequent, fierce and guilt-ridden. They generally ended with Peter trying to patch things up by 'seeding' their apartment with penitent gifts like Hermes purses and scarves, perfumes, Dunhill lighters and Cartier watches. The only thing neither could find was marital compatibility.

The most traumatic showdown for Peter was one whose immediate aftermath was witnessed by a couple of American friends who rang the doorbell of the Clarges Street apartment late one night. Over the entry-phone they were horrified to hear whimpers of pain, which they recognized as Peter's. Had he suffered another coronary? Fearful of what they would find, they gained entry and rushed upstairs to the apartment door. Peter opened it. His face was bleeding. He had cuts on his forehead, probably caused by the broken glass of a framed portrait lying on the floor. In another room was Britt Ekland, who was also the worse for wear. But the pain of his injuries wasn't what was causing Peter to weep. He picked up the broken picture and cried over the small, determined face of Peg Sellers, in front of which he had been in the habit, once a week, of placing a lighted candle of remembrance. Peg had fallen victim to a sidelong swipe – which Britt maintained was accidental – during a furious, mutually rancorous dispute.

After that, the split was inevitable. Britt Ekland sought temporary refuge with her family in Stockholm. When she returned to the Mayfair apartment, Bert Mortimer met her on the front doorstep and handed her all her belongings. This time her cases had stayed packed. The marriage was dissolved at the end of 1968. 'Mrs Britt Sellers, also known as Britt Ekland,' as her passport still stated ten years later, was advised by her lawyers to charge her husband with mental cruelty. Not the least injury she herself suffered, apparently, was the divorce suit. 'I felt [it] cast a stigma on me,' she sorrowfully recorded in her memoirs, amidst much else that offended her sensitivities, such as being rebuffed by Dino de Laurentiis when he was casting *King Kong*.

TEN

You Can't Film Despair

'Things seemed to go wrong too many times,' the British comedian Tony Hancock wrote in a suicide note four days after his marriage was dissolved in mid-1968. Then he swallowed an overdose of barbiturates and washed it down with vodka. Hancock's death, all alone in Australia, haunted Peter Sellers in his few hours of nightly sleep after his own divorce and his return to lonely bachelorhood.

'Pete, you all right?' Dougie Hayward would ask almost daily. A sigh. Then, 'Oh, I dunno . . . I suppose so,' from far away down the line. Robert Towne, the American scriptwriter of such films as *Chinatown*, was in London. Hayward would call him and say, 'Get over to Peter's flat in Clarges Street, sit with him for a bit. I'll take over at one o'clock.' The two friends shared the 'suicide watch' on several days every month. Peter was deeply depressed. But they noticed, at first with suspicious surprise, then with resigned understanding, how it took only a phone call from Princess Margaret to rally him and send him off elatedly, in the latest car for an evening's or a weekend's entertainment. 'What am I doing sitting here?' he'd say to the men to whom he'd been talking in tones of the last confession a mere half-hour earlier. His manic states had now become as alarming as his depressive ones: he shifted from one to another in seconds, sometimes in mid-sentence. His concern for his health had become that of a hypochondriac. He preferred to wear black, because of its slimming effect, 'Although,' said Hayward, 'he already looked unnaturally slim, *wasted*, if you know what I mean.' Black shirts and sweaters now replaced the rainbow voiles from the Deborah and Clare shop in Beauchamp Place, Knightsbridge. The only relief in these flattering but rather melancholy ensembles were gold chains or a medallion with some mystical inscription on it. Diet came to dominate every menu he opened, and if his mood hadn't been so piteous, the consequences might sometimes have been hilarious.

'Chef,' he once said, after supper at the Dorchester, 'I've just had the best steak tartare in my life. Haven't I, Bert?'

'Terrific,' said the faithful Bert, glad Peter had been pleased.

'Chef, it was absolutely superb. Tell me how you made it.'

'Nothing special, Mr Sellers. Just good meat, anchovy, oil, a raw egg. . . .'

'A raw egg? I don't believe it!'

'Yes, Mr Sellers, raw egg, to bind it together.'

'You put raw egg in my steak tartare without telling me? I've eaten *raw* egg!'

'Yes, Mr Sellers, but. . . .'

'No "buts", I've got a pain here. My cholesterol . . . What's it done to me? Are you all right, Bert? I want the manager.' Later, to the restaurant manager: 'I've been given a raw egg. I want this chef out of my life.'

To be fair to Peter, he was a dreadfully sick man most of the time. The medication he consumed so compulsively set off its own alarms in the very metabolism it was meant to calm. His increasing neurosis over any minor ailment – a cold, a cough, the mouth ulcers that, psychosomatically, he felt coming on as he entered a new role – led to his feeding himself indiscriminate mixtures of such pharmaceutics as Lem-Sip, Night Nurse, Benylin, Liquid Anbesol, and a plethora of proprietary cold cures and headache pills. He took them the way a child eats a bag of sweets.

Spike Milligan warned a television director, Tony Palmer, who was proposing a BBC documentary on Sellers's elusive personality, that 'you can't film despair, so why bother?'

However, Palmer did bother and early in 1969, a few weeks after Sellers's divorce, gained his grudging co-operation. He had to yield to Sellers's insistence that the television crew would shoot him over a six-month period, instead of the customary two months allocated to such programmes. In the event, the fifty-minute film took all of nine months to complete and emerged as so harrowing and bleak an account of loneliness that the BBC were at first reluctant to let it be transmitted. As one executive put it, 'Can you imagine people tuning in to see a funny Peter Sellers, and finding *this*?'

'He sees himself,' said Milligan, who narrated the programme, 'as a clean person in a colony of lepers. Can't afford to mix with them too much if he's to come out alive.' But Palmer concluded that Sellers's real fear was coming out of the programme as a totally uninteresting person, if he had to appear as himself. It was the old story of never being pleased with what he saw in the mirror and seeking an escape route via whatever film character he portrayed, only now film companies were so wary of him that the supply of characters in which he could take refuge had dried up. Instead of the major Hollywood studios beseeching him to give the nod to their film scripts, he was now obliged to go out and do a selling job on himself, and it was a bad time for the majors to buy. A financial crisis brought on by their own unrestrained budgetary inflation and poor box-office returns meant that they were all drastically curtailing or abandoning their British production programmes and recalling their funds. The virtual redundancy of American screen censorship, both lay and religious, which had once been so restrictive, now made it attractive to American companies to film indigenous movies with audacious themes.

Peter was developing a treatment of Terry Southern's satire *The Magic Christian*, concerning an omnipotent prankster, Sir Guy Grand, who uses his millions to play preposterous jokes on mankind; he deflates the pompous, upsets the complacent, punishes the avaricious and slays some of today's most sacred cows. This vision of the world as a kind of film set, where the star is a Christ-figure with an inexhaustible purse, was one that held a great allure for Peter. Revenging himself by surreal pranks on the world's gallery of rogues and rascals was an extension of *The Goon Show*'s sadistic elements. He co-opted Terry Southern and Joe McGrath to work on the screenplay with him – he felt a little guilty at the way he had allowed McGrath to be treated in the *Casino Royale* débâcle. True to his hankering for reassurance from the few people he respected, he asked the Boultings their opinion of the finished script. And true to themselves, they were brutally blunt. 'Peter,' said John Boulting, 'if ever I smelled disaster, this is it. It's a bad script with only one possibility inherent in it – of becoming a worse one if you make the picture. The only way to handle it, is not to do it.' Sellers ignored the advice and did not speak to the Boultings for a year.

The problem of financing the film was solved by taking the project to a new outfit that was impatient to get going, called Commonwealth United. This organization, by an irony that Terry Southern would have appreciated, was one that embodied the speculative fantasies of financier Bernie Cornfeld: it was the film-making wing of Investors Overseas Services, the multinational stock-dealing operation, which was shortly to suffer a spectacular crash. Thus one fantasist sold his fantasy to another – and as Joe McGrath remembered the initial salesmanship, the deal was done at a third remove from reality. 'Peter and I met with the Commonwealth United people,' he said. 'They said to me, "How do you see this? What kind of character is this Guy Grand fellow?" I looked at Peter. He said to me, "Go on, Joe, show them." *Me* show them! I was only going to direct the picture; he was going to play the role, if we ever got it set up. Anyhow I did the first thing that came into my head, which was an imitation of Peter doing Inspector Clouseau, while he sat there with a straight face. When I'd finished, the Commonwealth United people said, "Great!" and shelled out fifteen million dollars.'

The film was a disaster. Many of Sir Guy Grand's jokes lost their point in the farcical elaboration: the only moral of the story now appeared to be that every man has his price, which certainly seemed true of almost every star name or celebrity (including Yul Brynner, Roman Polanski, Laurence Harvey, Raquel Welch and others) who were sucked into the maelstrom.

What is interesting, though, is that even amidst this comic anarchy, Peter insisted on creating a character based on recognizable reality. Having exhausted the possibilities of playing Sir Guy as an upper-class Major Bloodnok, an orotund W. C. Fields, or a George Bernard Shaw with red hair, beard and knickerbockers, he finally opted to play him as a boozed version of Britain's Prime Minister of plenty, Mr Harold ('Most of our people have never had it so good') Macmillan. Ringo Starr played Sir Guy's son. Sellers blamed the backers for much of the mess. He alleged that they lost their nerve over the more outrageous gags. Out of patriotism or, more likely, concern for the IOS image, they refused to allow the film-makers to shoot the scene of Sir Guy gloating over people prepared to wallow in muck for a fortune in dollar bills at the foot of the Statue of Liberty – thereby cueing the joke on the famous plea about sending 'your poor, your tired, your huddled masses' for succour: 'I'll sucker them all right!' says Sir Guy. They forbade shooting on that sacrosanct location and compelled Sellers and McGrath to substitute a much less emetic finale at St Paul's Cathedral.

The film reportedly pleased Bernie Cornfeld, who had some characteristics in common with Sir Guy, but it failed to win Peter the new audience of informed young people he had hoped for. And the only profit he made from his association with the project came from the sale of his Elstead house to Ringo Starr for £60,000.

By the end of 1969, Peter's acceptance price for making a film had decreased from a million dollars to $400,000 and he had agreed to do *Hoffman*, an oblique comedy about a middle-aged bachelor sinisterly, yet pathetically, pressing his affections on a girl from his office typing pool whom he has lured to his apartment. It was part of a varied but economically budgeted production programme which Bryan Forbes had had to set up quickly – perhaps too quickly – when he was appointed production chief at EMI's Elstree film studios and given the impossible task of reviving the wilting British film industry.

Hoffman proved agony for Peter: there was too much of himself in it. He played the role without make-up, either physical or vocal. He had told Tony Palmer during the making of his television film, 'I suppose there are many men like me – this strange brigade of pudding faces who melt into the crowd. Some of them sit in subways. Some of them are faceless.' His Hoffman was such a face in the crowd. When he saw the finished film he begged Bryan Forbes to have it destroyed. Forbes said he had no power to order this, and before the première, Peter again broke the sealed-lips protocol of disappointed performers and went on record as saying how terrible it was. Failure cut him to the quick: each remark he made was a cry of self-inflicted pain.

His depression was also linked to the middle-age of the emotions he was passing through. Legally a Swiss resident with a limited number of working days permitted in Britain, he spoke of moving to Rome. 'That place always gave me most happiness ... [for] in Italy they don't have the same preoccupations as we do. They don't care about age, for one thing. Here and in the States, we're obsessed by it. In America, you're a senior citizen at fifty-three – imagine!' He was then forty-four and not ready for that kind of retirement.

What pulled him out of this decline was the offer of a role that seemed a remedy for his emotional and professional *angst*. The Boulting Brothers had done a deal with Columbia Pictures to adapt, produce and direct the stage comedy *There's a Girl in My Soup*, which the film company had bought some years earlier without ever having decided how to turn it into a film. What now made it viable and attractive was the availability of Goldie Hawn, a comedienne being spoken of as the new Marilyn Monroe. She was to play the dumb blonde who drops into the automated love-nest of an ageing playboy and drives him to such distraction after he's taken her to bed that he is compelled to take her to wife. The Boultings wanted Sellers to play this punctured Romeo, but Mike Frankovich, who headed Columbia's British production company, replied that Sellers was bad news. 'Look at the way he loused up *Casino Royale*. Personally, I think the guy is very funny. But New York would never go along with him – they're still smarting too much.'

'Mike,' replied the Boultings, 'we think we can control him this time. At times, Peter may hate us, but he respects us. Before he louses things up, he'd have to think we were perfect shits. And *that*, he knows we are not.'

However, Roy Boulting admitted to feeling a quickening of his pulse when Sellers, on the first day's shooting, demanded the removal of a script girl from the set. 'I caught her looking at me,' he said. 'I tell you, Roy, she really hates me. I don't want to see her again.'

Roy's mind worked fast. 'Peter, if you really believe that, of course it will be done. But first there is something you should know about that girl. . . .' He ransacked his thoughts. What was it Peter should know? Then it came: 'That girl especially asked to work on this film, because of her intense admiration for you, above all other stars. She cannot keep her eyes off you.' Half-an-hour later, Peter was over talking to the girl, who was flattered but slightly non-plussed by his effusive attentions. Roy Boulting had emotionally re-positioned him: he was now at the centre of the girl's world, instead of the target for her bad vibrations.

Sellers's fee for the film was $350,000, plus a share in the net profits: well below *Casino Royale*'s million-dollar fee, but at least it was work. His performance soared with his new-found spirits. Goldie Hawn seemed to bring him up to pitch, just as Sophia Loren had once done. Though the film was no more than a situation comedy, it became a *pas de deux* performed by two instinctive comic players, each of whom had a marvellous sense of timing, a feeling for the undertones of the situation and a sharp eye lest the partner won a trick.

What few people realized was that, once again, Sellers had used a real person for a quick study of his character. 'He asked us how he should play the part,' said John Boulting. 'He didn't always take such advice, but it helped clarify his mind. My brother Roy said, "I think we can take you to meet someone like the character." In this, I must admit, there was an element of mischief. Roy and I set up a luncheon, so that Peter could study the man at close quarters. It helped that he was a top photographer, as well as a man with a reputation for enjoying life. "Peter," we said, as he came in, "we'd like you to meet Patrick Lichfield."' Thomas Patrick John Anson, 5th Earl of Lichfield and a cousin of the Queen, had the dashing appearance, the well-maintained good looks, the whole glossy magazine aura of the times and the Byronic hair-style that were to inspire one of the actor's most wholly likeable and well-rounded characters. It happened that one of the Earl's frequent companions was Britt Ekland, which may have additionally helped Peter to mix fantasy with reality. *There's a Girl in My Soup* sometimes gives those in the know an impression of parallax vision as they discern the real-life models in the guise of the fictitious screen couple.

The film's Press notices which ranged, on the whole, from excellent to indulgent, continued to raise Peter's spirits. 'They were what he always wanted,' John Boulting said, 'a little circle of friends pouring out their praise of him. Just like childhood. Peg was there in spirit saying, "Pete, luv, you're the only one that matters."'

At the time he was making *There's a Girl in My Soup*, Peter had a new woman in his life. Miranda Quarry, aged twenty-three, had been his companion on and off, for two years. She had worked as an assistant on the publicity for *The Magic Christian* and was clearly fascinated by the world of film-making; yet she herself, as the step-daughter of Lord Mancroft, a one-time Tory Junior Minister in Parliament, belonged to a world that was light-years distant from the Jewish show-business East End confraternities to which Peter's connections still anchored him. To be precise, they had crossed each other's path years before: once when Miranda was three or four and Sellers had seen her in the London square where he and his first wife had briefly taken an apartment; and later, when she was keeping debutante's hours at the florist's at the Dorchester, and used to make up some of the bouquets which the impetuous Peter sent to Britt Ekland's suite.

Friends speculated as to what the attraction was. It seemed to be one of opposites. Miranda was the intelligent deb, who spoke several languages, had a background of well-connected county families and loved the kind of country pursuits which usually made a bricks-and-mortar, city-bred lad like Sellers fractious and bored. Peter had never had much time for the upper classes. He would occasionally imitate the way such people talked when he was answering them back, or else he'd put on a horrible Cockney accent. Maybe he only did it to annoy. He saw them as 'characters'. For Miranda, Peter's film world was a turn-on, quite as much as it was a turn-off for him. She liked having things in common with the famous faces she moved among; he wanted to have nothing in common with the social set she inhabited. Many of her friends knew him only in his professional capacity, and expected him to be the 'funny man' and entertain them over the weekend. Baffled opinion, perhaps not privy to the couple's enjoyment of each other's company, assumed that Peter had once again felt the need to change his own life-style radically, take on the social coloration of a character he hadn't yet played and experience the country-house life through which his friends the Snowdons moved with the same enviable ease as they did in the world of the jet-set.

Sellers and Miranda Quarry were married on 24 August 1970, in a brusque, ten-minute civil ceremony which was decided on so quickly that the bride had to go shopping for her gypsy-style wedding dress on the very same morning. Bert Mortimer was best man and Miranda's two Pekingese, named Tabitha and Thomasina, were her 'bridesmaids', somewhat to the amazement of Aunties Ve and Do, who had looked around for the usual attendants on hearing Miranda say she was going to fetch them. Somewhat more in Peter's style was the choice of the Jermyn Street discothèque, Tramp, for the wedding reception.

Peter's customary attack of indecision occurred immediately after the wedding announcement. He had telephoned Selinger and asked plaintively, 'Den, how do I get out of it?' 'He was a total law unto himself,' said Selinger indulgently. Another of his intimates recalled Sellers being asked to walk the 'bridesmaids' after the ceremony. He hated small dogs and perhaps it was this experience of walking them round the block which made him wonder if he should ever have married again. He also hated to feel that, however innocently, he was being imposed on; this moment was rather like one at the end of *Only Two Can Play* when the little Welsh Don Juan realizes his glamorous mistress is taking him for granted. There may have been deeper reasons. One of Peter's later co-stars is convinced that by now he had developed to a pathological degree his self-punishing habit of putting himself into situations where his worst instincts could come out and he could take a long, shuddering look at them. 'The *Virginia Woolf* syndrome,' she called it; 'If your mate is strong enough to take it, you find a new side to yourself. If not, you have another wrecked marriage to tidy up.' Shirley MacLaine discerned in some of Peter's extraordinary conduct during this period the efforts of a man to find his identity or, at least, to find out why he had been 'born again' after his near-fatal coronary.

If Miranda Quarry noticed such danger signals, she ignored them while pressing ahead with the acquisition of a beautiful country house in Wiltshire, which she and Peter intended to occupy when he was able to return from tax exile in the Republic of Ireland. Bert Mortimer, however, had his doubts about Peter's qualifications for country life. They were confirmed one weekend when the new Mrs Sellers called him anxiously from the shires. Peter had taken to his bed. No one could rouse him. He was growing weaker and weaker, and calling for Bert in a hoarse voice. It was as if his mind had gone. 'I got down to this beautiful house in next to no time,' said Bert, 'bounded up the elegant staircase and into Peter's bedroom, where he was lying under the sheets in a four-poster. "What's up, Pete?" I asked. "Is it your heart?" He opens his eyes. He looks up at me. Then he gives me a wink and whispers, "It's all a put-on. I can't take any more of this boredom. What I've suffered! Get me out of here, Bert. Get me away from these people."'

When Peter and Miranda left for Ireland in March 1971, after a huge show-business party at the San Lorenzo restaurant in Beauchamp Place which Peter and the other stars of the previous decade had helped make famous, it signalled the ending of the 1960s – the final knell. For all its overcrowded, enforced gaiety, the party was a sad affair. The guests included Warren Beatty, Shirley MacLaine, Princess Margaret and Lord Snowdon, and Nanette Newman and her husband Bryan Forbes, who had resigned just the day before from his job as EMI's film chief. Even Britt Ekland made an appearance. Sellers and Spike Milligan busked briefly on the pavement outside. A silver collection was taken among the guests for the Irish emigrant – it raised fifty pence. Emerald balloons and streamers decked the place, despite Sellers's dread of the colour. Perhaps this explains his low spirits.

He did not fly directly to Ireland, for he hated house-moving just as much as Miranda loved house-making. He let her precede him with her Pekingese, her Yorkshire terriers, four white-and-yellow parakeets and a parrot. Instead, he left the house which he had rented temporarily in Chelsea's Cheyne Row and flew to Austria for a holiday. When he walked into his Irish home, Carton Castle, some three miles outside Dublin, all was ready for him – 'Like a transformation scene,' said his new secretary Penny Heath-Brown. He and Miranda did not actually occupy the whole castle. They used what was called 'the stable wing', but to the uninitiated visitor, surveying Carton's extensive grounds, pheasantry and gardens, it looked as if Peter had once again gone wild and bought the whole shooting match. As it was, he had the appearance of landed affluence, without the need to pay for its up-keep, which was just as well, for he was beginning to have doubts about whether he could afford to do so.

To Bert Mortimer, living in the gate-lodge, which he found 'very mildewed indeed', it seemed strange that Peter was sometimes actually short of money. He told Bert that he'd have preferred to go and live in California, 'so that he could pick up some work'. Penny Heath-Brown attributed Peter's principal income to his *Pink Panther* residuals, but Bert knew enough about films to understand that the percentages which a star drew from even such authenticated box-office hits could take quite a time to reach his bank account. 'Sometimes Peter was down to his last few thousands,' he said. After one or two visits to his business affairs adviser in Switzerland, Peter would return in extremely thoughtful mood, contrasting perhaps his own restrained life-style with the evidence of comfortable living which Geneva offered. Peter began taking a much closer personal interest in his investments. At Miranda Quarry's suggestion, he sought the services of Denis O'Brien, a Canadian business adviser, investment manager and lawyer who operated in London and elsewhere, managed George Harrison's affairs among others, and had a reputation as a very tough operator indeed.

As the weeks went by in the damp backwoods of Ireland, Peter became increasingly morose. 'It was a bad, bad time,' said Penny Heath-Brown. Miranda, who was an excellent cook with a penchant for Robert Carrier's gourmet recipes, looked after the meals, a lady from the village did the cleaning, and everyone made strenuous efforts to fill the place every weekend and keep Peter entertained. Lord Snowdon, Brother Cornelius and Spike Milligan would fly over from England; so, too, would Lorenzo Berni, the San Lorenzo restaurateur with whom Peter intended opening a Dublin eating-place, though this came to nothing despite the efforts of one Dublin publican to get him to buy his tavern by filling it up with his drinking cronies on the night Peter went to assess its prospects.

'We all used to eat more than was good for us,' said Penny Heath-Brown. 'Supper would be at 10 p.m., so as to make the night seem shorter. We'd have Irish friends and neighbours in, like Edna O'Brien, Kevin McClory, the film producer, or Siobhan McKenna. We'd run movies, in particular *The Producers*, which never failed to put Peter in a good mood. After supper, he'd get out his ukulele and do his George Formby act for us. He was very, very proud of his father for teaching him how to play it, particularly one tricky, three-stroke movement. When he did it and we all broke into applause, his dear old face would beam with pleasure. He'd be like a child. Other nights we'd play with the ouija board, receiving spirit messages, we supposed, and would then spend hours – you know these Irish telephone exchanges – ringing round the world to confirm with friends what the board had told us.'

Peter kept up his exercises with his see-saw balancing board, his chest-expander and the portable bar on which he did chin-ups, but the tedium of daily routine soon began to tell on him. 'When he felt depressed,' said Bert Mortimer, 'he'd shut himself away from everyone and go to bed, take long walks alone or go out shooting rabbits. We'd drive over to Dublin for a little shopping, a round of the camera shops. But nothing constructive. I'd say to him, "Pete, why not learn French now you've got the time." He'd get all suddenly excited. We'd drive to Dublin at once, buy all the language courses, the tapes, the films, etc., maybe spend three or four hundred pounds. Then his interest would lapse as quickly as it had begun, the stuff would be locked away, maybe given away.'

Spike Milligan's visits cheered him up, but friends noticed how their attitude to each other had subtly changed. Beneath the friendly sparring matches and the old *Goon Show* routines, there was now a sense of how experiences can turn intimates into strangers.

Sellers hankered visibly after the irrepressible innocence of the old days. This showed itself in the delight he took in composing introductory messages for the answering devices he had fitted to the Carton telephones. He devised voices – like the bibulous Bloodnok or a high-pitched Chinese laundry man – then spent hours ringing up his friends around the world to beg them to call him back 'as I've done a new voice'. His act was now a token of his loneliness as much as of his inventiveness.

His worst days were the ones on which he received Denis O'Brien's reports on his investments. After one such report, he said gloomily, 'We'll have to let the servants go.' Money worries, in fact, began to cloud his days and nights. The details of these are unlikely to emerge; but the attempt of his Swiss-based business manager to reconcile Peter's extravagance with the moods of an investment market that was shortly to be plunged into turmoil by the oil embargo 'war' of 1974 certainly contributed to them. Peter was literally paying for people's general inability, or unwillingness, to say to him the three phrases 'You can't,' 'You mustn't' or 'No'.

It may have been this which so depressed him on one occasion that he took to his room for several days on end, emerging only at nights to eat make-shift meals in the kitchen when the rest of the household had retired. On the third day he made a sudden re-appearance. 'We got a shock,' Bert recalled. 'He hadn't shaved himself for several days, but he had cut off a lot of his hair, in a very rough, uneven fashion. Some of it was quite short, other parts he had left long and straggling so that it looked as if he had gone bald in a very patchy fashion. He didn't give us any reason why he'd done this. "I was just so depressed," he kept on saying. He had to wear a rather nasty gingery wig until his hair grew again. He looked a bit like Dr Pratt.' The bizarre incident recalled the penitent mood of Sellers's ancestor, Daniel Mendoza, who after his defeat by an American rival because of his long locks, had cut his hair to scalp level.

The tedium of Irish life caused him to say 'Yes' even more impetuously to film projects that he should have rejected. Neither *Where Does It Hurt?*, nor *Alice's Adventures in Wonderland* – in which he played the

March Hare and condemned the film as 'lousy' before it opened – brought him any substantial benefit.

He was in Rome in November 1971, when he heard that Miranda had fallen ill with meningitis and was in a dangerous condition. He did not hesitate this time, but risked a large tax bill by returning to London to be at her side – though the Treasury eventually gave him compassionate dispensation. Fortunately she made a slow, but complete recovery. What did not recover, however, was a marriage to which he realized he was ill-adapted, despite his wife's efforts to make it work.

Miranda spent her convalescence preparing their Wiltshire home; unhindered by tax rules, she could come and go between England and Ireland as she liked. 'I am living here in Wiltshire because it is quiet,' she said in mid-1972. 'My animals keep me company and I read and write a lot. I've a lot of planning to do and at the moment I'm designing a water garden which will be rather beautiful.' Placid, contemplative pursuits, no doubt, but hardly ones calculated to hold Peter Sellers content at home.

At that moment he was in Guernsey – outside British tax jurisdiction – filming *The Blockhouse*. This was only the second 'straight' role he had played, as a man entombed with seven companions in a bombed Normandy blockhouse at the close of the war. They have plenty of food, even a wine cellar; all that's missing is a way out. It sometimes reminded him of the situation in which he now found himself.

He seemed to have everything; yet his marriage and his investments appeared to him to have become a trap, instead of a refuge. As if to return to basics, he took up vegetarianism and yoga. The savoury roll made of yeast, vegetables and milk, and the exercises illustrated in Swami Vishnadevananda's manual, introduced him to a more tranquil existence than any that Ireland offered – or so he claimed. 'Ireland was a disaster ... I'm surprised I survived it ... All that green ... An unlucky colour.'

His obsession with yoga at this time reflected his innermost cares – those of growing old and being lonely. 'In yoga,' he said, with the certainty of the enthusiastic novice, 'there is no age problem.' And again: 'The one thing yoga does for you is ensure that you do not get lonely. If you feel lonely, you sink into yourself; you withdraw into yourself from the outside world and sit in a state that in Sanskrit is called *satchinananda*. It means existence, knowledge, bliss.' It had more practical uses, too: 'Mentally, I shut my wives off completely, unless their lawyers' letters come creeping in.'

He claimed his problems were lightened extraordinarily whenever he stood on his head, but seeking comfort, his thoughts turned backward in time, and he told friends he felt far closer to his late father now that he was going through the traumas of failure – the disappearance of the big film offers, the sneers of columnists who formerly had fawned on him for interview privileges, and the friends who never called him now. 'Do you know,' he said to the British journalist Clive Hirschhorn in January 1973, 'I only have two real friends in the world [Tony Snowdon and Evelyn de Rothschild]? I mean people I'd trust with my life. There are dozens of hangers-on, of *schleppers* as they say in Jewish. A star, you should pardon the expression, is never short of *schleppers*. [They] are like the tides of the ocean. If you make a hit film, they come in and almost drown you. If you make a flop, they recede into the distance.'

One reason why he accepted the leading role in *The Optimists of Nine Elms*, which Anthony Simmons directed on location in the slums of London early in 1973, was the reminder that Sam, the old street-busker with his trained dog and antique horn gramophone in a perambulator, held for him of his father Bill Sellers. Sam's voice, though, was one Peter borrowed from a gardener he had employed at St Fred's, who used to mispronounce his words and would say 'pernament' for 'permanent'. Sellers now found age and failure touching because of the redeeming charity they inspired in him. He even expressed a hankering for the old music-hall days. At least there had been people out in front who were quick to tell you if they didn't like you, instead of *schleppers* who showed their disdain only when your act ran into trouble. 'Den . . . Den, would you ever come back to me?' he asked Dennis Selinger, who, however, indicated he had enough on his plate. 'Then do us a favour, Den,' he'd say, half-jokingly, 'ring up Ernie Cash and see if you can get me a split-week's engagement at Biggleswade.'

Wearing his *Optimists* make-up and costume, a straw hat, a flapping coat that echoed King Lear adrift on the stormy heath, and a false nose that had been dipped into all brands of tipple in its time, Sellers took time off between the shots to busk the queues outside his old training school, the Windmill Theatre, passing unrecognized, but not unrewarded. He looked a little like Dan Leno, who, he believed, was one of the spirits presiding benignly over his career. In the film he painted the character in sepia, side-stepping every pitfall of lachrymose sentimentality, wearing his battered pride like the rows of patriotic Union Jacks sewn inside his overcoat, strumming his banjolele as he remembered his father doing, and calculating the character with such a fine sense of independent existence that there is genuine suspense as Sam hesitates for a split second between popping the left-overs into the dustbin for the refuse men or into the frying pan for his next meal. Out of the depths of his own misery, Sellers dredged a precious truth about the come-down that lies in wait for those who once topped the bill.

His gratitude to loyal friends made him warmly receptive to the Boulting Brothers' proposal that he prove to the world that none of his virtuosity had vanished by playing six roles in their next film, including a French president, a Japanese prince, a British Intelligence officer and Adolf Hitler.

Soft Beds and Hard Battles, a comedy set in a Paris brothel, is now admitted by the Boultings to have turned out 'a ghastly film', but they are generous enough to attribute this to their own shortcomings in the script and direction rather than to the impetuousness with which Sellers set off in pursuit of Liza Minnelli in the middle of the production.

'Peter was sitting three seats behind me,' John Boulting said with a resigned sigh, recalling the concert at London's Festival Hall in May 1973, where Liza Minnelli was singing. 'He had his camera. "I've come to take pictures," he said. Even then I had a twinge of anxiety. We were half-way through the picture. It had looked good in the script, but somehow it wasn't coming together in the shooting. Peter had a half dozen roles to play already – we certainly didn't want him entering into a seventh with Miss Minnelli. At the interval, he kept saying to me, "A great artist, isn't she?" I sat through the second half in a very anxious state of mind. At the curtain, I turned round, but Peter's seat was empty.

'I got to Shepperton Studio on the Monday and said to John Dark, our production supervisor, "You know, it wouldn't surprise me at all if Master Peter hasn't gone for Liza Minnelli." Johnny laughed. "A bit late with the news, aren't you? She's with him in his dressing-room at this very moment." It was 6.30 a.m.'

Though there may have been genuine mutual attraction, it was a richly self-serving relationship, too. Each was dazzled by the other's talents and celebrity, and not averse to the publicity engendered when two stars start openly satisfying their curiosity about each other's private life. Sellers, forty-seven, was still married to Miranda Quarry. The twenty-seven-year-old Liza Minnelli was believed to be engaged to twenty-one-year-old Dezi Arnaz Jr. 'Peter is a genius,' she declared to John Boulting. He was no less forthright. 'At last I've found the sort of woman who will come and take care of me,' Peter told his producer. Boulting, who had to take care of an expensive film, looked increasingly anxious. Within a short time the relationship had disrupted the schedule. Together the lovers attended Sir Noël Coward's memorial service and were mobbed. Together they visited the pleasant Hampstead home of Sellers's first wife, Anne Levy. 'She is a charming person,' said Mrs Levy, remaining commendably cool and unflustered by the unusual permutations of wedded and single individuals who were assembled in her sitting-room. 'She added, 'She might be just the one to help poor Peter settle down and find whatever it is he may be looking for.' Together Liza and Peter stood on the threshold of his temporary London home in Eaton Mews North and he hinted to the mob of reporters that, yes, marriage was imminent.

'By this time,' said Roy Boulting, 'the film studio was under daily siege. Moreover, the nightly courtship was showing up in Peter's work. Action had to be taken. I went to Liza and said, "Look, Peter has a heavy make-up call every day at 6.30 a.m. He can't go to Tramp every night with you, cover the disco scene before he goes to bed and snatch only an hour or two's sleep before reporting to the studio. He just can't cope, Liza. Nor can we." – "Roy," she said, "it's not my fault. I do a pretty good spaghetti. I'd just love to stay home and feed Peter. It's *he* who wants to hit the town every night."

'In desperation, I said to John, "Can we change the shooting schedule so as to give Peter a week or ten days to get this thing in perspective?"'

Peter and Liza used this unexpected sabbatical to do everything but plight their troth to each other wherever reporters stopped them. 'We're madly in love,' he told the Press who were picnicking in their dozens on the grass outside Shepperton's gates. 'We're as good as married,' she said as the caravanserai rolled on to the Savoy Hotel, where hardly anyone noticed a small, silver-haired man delicately picking his way through the crush to insinuate himself thankfully into the lift. It wasn't often Charlie Chaplin escaped attention.

The Boultings' ploy paid off. 'Two weeks later I arrived at the studio,' said Roy. 'Peter was already in make-up. Despite the thick pancake greasepaint he was wearing for his Japanese prince, he looked very grey, deflated. ... "Do you know what's happened?" he said in a voice so low I could hardly catch it. "Peter, I can't think," I said, feeling a frightful hypocrite. "Liza and me. It's all over. We've split up." Thus ended the great affair. Both of them decided to go on entertaining people, rather than each other.'

What Liza Minnelli probably didn't know was that Peter had been playing a double role all the time they were together. In his house there was a cardboard box labelled 'Titi'. In this were kept some of the personal belongings of Countess Christina (Titi) Wachtmeister, a twenty-five-year-old model and the daughter of Sweden's envoy in Washington, who had been Sellers's regular girlfriend before Liza Minnelli had filled his viewfinder at the Festival Hall. Sue Evans, Peter's newly engaged secretary, had had the task of hiding the 'Titi' box whenever Miss Minnelli paid a visit. When Titi Wachtmeister rang to say she was dropping by, a box labelled 'Liza' had to go into temporary concealment. As usual, life wrote a better scenario for Peter Sellers than some of those he filmed.

The episode had one unforeseen effect on Peter. Though it had nothing directly to do with the Boultings, who gritted their teeth and finished a film they would now prefer to forget, their indulgence of Peter's romantic whim by re-arranging the shooting schedule once again provoked his urge to take over and call the shots when he felt that those around him lacked confidence in what they were doing. There was always a part of Peter that hated his own indiscipline – and by extension, those who tolerated it.

The international film scene was no easier in 1973. Agents had begun scouting for investors in well-funded businesses outside the familiar territory of conventional Hollywood. Peter gave one or two interviews that year which suggested he was strongly in thrall to an Adolf Hitler role – he even had himself made up to resemble the Führer. Behind his frequent allusions to the dictator ('They should have a Eurovision Hitler contest') lay a project entitled *The Phantom vs. The Fourth Reich* which had been inspired by his American agents. They had won the interest of King Features, a comic-strip syndication company, in investing money in a film about the Phantom, the mysterious hooded figure of justice, in whom they owned the copyright. Sellers would have played a ninety-year-old Hitler as well as his fictional son Heinrich. ('He never had a son,' said Peter, 'but Heinrich would have been his name if he had.') Unfortunately, perhaps, the head of King Features died suddenly on vacation at the top of a ski hoist; his successor vetoed the film project, believing it was safer to invest in coloured stills than go into moving pictures, thus missing a chance to anticipate the market in comic-strip nostalgia which *Star Wars*, *Superman* and their like were to tap so lucratively a few years later.

Peter was again thrown into the depths of despondency, and in this mood became susceptible to any film whose nature, however freakish, guaranteed him the work which had become an indispensable part of his existence. One of these was *Ghost in the Noonday Sun*, and it led to the biggest catastrophe of his career since *Casino Royale*.

'It was a poor boy's version of *Treasure Island* with Sellers as a Long John Silver pirate chief,' said Wolf Mankowitz, who had initially declined to touch the project with a gangplank and had then yielded when asked to name his price for making such an imprudent connection. Strangely, too, Peter had sent word that he admired Wolf; paradoxically, Mankowitz confirmed his confidence in those who took a tough line with him.

As for Peter, the film offered literal escape into latitudes – the location was Cyprus and surrounding waters – where he would be away from Miranda Quarry's divorce-court action and where some of his old mates could be around to comfort him. A call to David Lodge ensured his presence. 'I think it will be an enormous bloody giggle,' said Peter. 'Spike's in it, you know.' It quickly turned into an enormous catastrophe that left its backers, Columbia Pictures, feeling shanghaied again by a man whose bankability, not to say sanity, they had already once had grievous cause to question.

'It was a case of the wrong people in charge of the right people,' said David Lodge with a measure of charity. 'It was left to everyone to pull comedy out of chaos. Peter stepped in to protect himself as much as salvage the production – and got no thanks at all. Anthony Franciosa and he didn't get on at all well together. Franciosa was playing another swashbuckler, but no one had told him he was supposed to be burlesquing Douglas Fairbanks Sr. On my first day, we were all being made up on the waterfront, a bunch of ugly mugs being rendered even uglier, when a car screeches to a halt. Out jumps Franciosa, white with rage, and screams at us, "Where's that fucking Sellers? He's truncated my fucking part!" What an opening line! We all looked at each other blankly. Some of us, like me, had just arrived and didn't know what was going on – and some of us didn't even know what Franciosa was talking about. "What's *truncated* mean?" asked one of the co-stars. I began to get the idea that Peter was up to his old tricks.'

The location would have tried the patience of a monastery of penitents. 'We had this horrible old pirate ship. They'd equipped it with a huge mast, which caused it to tilt sickeningly with every little movement of the sea,' said Lodge. 'We had to have it moved round to suit the sun. We were *always* in the sun. There was rotten fish in the galley and no loo. Anyone who needed the loo had to jump into a dinghy and be rowed to the loo boat. Meanwhile Peter would loll aboard his private yacht, in the shade, drinking iced champagne, and calling crossly to Peter Medak, who was directing, "Are you ready yet? Are you *sure* you're ready for the shot? Because I'm not coming aboard till you are bloody ready." Most days we were all rowed ashore looking green and red respectively from seasickness and sunburn.'

Amidst all this Peter vanished to London to attend Princess Anne's wedding. He was joined on his return by Titi Wachtmeister. The film crew prayed her presence would calm troubled waters. It had the reverse effect. One night an enormous argument blew up a storm in the hotel dining-room: shouts, tears, exit Peter. A nice, middle-aged couple, nothing whatever to do with the film business but sympathetic towards the girl who had been left in tears at her table, invited Titi to join them. Suddenly the doors swung open. In walked one of Peter's assist-ants, carrying a Vuitton suitcase overflowing with clothes. It was unceremoniously dumped on the couple's table, amidst the fish, spaghetti, wine and mineral water, leaving the nice couple speechless. Titi Wachtmeister did her best to summon up an adequate explanation-cum-apology, 'This always happens when I go out with that man.'

On another occasion, his assistant Sue Evans found a handful of jewellery thrust into her hand with the order, 'Put these under the hammer.' Auction them or hit them with a hammer, she wondered. She decided to do neither, but judiciously hid them and the next day a rather nervous Peter asked, 'Er ... have you still got Titi's things?'

'He could be genuinely regretful,' said Sue Evans, 'but this was a bad time for him. He felt he had so little going for him that saying sorry would only diminish him further. Once you understood Peter, it was easy to forgive him. To outsiders, he must have seemed intolerable.'

To Columbia Pictures' executives, seeing their movie sink with the treasure aboard, he was a bastard. Their distress rose like a rocket signal. Peter eventually lost his temper with the two producers – one English, one American. He not only ordered them off the location, but off the island of Cyprus. Spike Milligan assumed the helm; but it was far too late to do anything to save the movie. On the very day they were due to shoot an important sea sequence, a storm halted production for a week. It was never resumed. To this day the largely unedited reels of *Ghost in the Noonday Sun* sit in a film vault gathering dust, more treasured for their write-off value than any expectation of profit they represent.

In three years Peter Sellers had made *The Blockhouse*, *A Day on the Beach* (undertaken in Denmark for a protégé of Roman Polanski) and *Ghost in the Noonday Sun* – and none of them had been released. 'There was a part of Peter that always feared he would end up where he had begun,' said Sue Evans. At the end of 1973, it seemed to him that this fear was more than justified. He sent a Christmas cable to this writer which ended, 'Cannot see anything on the horizon that will bring me much cheer. Except the Kosinski book. Am trying to get *Being There* under way. Love. Peter.'

ELEVEN

A New Couple

About a year after his short novel *Being There* was published in 1971, the Polish-born author Jerzy Kosinski received a cable. 'Available my garden or outside it. C. Gardiner,' it read. There was also a telephone number. Kosinski is a novelist, whose own life story, which included being struck dumb by the war horrors he survived as a child in Eastern Europe, and a marriage to the wealthy widow of an American steel magnate, has provided inspiration for his fiction on more than one occasion. However, *Being There*, at that time his only comic novel, is an allegory of American society, which worships the appearance of things rather than their substance and views the world as a real place only when its image has been authenticated on a television screen. The book's hero, a simple-minded fellow named Chauncey (or Chance) Gardiner, has never set foot outside the walled garden of the millionaire whose plants he tends. All he knows of life comes from what he has seen of it processed on the television screen, yet at the end of the story he is well on the way to becoming President of the United States.

Kosinski, a man who loves the intrigues that make up daily existence, called the telephone number in the telegram and found he was talking to Peter Sellers. Sellers had one burning request: at last he had read a book that expressed everything he felt about himself and about life – a matter that had been an enigma to him. He wanted to turn it into a film. Like Chance, he had become a celebrity in a way he could scarcely begin to comprehend – just by 'being there', it seemed, or presenting facets of himself on which others could project their own feelings in a way that confused his image with reality.

'Since Sellers's heart attack,' Kosinski later told the American journalist Aljean Harmetz, 'he sees his life as dictated by chance' – in the same way that Gardiner's is when Fate introduces him to one of

Washington's power-brokers and makes him into that desirable candidate for office, a celebrity without any embarrassing background.

It would later be said that Sellers had seen the part as his all-out bid for the Academy Award 'Oscar'. In fact, his was a far more obsessive quest than this. It was seven years before he was finally able to make the film. To him, it was like the search for the Holy Grail, the vessel used by Christ at the Last Supper which supposedly disappeared from sight when approached by someone not of perfect purity. Peter felt that playing the part would purge him of the coarse and exploitive roles he had taken in other films. He would finally achieve the perfection that had eluded him. But the role at that time, in 1972, unfortunately proved elusive for reasons that were rather more mundane. Kosinski rather fancied himself as the screen's Chance; he wanted to direct and star in his own screenplay. (Later, he actually played a leading role in Warren Beatty's film *Reds*.) Then again, Sellers's faltering career made it impossible for him to get a major film company interested in what was already considered a rarified (and therefore risky) project.

Peter already had Hal Ashby in mind, the director who had just made *Harold and Maude*, which he had loved. Shocked to find it tucked away in a tiny London cinema, neglected by its distributors, he had even offered to pay for Bud Cort and Ruth Gordon to come over to England and help him launch it properly. It was the same situation as *The Producers* all over again. Nothing came of this; but Ashby was grateful. 'I can't raise the money, either, to do *Being There*,' he told Peter. 'But let's make each other a promise: whichever of us gets "hot" first will help set up the picture for the other.'

Over the next few years Peter lost no opportunity to remind Kosinski that Chance Gardiner was ready and willing, if not exactly able, to play the part. He would write letters to the novelist signing them, 'Chance', and send him cables couched in the simplistic allegories which the character composed when drawing lessons for life's conduct out of horticultural wisdom. He even played the simple-minded Chance whenever they were together. On one occasion, sitting in front of a television screen that wasn't switched on, Peter rebuked a waiter for walking across his line of vision; the man apologized. (It was the arch little game he had once played with the Jardin des Gourmets waiter for the benefit of Canon Hester.) Another time he moved the guests at Kosinski's party to one side of the room so that he could keep an eye on the television – this time the set *was* working. What finally won Kosinski over to assigning Sellers the right to a pre-emptive strike at the role was an incident that happened, appropriately enough, amidst the wilting greenery of a mutual friend's sun-baked Malibu garden through which the two men were strolling. Suddenly Sellers stopped. In full view of Kosinski, he 'became' Chance the gardener. Just as the Boultings remembered seeing Sellers's physical bearing alter eerily when he played Fred Kite, Kosinski now witnessed an older, heavier-looking man in front of him, who stooped with a stiffness in his limbs, picked up a hosepipe and watered a little shrub that was dying from drought. 'His face was utterly serene. It was as if I wasn't within a hundred miles. He had stepped into his own world. He *was* my Chauncey Gardiner.'

But he was not yet up there on the screen. What enabled Peter Sellers to achieve his dream role was a stroke of luck as providential as anything in Kosinski's novel: Inspector Clouseau came to his rescue.

Apart from a cameo appearance in Spike Milligan's film *The Great McGonagall* – he played Queen Victoria in drag on his knees, 'because she was a very small woman' – Sellers's film career appeared to be at a dead end. No major offers were coming his way. His last seven films had either not been released or were commercial disappointments. His marriage was dissolved in September 1974, in an undefended suit. Miranda Quarry was granted a decree on the grounds of irretrievable breakdown: Sellers agreed to pay an undisclosed sum, reported to be about £30,000. What almost no one except himself and his closest advisers knew at the time was relatively how little money he had left in the way of savings and investments. It fell to Denis O'Brien, his new business adviser, agent and lawyer, to break this news to him. Investments made in good faith in earlier years had turned out poorly. The international financial crisis of 1974, the year of the Middle East War affecting the West's oil prices, savagely reduced the value of his remaining stock and property assets. Perhaps his own personal spending had not been extravagant; but the bills charged to his foreign-based companies strained even their capacity. For almost a dozen pictures, his fees had been paltry in comparison with the hundreds of thousands of dollars he once commanded. He owned percentages in certain film profits, but only the two *Pink Panthers* generated a substantial cash flow. This income came in slowly, and much of it was spoken for in advance. His personal bank account was once so low that he had to borrow £1,000 from friends to pay his aides. His celebrity alone enabled him to maintain the illusion of wealth that was popularly believed to be an inseparable part of stardom.

Denis O'Brien realized that Sellers needed to generate cash quickly and concluded a three-picture deal with producer Walter Mirisch, which brought his client an immediate and welcome advance. Peter also agreed with uncommon alacrity when an approach was made to him and Blake Edwards to bring Clouseau back to the screen – the small screen this time, as a twenty-six-part situation-comedy series for television, to be produced by Lord (Lew) Grade, entitled *The Return of the Pink Panther*. Blake Edwards, with movies like *Darling Lili* and *The Tamarind Seed* thankfully behind him, was anxious to demonstrate his own box-office credibility. The need felt by both men to prove that they could once more deliver the goods made them forget their intermittent enmities. It was soon apparent, however, that no power on earth (or script-page) could hold together the highly fissionable elements for the length of time a television series would take to make, so they decided to do it as a feature film.

Each *Panther* movie was progressively more successful than the last and *The Return of the Pink Panther* in 1975, spectacularly confirmed that Peter Sellers in the right film was still a formidably bankable talent. This provided all the muscle he needed to press ahead with setting up *Being There*, though that still took four more years.

The Return of the Pink Panther was the first film that introduced Clouseau's oriental houseboy, Cato (played by Burt Kwouk), whose precipitate attacks on his master became a staple and fondly awaited ingredient in all subsequent *Panthers* – and one which particularly appealed to Blake Edwards's relish for sadistic knock-about. To see Peter take to physical farce so exuberantly, frequently 'uncovered' by stunt men, one would have imagined him to be in the prime of health. His heart was indeed holding up amazingly well after the battering it had received in 1964 and the strains he continued to put on it. But his health now held an unhealthy fascination for him. On a visit to South Africa in February 1974, he persuaded Dr Christiaan Barnard to let him photograph a heart operation. 'I managed to survive it without fainting,' he reported, 'but I don't know how he put the fellow together again.' The ostensible purpose of his visit was to have a holiday and take photos for a magazine spread. He and Barnard went off to stalk wild game with cameras in a Rhodesian national park and it was on one of these forays that an enraged bull elephant charged the truck carrying them. Peter immediately put his yoga to the test by chanting a mantra that his swami had taught him for success in his film work. It appeared to work equally well on maddened pachyderms.

In the aftermath, he immersed himself increasingly in Eastern philosophy, perhaps encouraged by its effectiveness on safari. His whole home environment reflected this: the carpets were earth-coloured and the walls saffron to match his swami's robes. Even when he was meditating on worldly things like Press interviews, he took up a cross-legged and bare-footed posture on the floor. He had taken to wearing brown-tinted spectacles and this increased the air of remoteness that sometimes descended on him and was accepted by some interviewers to be a sign of transcendentalism. He was wont to say, 'Yoga has given me a tranquillity I wouldn't have thought possible.' This was not always the case, though. Sue Evans, who had started working for him in 1973, recalled the doorbell ringing at the Pembroke Place house where she and her stage-director husband Frank Evans were living in 1974. It was late at night. At the door stood a distressed Peter begging to be let in. He had just seen the occult horror movie *The Exorcist*, and been so unnerved that he couldn't face a night alone in his own home. It was the faithful Bert's night off; and Peter was like a little boy wanting his mother. 'Could I possibly stay with you tonight?' he asked the Evanses. In fact, he stayed about ten days with them. He found Sue Evans's sympathies very appealing at a time when his mother's death, his own divorce, and his heart twinges exposed him to loneliness and intimations of mortality.

'Only to certain people could Peter expose any kind of weakness,' she said, 'and I suppose I was one of them during these months.' Not long before this, when Sue had got married, he had taken it as a personal rejection and had composed a telegram (which friends stopped him sending) which said to Sue in effect, 'Sorry, but I feel your loyalties will be divided. Better stop working for me.' Sue Evans, hearing about it, had taken another job briefly, but, like Peter's other aides, found herself re-engaged almost by default. 'On Boxing Day 1974, he came round for dinner. After nearly eating us out of house and home, he said suddenly, "Sue, why did you leave me?" – "*Leave* you? You fired me." – "Fire you? Oh no, no ... I'd never do a thing like that."'

Sue Evans's working day would begin with a phone call from him, usually at eight in the morning. She had to tell him what he was supposed to be doing. Even when he was in America and she in London, he would call her to discover the day's programme. 'I would then open his mail and sometimes have to decide what to tell him and what not to – bad news was very upsetting. If I felt he'd be depressed, I'd try to sort the matter out myself, or keep it from him for a few days. Any form of pomposity made him flare up instantly.' Sellers's entry in *Who's Who* carried no mention of membership of any gentleman's club in London. 'Forms, proposers, seconders ... they always irritated him. It wasn't arrogance or self-importance, but that old, old hatred of officialdom.' The perfectionism Peter strove to apply to his movie-making also made for difficulties in his working relationship with his assistant. 'He felt he should be dictating letters simply because someone had once said to him, "You should dictate letters." He'd mumble, mutter, pace up and down, and if he did get through a paragraph, he'd usually look at it, say, "I didn't mean that", and start again. I'd sometimes take it on myself to change the text before the letter was sent. Peter invariably pushed the worst side of himself to the forefront, as if he wanted to throw the first punch. He fretted over minute things. If his signature on a letter dissatisfied him, I'd have to do it all over again. If he didn't sign in the right place on his fan photos, we'd begin again on a fresh batch. He was superstitious. That's well known. But I often thought, it was only when he remembered to be!

'Oddly enough, when he got a telex cabling machine installed in his Swiss chalet, it was all different. He enjoyed composing cables to his friends and enemies. He worked them up like a film script, improving them with sharp Goonish jokes or barbed retorts to imagined or actual offenders. They were a form of therapy.'

They were also a form of humour in which Sellers's skilfully playful side could find full scope. To one of his friends, Mo Rothman, the world-wide distributor of most of Chaplin's films and an associate of Blake Edwards, Sellers waxed lyrical in the style of his favourite bad poet. 'Ode on a Birthday Rose after William McGonagall,' he telexed, and continued: 'Oh, Beautiful Rose which has arrived today/Without the slightest delay or dismay/Very appropriately on my birthday/And has taken any feeling of gloom completely away./It arrived with good wishes from a gentleman named Mo,/And for to find a finer man a long way you would have to go./So three cheers for the Rothmans on this happy day/And I hope his travels won't take him too far away – *Oy-vey*!'

The same recipient got another telex 'which I may send to Tony Adams' (Adams was Blake Edwards's executive producer). Reading it, one understands what sparkling company Sellers could be when the right mood was on him.

'Following your phone call at 3.30 a.m., asking my advice regarding choice of schools for your son, I strongly advise you to send him to Cretinby. A difficult place to get into and harder still to get out of. Ask that the headmaster send you his brochure. The fire escape does not look very safe in the photograph of the school, but it's a lot safer in the picture than it is in the building. It is used every week. The school, of course, is co-educational, but the boys and girls do not share the same curriculum. They have separate ones built to segregate the sexes. The headmaster goes round with a crowbar and pries them apart. There are two types of pupil, Category A and Category B. At mealtimes the Category A get priority, the Category B get food.... Apparently the headmaster has no syllabus of his own and does not think it is anyone's concern how he chooses to spend his leisure. In my opinion this is an outworn shibboleth, but it was knitted by the carpentry class and has not worn at all well. My advice, Tony, is that instead of hawking the boy round to Eton, Marlborough, Charterhouse or Repton, send him to Cretinby. The teaching is on the Montessori system, but you will, of course, prefer to pay cash. Besides, it's in the heart of the swamp country.'

It would be hard for anyone to harbour rancour very long after receiving a diverting telex like this: it was often a form of making amends without having to apologize.

Sellers found Sue Evans indispensable – until the day he met Lynne Frederick. 'And then,' Sue Evans is the first to admit, 'when Lynne was around, I was redundant. Lynne was the first woman who really understood Peter's needs and was prepared to sacrifice a lot of her own life to care for his.'

Lynne Frederick was just twenty-one when they met. She was an attractive brunette with a sense of high definition to her personality, which the only child in a family, conscious of his or her singularity, sometimes develops early and enduringly. Her parents had separated when she was two years old: her father was then in America, while her mother, Iris, worked as casting director for one of Britain's independent television companies. This disrupted infancy had helped Lynne acquire an early self-reliance and an aptitude for handling difficult situations that was precocious for her years. She was making a reputation for herself in television and shortly she would move into big budget movies. She was also a client of Dennis Selinger. 'It was like history repeating itself,' Selinger later said, recalling how Peter had met Lynne Frederick through him in 1976, just as he had met his first wife, Anne Hayes. But as Lynne recalled the event, it was not quite like that.

'Nobody at Dennis's supper party realized Peter and I had never met before. I had to introduce myself. "My name is Lynne Frederick." – "My name is Peter Sellers." – "Yes, I know" – "You do?" Very stiff, stilted dialogue. We sat opposite each other at table and he stared at me throughout the meal. I was in love with him right away. I'd seen those eyes, like the ones of a nervous little nine-year-old boy. His hands shook slightly as he ate.' Analysing Peter's attraction for her, Lynne later concluded it lay in the surprise she felt at that first meeting. 'He was not the kind of person I expected. I'd thought of Peter as self-assured laughing, joking all the time – in short, the public image of the comic actor. Instead, I found him shy, lonely, desperately insecure.'

When dinner was over, Peter pleaded with her to come back with him to the apartment he was renting in a luxury Thames-side tower block called Roebuck House, where he lived below Lord Olivier and had the international arms dealer Adnan Kashoggi as a neighbour. 'But Dennis wouldn't let me go alone,' Lynne said. 'He saw me being gobbled up. Eventually he agreed, if he could chaperone me. Peter didn't as much as put his hand on my knee, but wore his "little boy lost" expression as he showed me the views over the river without ever losing his view of me! To tell the truth, I felt this was his technique with every new girl – making himself out to be vulnerable. But I found it endearingly child-like.' The visit ended at about 2 a.m. At 4.30 a.m. the same morning, Dennis Selinger was wakened by a call. Peter said, 'I need Lynne Frederick's telephone number.' – 'Good God, Peter, it's not even daylight. You can't phone her now. Anyhow, I haven't got it – it's on file at the office.' – 'Then get up. I'll meet you at the office.' Peter persisted in this vein for an hour. When it was just about a reasonable hour of the day, Dennis Selinger called Lynne. 'Shall I give Peter your number?' – 'Well, he'll get it from somewhere.' But Selinger was still chaperoning her in spirit. He told her, 'You can call Peter between one and two o'clock at San Lorenzo.' She did so and immediately he gabbled, 'Where are you? What's your number? When can we meet?' Lynne said later, 'When Peter found something that was unattainable, he had to have it immediately.' But this time he did not get it. Two days later he asked Lynne Frederick to marry him and she said 'No'.

'How long did you take before you asked Britt Ekland to marry you?' she asked.

'Britt was a mistake.'

'If that was a mistake, why repeat it? You're asking me after only two days. I could turn into another mistake.'

So they waited. And while they waited, with Peter calling her almost daily, he wasn't idle. He quickly turned out *The Pink Panther Strikes Again*, which opened to seasonably amiable reviews just before Christmas 1976. Although it was a long-winded movie, and was self-indulgent about how much of any one gag it should feed the audience, Clouseau's ridiculous attempts to keep his dignity in balance, when all the rest of him is leaning every which way, saved many a scene from tedium. 'Peter kept tinkering with his French accent till it very nearly became unintelligible,' said Lynne Frederick, who was independently pursuing her own movie career. But the efforts produced Clouseau's semantically exotic pronunciation of the word 'hump', uttered as if a German umlaut had intruded on an English vowel and come up against an over-refined French accent. The 'hump' gave rise to one of the zaniest scenes in all the *Panthers*, when the helium-filled Hunchback of Notre Dame disguise that Clouseau has adopted over-inflates and carries him up, up and away over the roofscape of Paris like a hilariously obscene bit of mutated humanity from Bosch's *Garden of Delights* painting.

He also appeared in the Hollywood-made movie *Murder by Death*, Neil Simon's parody pastiche of detective thrillers, playing the epigrammatic Chinese sleuth, Sidney Wang. This had less happy results, as far as he was concerned. When the film came out in the middle of 1976, Peter and Lynne went to see it. He hated what he saw of himself and he disliked the film even more. Over a long dinner with Lynne, he composed a letter to producer Ray Stark calling his film 'the epitome of 8 mm home movie-making', a preposterous view with no rational basis, but he was inflexible. He later decided to sell his percentage in the film and he was bought out for around $1,300,000.

During the first eleven months of their association, Peter and Lynne got to know each other very well indeed. What she learned might have scared off any other young woman not so convinced – and *affectionately* convinced, too – that here was a man who needed to be cared for as well as loved. By happy chance, she had a strong protective nature and a preference for men mature enough to have experienced the world, yet vulnerable enough to welcome a soothing touch on the bruises it has left. Peter had found his girl, someone young enough to be sexy, yet old enough in spirit to be a mother-figure. They were married in a secret five-minute ceremony in Paris on 18 February 1977, and left at once for a honeymoon in the South of France.

Peter had kept his increasing concern over his heart pains a secret from Lynne. The only sign she had before her marriage of just how ill he might be was his need to carry nitro-glycerine ampoules wherever they went – 'at least that was all he let me see,' she said. 'He'd put one under his tongue whenever he felt a twinge. Naturally, I was anxious. But he assured me it was a natural precaution with his medical history.'

However, she had noted how preoccupied he was with seeking some kind of cure for his heart troubles. They went to South Africa in September 1976. Peter had begun experiencing very mild heart pains and he wanted Dr Christiaan Barnard, with whom he had gone on photo-safari two years earlier, to examine him. He was considering undergoing an angiagram to determine the condition of his heart in preparation for possible by-pass surgery. It was all done in great secrecy. The appointment was fixed, the room in the Cape Town clinic booked and Peter was to check in on the Monday under an assumed name. On the Sunday, his nerve failed him: 'I'm just so scared, Lynne. I can't go through with it. Let's get out of here.' They flew off that same day. For a long time he thought Dr Barnard would never forgive him; but the two subsequently ran across each other when both of them were in Judea, and Barnard told Peter that he had felt only sympathy, not anger, over his unannounced retreat.

Still in search of any means of treatment that would give him reassurance without unbearable emotional strain, and accompanied by Lynne, Peter flew to the Philippines in October 1976. Peter had heard about the so-called psychic surgeons of Manila, who were reputed to be able to perform major operations without the use of instruments or anaesthetics. Lynne was permitted to remain with Peter during the 'surgery', which was performed over a period of ten days in their hotel suite. She was even allowed to take photographs of them at work. 'The two surgeons wore short-sleeved Filipino shirts, so they had nowhere to conceal any material,' she recalled. 'They laid a white towel on Peter: some sort of x-ray, since shadowy areas seemed to appear on it, allowing them to carry out a diagnosis. They then began massaging his skin. Suddenly blood appeared – and their hands seemed to slip under his skin and enter his body. All this time Peter was completely conscious of what was going on and feeling no pain at all. He reported he could feel their fingers exploring his internal organs and seeking any malign entity, like a blood clot. They brought out what looked like a dozen of these and put them in a kidney tray. Each time they finished, they smoothed the skin back into place and left no sign that anything had ever entered it.' Lynne was well aware how controversial, not to say suspect, such techniques were considered to be. Reputable medical associations gave no warranty of respectability (or even effectiveness) to what many condemn as a clever conjuring trick practised by charlatans. In fairness, it must be added that Sellers was not charged anything and his name was never used (except by himself in later public comments on the 'operation') to advertise the surgeons' services. 'He did seem to show improvement,' Lynne said, 'but it lasted only a couple of months.'

Soon the additional medication Peter had been taking before their marriage made its effects visible. This drug, called Inderal, was intended to decrease his pains by calming his heart, making it work more slowly by cutting the beat to about half its normal rate. It had undesirable side effects, however. Peter complained that the drugs he was taking 'make me feel I'm living in a fog, a shroud of cotton wool'. They did lower his blood pressure, but he began suffering from what is known as the Stokes Adams condition. Fainting fits came without warning. One of these was very alarming.

The couple had recently bought a new home in Port Grimaud – the artificially created 'Little Venice' in the South of France, with its waterways where riparian dwellers could moor their boats. They drove over to view it from St Tropez. 'As Peter got out of the car to open the front door, he said he felt a little dizzy. I watched him. I was a little anxious. But it might have been attributable to the long drive we'd done. He was about to insert his front-door key in the lock, when I saw him collapse, suddenly and totally. As he fell, he struck his head hard against the stone portico of the house. This injury remained with him as a long scar running from his right eyebrow into his hairline. Make-up usually hid it. But if you knew its position, you could locate it in some close-up shots.' Another time they were eating at La Ferme, a restaurant above Nice. 'In the middle of a sentence, Peter broke off. I looked up from my food. He was staring at me. "What's the matter, my darling?" Instead of replying, he just toppled sideways.'

Because of the risks these fainting spells involved, he was advised to give up his beloved life-long affair with one new car after another: his driving days were over. This depressed him greatly and contributed to his restlessness.

So it was an anxious Lynne who, on 20 March 1977, boarded the Air France flight from Nice to London with her husband. They were about thirty minutes from London when Peter complained that he felt dizzy. By this time Lynne was used to taking his blood pressure with an instrument that accompanied them everywhere. 'It had plummeted very low. His heartbeat had been cut from seventy-two to thirty. He was sweating profusely. He had gone grey. His eyes began rolling upwards. It seemed to me it was more than a fainting fit. I sought help from the Air France crew, but they weren't any too bright, so I cried "See if there's a doctor aboard." There was, fortunately. Peter's pulse was now thirty-two and the doctor believed he had suffered a minor heart attack.'

He was hastily examined on landing, then rushed across London to Charing Cross Hospital. The hospital put out a preliminary bulletin which at first confirmed that he had had a 'moderate' coronary attack, but within hours this was denied. Sellers's 'indisposition', as it was now called, was attributed to some recently eaten oysters. Behind this revised diagnosis, which didn't allay Press suspicions, lay a crisis which

Peter's advisers had decided must not be made public. A film star can make his millions only while he remains healthy, or appears to do so, or at least while he retains the confidence of the production companies employing him that, even if not in prime condition, his general state of health will be insurable. The news that was broken to Lynne Frederick within minutes of Peter's examination would have resulted in potentially damaging world headlines if it had been made public there and then. Medical examination suggested that Peter had not suffered another coronary: his fainting spell had been caused by an extreme reaction to his Stokes Adams condition. But his heartbeat was very erratic and his condition so serious that, in the doctors' opinion, a pacemaker ought to be implanted immediately in order to regulate the functioning of his heart.

This was done. Peter's pulse rate stabilized at 71.2 and six hours later Lynne was able to say to the newspaper reporters, with perfect truth, that 'he's sitting up in bed drinking a cup of tea ... very puzzled about what's been happening to him.' Even Sue Evans, who was in London and had rushed to the hospital on hearing the news, was startled at the swiftness of his recovery. She had steeled herself for the most alarming news when Lynne met her and said, 'Sue . . . and then broke off, as if she were unable to find the words. Then she had continued, 'Sue, would you mind going down Earl's Court Road and finding a Chinese takeaway that Peter remembers?' Sue burst out laughing with relief. 'It was so typical of all Peter's recoveries. He could be terribly ill, but he turned it into a jesting matter. He always recovered.'

The couple resumed their honeymoon ten days later, but both had been deeply affected by what had happened. The condition of Peter's heart had remained stable for ten years following his Hollywood coronary in 1964, then he had begun to experience renewed symptoms of malfunctioning, which was when he should have had his angiogram examination. The recent attack was evidence of how the organ was deteriorating, even though the pacemaker actually caused an improvement in his general metabolism, since medication was no longer needed to the same debilitating degree. All the same, Peter Sellers had an extraordinary run of bad luck – it can be called nothing else – where his pacemaker was concerned. The pacemaker that had been inserted in March began to go on the blink in April. Peter hastily checked into a St Tropez clinic and the defective mechanism was replaced. This second one started going wrong almost immediately, when the wire leading directly into his heart muscle became detached. The pacemaker was replaced by a third one at the end of April because the wire broke. He had to be rushed back to the clinic in May and this time the pacemaker that was implanted in his body was the one that functioned until the end of his life. But four operations inside three months was a scarcely bearable strain; and all of them had to be kept a close secret lest the publicity impair his earning power or the willingness of film-makers to risk employing him. 'A blood check, normal in such cases', was usually the accepted explanation if anyone noticed his presence in the clinic.

As for Lynne, she now had to accept that 'looking after' Peter was going to be a more strenuous commitment than simply accommodating herself to his mercurial moods, offering him reassurance in his work and being a caring partner in their marriage. 'He wouldn't have brought himself to ask me to give up acting,' she said, 'but it became obvious to me that my career must be Peter. He was a full-time undertaking, a twenty-four-hour-a-day commitment.'

They moved into their £60,000, three-bedroomed Port Grimaud home, which had a rose-coloured dinghy moored at the door called – what else? – *The Pink Panther*. Soon, however, it was high summer and Port Grimaud, which had been so quiet in the off-season when they had bought the house, was over-run by holidaymakers and day tourists. Peter detested crowds, so they moved back to London and later sold their house.

Shortly after the insertion of the pacemaker, Peter's loyalty to yoga waned. 'After all, what did it do for me?' he said. 'I obeyed all the instructions. I said my prayers regularly. I did all the exercises for peace, tranquility and happiness. And all that happened was that I got steadily worse.' Yoga's spiritual concerns were replaced by a constant watchfulness over his physical condition, but to Lynne's anxiety this became increasingly morbid. His attempt to come to terms with the emotional aftermath of having a pacemaker's alien presence in his body proved painful. He was desperately anxious that people shouldn't think of him as physically incapacitated, so he wore a track suit, gave the impression that he went jogging and was photographed as if he had just returned from a brisk run. At other times, in public, he would crack a joke about being 'the partially bionic man'. (News of his first pacemaker had, of course, eventually leaked out.) But all this was whistling in the dark to keep his courage up; in private he was more morose. 'In some book he'd read,' said Lynne Frederick, 'he'd picked up the phrase "a cardiac cripple" and now he began referring to himself as one.' It was not said as a joke, but in the increasingly embittered tones of a man whose body was failing him and robbing his life of potential and meaning. He felt that he was functioning at fifty per cent of capacity.

Denis O'Brien was continuing his efforts to strengthen his client's financial standing. He proposed investing some of Peter's *Panther* fees in a project to build a private club and hotel in the Seychelles – another partner was the Beatle George Harrison. O'Brien did not find Peter an easy client. He cautioned him against his extravagancies. He scrutinized the worth of a film deal in money terms, though these might be irrelevant to Peter's interest in it. Consequently he did not take kindly to Peter upsetting some carefully constructed deal which was intended to enrich him simply for what O'Brien considered to be a whim; nor did he like being told to agree to some other deal because the role in question appealed to Peter's imagination instead of to his bank account. 'It's not worth it, Peter,' he would say, but to Peter 'worth' was how he felt at that moment. Lynne Frederick had had no illusions about Peter's disorganized finances when she married him, but she soon became aware that the necessity to work, and not merely the welcome fees that went with it, was what really drove him on. She realized that his chief fear was not of death, but of the way his disintegrating constitution – 'which must have been that of a lion,' she said – might make it impossible for him to find work. But even work brought no surcease of worries. 'Psychologically, the more Peter knew about himself, the harder life became for him. It wasn't just himself he worried about, either. In my opinion, if any one thing killed him, it was worry about the number of people depending on him when making a film. But what solution was there? Quit working? If he'd done that four years before, he'd have died four years earlier. No, he just had to press on – and hope.'

The Revenge of the Pink Panther, released in mid-1978, was the fifth in the series to star him; he was paid $750,000 plus ten per cent of the gross. It was reminiscent of *Tom and Jerry* material with Sellers, as the dignified mouse, unconsciously eluding the swipes of a big bad Mafia cat; but he did it so nimbly – astonishingly so, considering his ill-health – that one didn't sigh too much for a better mousetrap. Some gags were as good as anything he and Blake Edwards ever invented. Standing in a suit that is still smouldering from a bomb outrage, he manages, like a human match, to ignite a document which is handed to him and he then spreads the conflagration over the carpet and the desk of Inspector Dreyfuss (played by Herbert Lom), another of the characters whose guaranteed re-appearance was one of the reasons for the series' tremendous popularity. (The public may know what they like; it's even truer that they like what they know.) Venturing half-clad too near an electric fan placed at navel level, a sudden 'ping' alerts Clouseau (and the audience) to the agonizing possibility of involuntary castration. The series had coarsened, but somehow he had preserved his finesse.

By now, the customary way of finding a film for Sellers was to try and interest him in a project. If he said he liked it, it was then developed with his talent for mime, impersonation and humour very much in mind. The script might undergo innumerable changes by many hands, and some thumbs. For the first of the three-picture deal which was made to get him some ready money, Walter Mirisch wanted him to play the dual roles of king and commoner in a comic remake of *The Prisoner of Zenda*. He believed it was perfect for Peter's multiple talents. Peter thought it a promising idea at first, but the completed script thoroughly displeased him: in his opinion, it was too broad, too vulgar. His mind was full of the subtle resonances of *Being There*, which seemed, in Hollywood parlance, to be nearing the stage of a 'firm maybe' now that he and Hal Ashby were both 'hot' talents. Ashby had directed *Coming Home*, that benign binding up of the Vietnam war wounds with Jane Fonda and Jon Voight which was to win both stars acting 'Oscars' in 1978. The *Zenda* script underwent several re-writes, which didn't improve it in Peter's opinion. He decided not to do it. He was then informed, in brutally simple terms, that he had already signed to make it, he had had part of his $425,000 fee advanced to him, and he would be held to his contract. If he still refused, he would be sued. A sum of around nine million dollars was mentioned as both the movie's estimated cost and the likely extent of the claim against him. Peter's attitude was a belligerent, 'Go ahead and sue.' His lawyers were less truculent: 'Peter, you don't have anything like nine million dollars to pay the damages, if you lose the case. A law suit of this magnitude will wipe you out. Not to mention the damage it will do to your career by showing you as going back on your written word.' An injunction might even be slapped on him, preventing him from working on any other film until the case came to trial. That would kill forever the prospect of filming *Being There* and might literally kill him if he couldn't work. Peter surrendered to the inevitable.

The signs of age and ill-health were increasingly evident. To tone him up, he underwent minor cosmetic surgery in Los Angeles to take up his slack jowls and lift the drooping skin between eyebrow and eyelid. It was done in a morning. He was later slightly annoyed to find Jerzy Kosinski referring to *Being There* as the reason for this rejuvenation. Kosinski had started to think Peter might be a little too old for Chance.

'Well,' said Peter, reasonably, 'you could have avoided that by saying "Yes" earlier.'

In mid-July 1978 he flew to Vienna with Lynne, who was to play Princess Flavia in *The Prisoner of Zenda*. He was anxious only to get the film over and done with, which was not the best mood in which to start what needed to be an adroitly handled comedy. But as usual he had put hours of work into preparing his own roles: the Cockney Hansom-cab driver Sid Frewin, who is the King's double, was easy enough; for the 'silly idiot' Ruritanian monarch, he 'borrowed' a plummy voice he had last heard in the mouth of a friend of Miranda Quarry's at a country-house weekend.

Because Peter hated large gatherings, it came as a great surprise to Lynne when she discovered that he had organized a party for her birthday soon after their arrival in Vienna. He invited about thirty friends and film people, including the distinguished musician Anton Karas, who had composed the theme music for *The Third Man*, to serenade Lynne on a zither. The buffet left no tin of caviar unopened. It seemed to be his way of making up to her for the burden of responsibility that his precarious health was increasingly imposing on her.

Lynne, who recognized his deteriorating condition, was more vigilant than ever. He had become totally unpredictable: his mood would change four or five times a day, somehow always out of kilter with events. 'You had to be totally prepared for his moods and ride them out – like surfing on a wave that continually altered volume and direction under your feet.'

Perhaps her own parents' broken marriage and her early separation from her father made her exceptionally sensitive to Peter's relations with his three children by Anne Hayes and Britt Ekland. She realized that not only did he have no natural talent for being a father, but also he was deeply hurt by what he considered to be his children's attitude to his own struggles, set-backs and successes. He had gained the impression, rightly or not, that they even regarded his well-publicized life as an embarrassment. Lynne felt that Peter's health was so uncertain that she should do all she could to bring him closer to his family. Thus, when Peter's fifty-third birthday occurred in September, she contacted Michael and Sarah Sellers and told them of a small party she was arranging for their father. Could they come to Vienna? She was sure he would be both surprised and grateful to see them. It is unlikely that Peter's family appreciated how ill he was, but, in the event, the children had previous engagements and were unable to be there.

The Prisoner of Zenda was not going well. Its first director was Stan

Dragotti, who had made a series of airline commercials with Peter in 1975 which upset some national sensitivities because of Peter's impersonations of grasping Scotsmen and Mafiosi Italians. But it seemed that Peter wanted a director who would stand up to producer Walter Mirisch. Richard Quine took over at Blake Edwards's suggestion. Quine, who had made a reputation in the 1950s and 1960s with comedies of wit and a certain elegance like *Bell, Book and Candle* and *How to Murder Your Wife*, found neither to hand in the comic kingdom of Ruritania. Uncertainty perhaps caused an even sharper exchange of fire between Sellers and Mirisch. If Mirisch suggested that Quine shoot a scene with three close-ups, Sellers, on learning of this from Quine, would decree it should be done in one long shot, and so on. The film was completed both over schedule and over budget.

Peter at this time was referring his on-the-set problems to a new agent, Martin Baum, of Creative Artists, in Beverly Hills, and he had engaged the law partnership of Rickless & Wolf to represent him in London and Los Angeles. His break with Denis O'Brien came in 1977 and was due to differences in temperament rather than to any disappointment in business deals such as the Seychelles venture, which had been affected by the sudden change of government there. O'Brien found his client's renewed extravagances unsettling. Now that the *Panthers'* residuals were rolling in, Peter was on a spending spree. He desired to buy a $90,000 boat. O'Brien pointed out the drain this would be on his re-organized finances and doubted whether he needed it or could afford it. Others might have had the sophistry or guile to say 'What a splendid idea, Peter' and then, while seemingly going along with his client's madcap notion, gently talk him out of it or divert him to lines that would show some return on investment (such as chartering). Because the financially prudent O'Brien wasn't encouraging over the purchase of the yacht, the relationship was terminated.

While *Zenda* was being edited, Peter's hopes rose slightly: perhaps it could be made to work in the cutting-room. As always, it was agony to him to think he would be trapped forever, on permanent public inspection, so to speak, in a film he knew was unworthy of him. A preview of an early assembly was held in a Universal Studios' screening room in the presence of Mirisch, Quine, Baum and Peter and Lynne. 'Peter kept muttering to himself all through the film,' Lynne recalled. 'He was never good at seeing himself in a new film for the first time – but this was worse than anything. Sometimes I'd even hear him swear. When the lights went up, we all sat in total silence for a second or two. Then Peter got up stony-faced. He walked to the door, turned round, and said to

Walter Mirisch, "I have only one comment to make. My lawyers will be in touch with you."' In the event, Peter wrote Mirisch a three-page letter suggesting changes and (he hoped) improvements. Although Mirisch did try incorporating some of these in another cut, it could not alchemize a leaden romp into a golden comedy. Peter behaved according to form in other ways. In a conversation with television journalist Rona Barratt, he spoke his mind forcefully about the picture and advised people not to go to see it. Walter Mirisch was reported to have said that he never again wanted to see, hear from, hear about, have to look at, or even be sent a cable by Peter Sellers. The other two films which Peter was contracted to make for him were dropped.

Peter did not mind: *Being There* was under way. Andrew Braunsberg, a producer who had met Kosinski through their mutual friend Roman Polanski, had persuaded the author that he could set it up. Lorimar, a relatively new but well-funded contender on the Hollywood scene, one of the so-called 'instant majors' which put a bundle of talents together into a deal, agreed to finance the Sellers–Ashby–Kosinski package and shooting was set to start in January 1979.

Peter's fee was to be $750,000, plus ten per cent of the gross domestic (including Canadian) receipts in excess of ten million dollars, plus ten per cent of the gross foreign receipts in excess of three million dollars. He had achieved his dream and found it had a golden lining.

In high spirits he and Lynne flew from New York to Geneva in December 1978: there was a chalet they wished to purchase in the Swiss resort of Gstaad. During the flight, Peter started sweating profusely; then his pains began. 'We suspected angina right away,' said Lynne, who began massaging his heart. 'It seemed to have gone bananas. It was racing away. By the time we landed, it was worse. It was beating at 110 or thereabouts, a condition called tachycardia. We rushed him into hospital in Geneva.' Tachycardia is such that, while it seems as though a coronary is occurring, there is an extremely fine line between the two conditions, on which medical opinion may easily disagree. But the pain apart, Peter's anxiety was almost unbearable. To be felled like this after all the years of planning, within weeks of beginning the movie for which, it seemed, his whole life had been one long rehearsal. Lynne determined to keep his illness a total secret, 'and by some miracle, helped perhaps by the fact that everyone's mind was on Christmas, we succeeded.' Fortunately Peter had passed the medical for his *Being There* insurance cover only a few days earlier. Even Marty Baum was kept in the dark, believing his clients were simply on an extended shopping trip. At the end of three weeks of enzyme tests, the evidence was still inconclusive whether or not Peter had had a coronary. 'How he pulled through that time, I'll never know,' said Lynne Frederick. 'Maybe if he hadn't had the greatest role in his life coming up ahead of him, he'd have given up his life there and then.'

The two of them spent Christmas in Switzerland and then returned to America in January – for *Being There*.

TWELVE

The Big Chance

Besides his ever-present fear of imminent heart failure, Peter Sellers was experiencing a deeper unease – a failure of artistic nerve. It had taken him over six years of tenacious lobbying of all concerned – writer, director, production companies – to get *Being There* set up as a film. Now that he was within days of playing the role of a lifetime, he realized that he didn't know how to do it.

'I thought I knew all about Chance,' he told Lynne, pacing anguishedly up and down. 'The truth is, I don't know the first thing. Lynne, you've got to help me find him.'

This time it wasn't just a matter of letting a spirit presence enter him; such receptivity took time, and he had only three days before Hal Ashby was due to begin directing him. He had to go out and 'find' the character. 'We spent a chaotic weekend feverishly putting Chance together,' Lynne recalled. 'If Peter found the voice, he felt all else would follow – so we tried imagining how Chance sounded. Peter tried out a whole continent of American accents, which I taped and played back. Chance had to have an American intonation, but because the character seems to come from nowhere – even the FBI, the CIA and the KGB can't trace his background when they try – he couldn't have an accent tied to a particular locality. One of Peter's voices would be too New Yorkish, another too West Coast, a third too Deep South. . . . To listen to Peter's repeated efforts was a little like watching a man unpacking a travel bag for something he fears he hasn't packed.'

Sellers later said he didn't realize the solution was literally staring him in the face. Wherever he went, he always found house-room for a picture of his favourite comedian Stan Laurel, either together with Oliver Hardy, or else in a small snapshot of himself and Laurel taken on that first visit to Los Angeles which had shattered his illusions in so many other respects. The picture was one of Peter's dearest treasures, one of the few truly intimate things he owned. The child-meek, transparently innocent voice of Chance, if one listens carefully, is first cousin to Stan Laurel's: the native Lancashire flatness curled up at the edges by an acquired American undertone.

Having found the voice, he tackled the walk with Lynne using a video-camera to record him walking across a room, along the corridor, sitting down, standing up. They would then watch the playback. 'Again and again he'd say, "Lynne, I haven't got it. I look terrible," and off he would go again, trying out another kind of step.' Eventually it came: a walk that suggested a man who took little exercise, was heavier than he should be, and who pursued his way through life, as he had done inside his garden, at his own unhurried pace. He'd already worked parts of Chance into his physique: for instance, he'd put on weight. After all, he said, Chance never went outside his employer's home, had his meals cooked for him, ate well and regularly, and lived life by proxy in front of the television screen. 'He's sedentary and solitary,' said Peter, 'even eats like a big child, which is basically what he is.' And so he *became* him. Lynne's last contribution was to take a pair of house-scissors and cut Peter's hair into 'a sort of high crew-cut' – the way the maid Louise had done for Chance in the book – though she described it as 'a Frank Sinatra style'.

When he answered his camera call, it wasn't Peter Sellers who ambled on set, but Chance the gardener, tranquillized by his own guileless view of the world and sedated against its terrors by the emulsified imagery which television had fed him.

Peter always acknowledged how much he owed to Lynne in this crucial 'rehearsal' period. Two months before he died he impulsively bought a paperback edition of Kosinski's novella and inscribed on the title page: 'For my darling Lynne who helped me achieve my greatest ambition – to play Chance. I adore you. Peter, May 1980.'

Sellers's role and the way he played it determined the feel of much of Hal Ashby's film. The film had to move at his speed, for instance, and this was 'deliberate', to say the least. He had to elaborate what was basically a single joke by passivity, that most negative of means. The comedy of *Being There* isn't released by the words themselves – though the solemnity of Chance's simple-minded observations frequently makes them sound droll – but by the space between the words as people react expressively to them. More of the movie depends on reaction shots than on punch lines. Peter had continuously to be doing nothing, simply 'being there', in order to precipitate the ironies of a media-manipulated world in which all trust and credibility are based on illusions and deceptions. Chance had to be kept totally passionless, yet made to appear omnipotent – his courage supplied by other people's lack of conviction. The movie showed Sellers as the screen's most brilliant minimalist; it was a white-upon-white composition whose powerful simplicity concealed its sustained calculation.

Shirley MacLaine found him 'a dream' to work with. Kosinski paid him the highest tribute that a creator could to his interpreter: 'Nobody thought Chance was even a *character*, yet Peter *knew* that man.' Peter himself confessed that he had sometimes felt 'abstracted' from the film in an unearthly way, as if he were standing by, looking at himself. It reminded him of the time he had 'died' on the operating table and seen himself revived, pulled back again from the spiritual state to the physical being. To the American journalist Mitchell Glazer, he confessed: 'The whole experience of *Being There* was so humbling, so powerful ... I'd often say 'Cut' (during the take). And people would come running, saying, "Is anything wrong? Don't you feel all right?" And I'd say – and I know this is a bit Chance-like to say a thing like this – but I'd say [in a guileless monotone], "Oh, no, no. I've never seen anything quite like this film before."'

To Shirley MacLaine, he unburdened himself with a disconcerting excess of fatalism. As often happens in the disorganized 'organization' of shooting schedules, the last sequence they shot together happened to be the scene of their first encounter in the film. Chance has had a minor accident due to her chauffeur's inattention; and this rich Washington 'samaritan' wafts him home in her limousine to be the convalescent patient, and later the house-guest, in the residence where her ailing husband (played by Melvyn Douglas) still pulls the strings of power. The two players had to sit together, cramped in the mock-up of the car's back seat, for a skilfully lit process shot in which night-time Washington was to be projected behind them. Enforced propinquity brought Peter to the strange confession about his death-and-rebirth in Hollywood. 'But I noticed that all the time we sat there,' said Shirley MacLaine, 'he was making small movements that suggested he was in pain, clutching his tummy under his top-coat, massaging himself. "What's wrong?" I finally asked. "Nothing, probably indigestion," he said. But eventually, as we sat there waiting for another take, he came out with it: "Shirley, I want to tell you, this is the same sound stage on which I first experienced that feeling, back in 1964, that all was not well with me." He didn't have to speak of dying to make me feel he was near to it – and he knew it. But what was troubling him wasn't dying. It was finding out why he was alive. I think he saw *Being There* as the clearest

205

statement about himself that he ever would or could make. Once it was done, it's my opinion that he said to himself "Why go on?" '

At the end of the day's shooting, it wouldn't be Peter who returned to Lynne, but Chance the gardener; and, just as his first wife had done, she found the transformation alarming to live with. It was as if his own body, in its debilitated state, didn't have the strength to take over when work was done and home life had to be resumed. He appeared to Lynne to have changed into a very old man, who sat there staring at her. He was physically present, but it was as if his astral soul inhabited another planet. When he was in a conversational mood, his need for reassurance was overwhelming: he made her promise never to leave him for anything. His tachycardia had implanted apprehensions into every hour of his waking life. 'The least little bit of breathlessness alarmed him. If anything he ate disagreed with him, he'd clutch himself and say, "Lynne, Lynne, it's happening. A heart attack!" People in Peter's state have reactions of this kind – it was only to be expected – but one had to learn to tell the difference between Peter's imagination and what might indeed be the real thing. The strain on me was terrible – though ultimately, and here I'm possibly exaggerating, I felt as competent as a cardiologist rushed in to do a "spot" diagnosis!'

Only a few intimates knew the strain Lynne was under. Sue Evans was one. Another was Michael Jeffery, a young man who had replaced Bert Mortimer when he left Peter's service a year or two earlier after some differences that still remain a mystery to him. Jeffery had been Peter's dresser on *The Prisoner of Zenda*; now he acted as his personal assistant.

On the weekends he had free from making *Being There* on location at the Biltmore estate at Ashville, North Carolina, where George Vanderbilt's huge, gloomy pile did duty for Melville Douglas's Washington mansion, Sellers would gratefully fly off by chartered aircraft to Grand Cayman Island in order to thaw out. Even there, worries intruded on him. Britt Ekland wanted to publish his love-letters to her in a book of ghosted memoirs ('a load of muck', he called it) and so he had to get his London lawyers to put a stop to this. Sophia Loren was on a tour of Britain to publicize her memoirs, which, paradoxically, hurt his vanity because his 'love affair' was not mentioned. Worst of all, he was aware that his precarious physical condition wouldn't let him show Lynne the full affection he felt she deserved: he had become impotent.

Marty Baum, his Los Angeles agent, was now the one to have to take the strain of Peter's constant telephoning at all hours of the day and night. Eventually he had to move out of his wife's bedroom and into a guest room to let her get some respite from Peter's harassment. ' "Difficult" is a fair word to use about him,' Baum said with commendable understatement. ' "*Very* difficult" is an even fairer way of putting it. At this stage he was desperately in need of psychiatric help. I've never come across such an extreme case as Peter's.' Baum had been Sidney Poitier's agent when that actor had voluntarily entered into analysis in the 1960s; and in his autobiography *This Life*, published in 1980, Poitier paid full and frank tribute to a nine-year experience that had sometimes left him quivering with uneasiness 'at the thought of what a perfect candidate I was for a mental institution'. Baum harboured much the same thoughts about Peter and on one occasion, after he had received an explosive cable from Peter, Baum composed a telex reply. It read: 'It might have escaped your attention, therefore I must point out to you that I am Jewish. There is a tradition among European shtetl [peasant village] Jews that when you want something really bad, never mention it, because if you do, a Cossack will take it away from you before you get it. That is my superstition about something I want very, very badly for you. All my love, Marty.'

Lynne, too, had been considering the possibility of Peter having analysis, but she was well aware that the suggestion would alarm and probably antagonize him.

On one occasion, Peter worked himself up into an extremely distressed state: he threatened to commit suicide. Opening a whisky bottle, he sloshed the liquor into a tumbler, then revealed a hoarded handful of Seconal tablets and 'dared' Lynne to give him a good reason for not swallowing them. It was a despairing cry for help and love, and it took all Lynne's power of persuasion, like a mother talking to a child, to calm him down.

It was at this juncture, at the beginning of May 1979, that Peter tried to take the pressure off; they had been inseparable since their marriage. His cumulative ill-health, which might have separated some couples, brought them into an interdependence none of his other marriages had ever produced. She had nursed him, sometimes literally, through the most intense acting experience of his career. He resolved to go for a brief vacation, accompanied only by Michael Jeffery, and thus allow Lynne a chance to unwind. He asked Sue Evans to come over from London and keep her company in the new Hollywood house Lynne had bought for them both.

He and Jeffery took off from Miami in a chartered Lear jet to fly to Barbados where Sellers had rented the house which the late Oliver Messel, the designer and decorator, had owned. Then he planned a move for Lynne and himself into a chalet he was acquiring in Gstaad.

As his aircraft entered the area known as the Bermuda Triangle, weather of unusual intensity began to buffet it. Oxygen masks were given out. Suddenly it plummeted from 41,000 feet to 28,000 feet at two or three times the normal speed of descent. Sellers thought, 'This is it.' Despite his recently acquired mistrust of yoga, he found himself chanting a Hindu mantra and praying for his life. It was a severely shaken man who landed in Barbados and immediately had a flaming row with some vexatious Customs officials. What did earthly goods matter when his spiritual being had been so nearly snatched from him? He proceeded to the rented house – and another row. The servants were all asleep and nothing had been prepared for the travellers to fill the void in their frightened stomachs. He was so furious that he didn't get a wink of sleep and the very next day, in a vile temper, he flew off to New York, abandoning his holiday. Another sleepless night followed as he and Jeffery, lodged uncomfortably in a hotel near Kennedy Airport, attempted to make a reservation, at short notice, for Peter's usual Dorchester accommodation. At that season, London was short of hotel rooms of the kind Peter required. Arriving off Concorde, they stayed at the Inn on the Park, where he wasn't accustomed to sleeping, and, predictably, sleep eluded him. He was in an irritable, insomniac mood when he indiscreetly spoke to a journalist, David Lewin, of the strain which his married life had been under during the past few months. He questioned how much longer things could continue that way.

For Peter to confess what was troubling him was always difficult. Fatigued, frightened for his health, and six thousand miles away from his wife, he had no sooner talked about whether it wouldn't be kinder to all concerned to have a divorce, than he bitterly regretted it. He realized that his marriage was one of the principal reasons (his work being the other) why he was still alive – Lynne was his mainstay. But it was too late. Lewin had printed the story in perfectly good faith and it was given the deserved prominence of a scoop. The first Lynne heard of it was when the other London papers began calling her, asking for confirmation or a comment. She was deeply upset and even more profoundly puzzled at what could have induced Peter to say such a thing. In vain he protested, 'I was drunk. I was dead tired. I didn't know what I was saying.' Now it was Lynne's turn to retire within herself and consider the situation.

Peter grew frantic, angry, pleading, tearful. He began pouring out his feelings in incoherent telex messages. Copies were sent to his London lawyer's office, where they were received with a mixture of sadness, resignation and sometimes downright incomprehension. Some messages were distraught and wounding, some piteous and contrite, and some were accompanied by professions of undying love and, on one occasion of misdirected repentance, a huge bouquet of flowers. It became difficult to tell in which order the messages and their mixed emotions should be read.

It was Lynne who had the more mature head on her young shoulders. Even so, her patience had never been so severely tested. At one bleak moment a separation agreement was drawn up, in which the terms were extremely beneficial to her, but her instinct told her that Peter's life would virtually come to an end if she were not by his side. He was long past the stage of any possible reversion to the state of unmarried self-sufficiency. The life-style of his 'bachelor' days was now totally impractical, so a reconciliation was effected, and paradoxically it strengthened the ties of love. As an earnest of his remorse, Peter agreed to his own lawyer's advice that the terms of the agreement should stay in force even though he and Lynne were together again. He continued to make her substantial payments. His reason for assenting to this unorthodox arrangement revealed much about his nature. His own insecurity was so massive that he dared not 'trust his instincts'. By assigning Lynne much else besides his love, by making her financially independent of him, and by entering into an agreement to keep it that way, he felt he was testing the strength of her affection. Love was the only thing that need hold her to him.

Peter sealed their reconciliation in characteristically playful fashion – his preferred way of apologizing – by sending her the following letter purporting to come from 'Nice and Friendly Telegrams Inc., Hollywood Office, 1525 Happy Buildings, Airport Road, South Reseda.' It read: '24 August 1979. To Mrs Lynne Peter Wagner Harding Frederick Sellers. Dear Madam, Our client Mr Peter Spotty Howard Sellers wishes us to inform you that he will never again avail himself of Rotten Nasty Telegrams Inc. Ltd. They have made him very ill, whilst we assure you that our service will have the completely opposite effect and make both Mr Sellers and yourself nice and friendly. We remain, Madam, yours very sincerely, Mr P. P. Charles Nice and Mr Sid Friendly, for and on behalf of Nice and Friendly Telegrams Inc.'

The following months showed how both parties to the arrangement put it in the background of their life and, indeed, their memory. There was so much to do together and each of them realized how little time there might be left in which to do it all.

Lynne and Sue Evans began furnishing the Gstaad chalet, which had been bought in the summer of 1979, and Peter came to feel more at home there than anywhere else. It stood on a hill, giving it a sense of apartness and solitude which he instantly took to. In the garden were plastic gnomes, which appealed to his Goonish outlook, and there was also a nuclear fall-out shelter, fairly commonplace equipment in Swiss residences above a certain income-level. He had a telex installed and played a series of *divertimenti* with the cables he sent all over the world. He had never been a man to acquire personal possessions beyond the expensive playthings like cameras, recorders, etc., but now with Lynne to guide him, he began collecting items of antique furniture, lamps and pictures. The days and nights in Switzerland were some of the most peaceful ones that Lynne could remember. She and Michael Jeffery would cook the supper while Peter, anxious not to get left out of things, concocted exotically mixed drinks. On bad days he might drink a little too much, though he was never drunk; on good ones, he would manage to walk the legs off the others as his moon-boots stamped through the snow to his favourite café. At Lynne's suggestion, Michael Sellers was invited to Switzerland to stay with his father. On the occasions he came, Lynne made herself scarce on extended shopping expeditions to Geneva. In these last months a closer relationship began to grow between father and son than either had known before.

In those months, too, Peter was drawn ever more closely to Lynne, despite their occasional rows. His erratic temperament could still spark off a quarrel and he had a child-like way of showing his displeasure. He would go round the house, upstairs and downstairs, taking down off the walls any framed pictures of himself and Lynne, then stump down to the garage and stack the whole armful in a corner. Later that evening, his mind would clear, and the pictures would be found back in place by sunrise. Forgiveness, too, would be begged in the hours between night-fall and dawn, when his self-scrutiny would often lead him to write to Lynne with unusual and touching clarity. 'Sunday, 3 a.m.', he once wrote, and continued: 'My only darling girl, Sitting here in the early hours, sipping some naughty Jack Daniels for my cold, I am thinking that not only are we truly meant for one another, but that it has taken all these years for me to find you. I will never leave you and I trust in God that you will never leave me, because my whole existence revolves around you. I know I have several annoying faults, but I am only a little thing, and I get all caught up. For example, the incident of the photographs of you in Gstaad. I love you so madly that when we have a row, I just don't think before doing things which I later desperately regret.

You know that's true of me, although it's something you would never do. Fifty years is a very long time and I seem to have wasted most of them, apart from those happy *Goon Show* days. If I had met you then, how different it all would have been. Perhaps when I have spent my time here I will know the answer. Only you know that basically I am really Bluebottle and nothing else. All this acting is brown paper and string. I will love you forever. Your Peter.'

Sue Evans, Lynne or his chauffeur Peter Greenwood now drove Peter on most short trips. When he travelled further afield, it was invariably by private aircraft or Concorde for the transatlantic journey. A propeller-driven Cheyenne or a Falcon or Lear jet with their armchair comfort and kitchen-cum-bar facilities took him back and forth to England. What he saw as the petty authoritarianism of London's Heathrow Airport had become intolerable to him; he had had so many arguments with testy Customs officials that he thought they 'saw him coming, so he preferred to have his aircraft touch down at more rural Stansted Airport, where it could be off-loaded in minutes and there were 'nice' Customs and Immigration officials who greeted him with a welcoming, 'Come on, Mr Sellers, let's see how quickly we can clear you through this time.'

All this was horrifyingly expensive. The bill for private air transportation in the last year of his life came to nearly $250,000 and made Elwood Rickless decide it would be cheaper for Peter to buy an aircraft which, when he wasn't using it, could be chartered to other people with a similar taste for expensive privacy. If anything, Peter was even more spendthrift than he had been. One day he and Lynne went to Geneva to buy him a new pair of spectacles. Something else in the opthalmic optician's shop caught Lynne's attention and, when she returned, Peter was preparing to buy some spectacle frames. She agreed that she liked them. 'They're a bit on the dear side,' he said. This unusual admission astonished Lynne, so she asked how much they were. 'About $5,000,' he said. 'You see, they're eighteen-carat gold.'

But why not spend the money? Marty Baum was keeping the telex lines busy with one deal after another. Baum attributed his success to an arcane process which he defined as 'giving credibility to what a picture with Peter Sellers in it could do at the box-office and then influencing the buyer to believe that such and such a project could realize this potential'. The figures on the agreements he made expressed the same sentiments in shorter but possibly even more impressive terms.

For making his next picture, *The Fiendish Plot of Dr Fu Manchu*, Peter was to be paid a million dollars, plus percentages of the gross receipts, after the film had regained its cost, which escalated from ten per cent of the first forty million dollars, twelve and a half per cent between forty and fifty million dollars, fifteen per cent between fifty and sixty million dollars, and finally twenty per cent thereafter. For *The Romance of the Pink Panther*, whose script he was co-authoring with writer Jim Moloney, he was to be paid $3,000,000 ($1,000,000 upon signature, of which $425,000 would be deposited in an interest-bearing escrow account) and equally impressive percentages on gross receipts from the first dollar the picture earned. Then there was an agreement for him to do a remake of the 1938 Preston Sturges comedy-thriller *Unfaithfully Yours*, about the orchestra conductor who believes his wife is unfaithful to him and, during a concert, devises in imagination three different stratagems, including murder, for dealing with the situation. For this, his compensation was to be $1,500,000, plus $500,000 guaranteed deferment (payable within one year of the film's release), all against ten per cent of the gross after the first dollar, escalating to twelve and a half per cent after the film had recovered its cost. This was a 'pay or play' arrangement, meaning that if, for any reason, the film wasn't made, he would still get paid. The only proviso was that he be insurable. No wonder Marty Baum would later say, 'If he'd had another year or two, Peter Sellers would have amassed great wealth.' In fact, at the time the last deal was agreed, he had barely a year left.

Sue Evans was 'terribly shocked' at what she saw when he arrived at Geneva to join them in Gstaad. 'He had turned into an old man. Previously he had been an attractive, fairly active man in his early fifties. Now he appeared smaller, because he had developed a stoop. He had become very forgetful. Half-way through a conversation, you'd become aware of his absence – it was as if his concentration were going.'

In September 1979, he flew to Paris to begin work on *Fu Manchu*, which had undergone the inevitable changes of director before Peter finally approved Piers Haggard, a graduate of British television. Differences of opinion were apparent early on, stemming chiefly from Peter's dissatisfaction with his own performance, particularly as the eponymous 168-year-old Oriental villain. He felt that he never 'got' Fu Manchu. The weight of the make-up – long black fingernails, contact lenses to change the colour of his eyes to a darker shade of evil, cheeks shrivelled into a simulacrum of venerability by a plastic overlay – anchored him to the commonplace caricature of oriental criminality. The compensation was the other half of his dual role: Fu's nemesis, the

Scotland Yard detective Nayland-Smith. Except for a moustache and a pipe, which he waved like a baton to conduct the great symphony of thought going on in his mind, Sellers wore no other make-up as Nayland-Smith – and was funnier than all the tee-hee in China. But it was an uncomfortable picture to watch. An ailing actor was so painfully in evidence. Its very story ingredients were ominous. For even more gruesome than seeing a prematurely old Sellers turned into a figure of total decrepitude by make-up was Fu's search for the Elixir of Life and his constant need to be sustained by receiving repeated electric jolts of the same kind which had kept Sellers alive in Los Angeles. Art was now imitating not life, but death.

Peter's frailty led Lynne to take a precaution she deemed already overdue. When he fainted one day after overdosing himself with patent medicines, she confiscated an array of pills, powders and bottles that would have set a pharmacist up in a small business. It was all for his own good. Yet, in the eyes of some uninformed people, she was cast as Regina Giddens in *The Little Foxes*, contributing to her husband's demise by withholding his heart drops!

As if all these burdens were not enough, Peter had another cause for worry in the release of *Being There*. The reviews were generally excellent to ecstatic. His skill as a serious actor was now put permanently beyond doubt. But he had discovered that Hal Ashby had decided to use some of the aborted out-takes – the scenes shot, but never used – as a background to the final credit titles. These consisted of shots in which Sellers, as Chance, muffed his lines on camera or broke down giggling helplessly at the end of a take. Though the effect was funny, it was also profoundly alienating. Sellers could not alter the movie, which was already on release in America, so his anxiety now concentrated on its European screenings. Its première would probably take place at the Cannes Film Festival, in May 1980, where he stood a good chance of being considered for the acting award. He already seemed assured of an 'Oscar' nomination – and, he hoped, the award – in the 'Best Actor' category. Something, he felt, had to be done about those out-takes.

'I must reiterate once again,' he telexed Hal Ashby, 'that the out-takes you have placed over the credits do a grave injustice to the picture for the sake of a few cheap laughs. It breaks the spell, do you under-stand? Do you understand, it breaks the spell! Do you hear me, it breaks the spell! I'm telling you how it breaks the spell and as I said in my previous telegram there's not much point in the film going to Europe as I saw it last night. I know in Vienna when you called me and I told you we were running over schedule [on *The Prisoner of Zenda*] you said, "I'll recast the part of Chance." It's too late now. For goodness sake, don't ruin what opportunities we have left.'

This cable was sent on 18 March 1980 and a few weeks later, when the Academy of Motion Picture Arts and Sciences voted its 'Oscar' awards, the fears implicit in the last two sentences were fully realized. Peter lost to Dustin Hoffman for the latter's excellent, though familiar, performance in *Kramer* vs. *Kramer*. Shirley MacLaine was not the only Academy member who felt that the presence of those final out-takes was what had cost Peter a small but possibly critical number of votes. They did indeed 'break the spell'.

He treated the loss of the 'Oscar' with little apparent of emotion, 'but deep down inside he was tremendously disappointed,' said Lynne Frederick.

She returned to Switzerland with Peter for a brief rest in November 1979, while shooting continued on scenes in *Fu Manchu* in which he did not appear, but there he suffered another coronary or tachycardiac attack. He checked into a Geneva clinic and was ordered to take a month's rest. The film closed down till the New Year. It might never have re-opened, according to Lynne, who was a production executive on it, but for Peter's obsessive perfectionism.

Even after it wound up, there ensued a wearisome wrangle, conducted largely by telex, with a series of disenchanted executives of Orion Pictures who were producing it. Peter sent them a cable in January expressing a sardonic sense of fatefulness. 'I very much regret your lack of enthusiasm for the film because, while I realize it is not of the *Animal House* genre, nevertheless it's an amusing film which will not be embarrassing or a total loss to you. Please heed my words and leave the film as it is.' Despite his pleas, *Fu Manchu* underwent a process akin to Chinese torture. Pleading pathetically in a later cable that 'if you allow the King George v telephone scene to be cut, you will without any doubt drive the final nail into the casket of yet another Orion film,' he continued. 'The movie, already doomed, will sink without trace ... *Fu Manchu* could just have scraped by, but now there is no hope whatsoever. I would advise you to endeavour to sustain the loss, however difficult, and retain the dignity still remaining for a once great company. Yours sadly and sincerely, Peter Sellers.'

Ill health, production disputes and personal disappointments all contributed to Peter's increasing instability of purpose. His periods of elation and depression succeeded each other at alarming speed. Sometimes he believed he had only weeks left to live. But then he would think of that old prophecy made over thirty years before in the ENSA lodgings by the pretty Irish nurse: 'You'll live till you're seventy-five.' This would buoy him and make him think of all the hopes he might yet realize. In one such mood, early in February 1980, he wrote to Lynne: 'Four years ago I met the most beautiful girl in the world. Three years ago we were married. The next twenty years will be some of the best. I love you forever, Peter.'

He suffered another tachycardiac attack in Ireland at the end of April while he was making three television commercials for a British bank. His fee was $200,000, 'money in my hand,' he said, recalling that this was the only meaning it now had for him. He cabled Marty Baum to relay the news of his recovery 'to all moguls and suchlike who may be staining their underwear'.

He had cabled Baum on 30 April: 'Have once and for all definitely decided I cannot attend Cannes Film Festival (where *Being There* was in competition, the out-takes now replaced by 'neutral' shots of a television screen suffering 'interference'). I cannot face all it entails. I should have married Marjorie Main.'

Almost immediately a second cable followed: 'Please disregard my previous telex. I've decided I will go to the Cannes Festival after all because I'm a man who makes up his mind and sticks to it. I have decided to marry Rudolf Nureyev.'

When the Cannes prizes were announced, the 'Best Acting' Award went to Michel Piccoli, a French actor in a Franco-Italian co-production, *Salto nel Vuoto* (*Leap into the Void*), which was shown in its Italian version. Kirk Douglas, who was President of the Jury, was clearly infuriated by the haggling and horse-trading that had gone on along the lines that 'it was time for the French to get a prize.' He swore he would never return to Cannes. Peter's lawyer, Elwood Rickless, who was present, told Peter that if Roy Scheider had got the award for his role in *All That Jazz* (a film which Lynne did not want Peter to see because of the grizzly presence in it of an open-heart operation), he would be justified in feeling hurt; he would, in Rickless's opinion, at least have lost to another performance of international magnitude. Kirk Douglas even left the official dinner where the awards were being presented as a mark of his indignation at the conduct of a few chauvinist jury members. He had supper with Peter and Lynne.

Going to Cannes and facing the assault and battery of the media was difficult for Peter. Only Lynne realized how much he suffered. Gallantly, if a little piteously, he still went through the motions of protesting that, if not exactly in the prime of life, he was still good for any number of years. Rex Reed, the American columnist, was in Cannes making a television documentary on the festival for producer Billy Baxter. Amidst an inhumanly overcrowded party – just the kind of event that Peter loathed – Reed interviewed the star of *Being There*. 'Every time I get a little cold,' said Peter, 'the Press says it's a massive heart attack.' It must have been one of his last public utterances.

Immediately after Cannes there occurred one of the most extraordinary periods in Lynne's relationship with her husband. She knew how disappointed he was; but now his thoughts took a deeper, darker spiral into depression and concern with death. The couple had been staying at the Hotel du Cap at Eden Roc and from there they flew, via Nice, to Brindisi and chartered a yacht to go cruising through the Greek islands in early June. However, Peter soon began to feel ill in body and mind. He became obsessed with the thought that he might die aboard the ship, out of touch with land, out of reach of home. 'In the last few years of his life,' said Lynne, 'he worried constantly over what might happen to him if he died outside England. As he spent most of his time abroad, this seemed a very real possibility. He had made me promise to get his body back home by any means, and again and again we'd gone over the instructions for his cremation – how he wanted the service, how he wished another rose tree to be planted in the same bed as the one commemorating his parents, how he wanted his ashes scattered near where theirs had been, but not on the same spot . . . .' Now in the middle of the Aegean he was rehearsing his death once again, putting Lynne through all the imagined possibilities she would have to contend with if he died that very night. 'How would you get my body ashore?' – 'By helicopter.' – 'Yes, but how would you get in touch with the helicopter?' – 'By radio-telephone, I suppose.' – 'Yes, but would I be in a casket, or just normal?' If the answers she had to improvise, in a calm voice, did not come quickly or convincingly enough to her lips, Peter would grow agitated. Above all, he wanted her absolute assurance that she would not permit him to be buried at sea. He also specified the people he wanted to be invited to his cremation. 'The memorial service, if there is one, is different,' he said. 'Anyone can come to that.' He was equally precise about those he did *not* want at the cremation. In short, he was torturing himself by the very clarity of his preoccupation with dying. He wanted to leave nothing to chance. His state of mind became so disturbed that the holiday was cut short and they flew back to Switzerland.

Peter had begun a haggling session with United Artists over *The Romance of the Pink Panther* script, which had been returned by one of their executives so mauled about that, as he said in a telex to Baum, 'following so closely on the nightmare of *Fu Manchu*, I ... seriously considered jumping overboard. Lynne's attempts to pacify me resulted in my telephone call to you.' He said the script needed 'very substantial re-writing' and he urged his agent to suggest Lynne as the forthcoming film's executive producer. 'She most certainly has the talent to do it with the help of a good "line" [on the spot] producer.'

He returned to Gstaad to work with Jim Moloney on the revised script and the ambience seemed to have a salutary effect on his spirits for, on 16 July, he was cabling Baum again: 'Script on way to you by courier. No joking, I think it's bloody terrific and I hope you will. All the best. Peter Shakespeare and Jim Bacon.'

The high spirits of this cable were deceptive. Peter's mood was far from jubilant. He had already taken one of the most fateful decisions of his life, a decision he had postponed for too many years, and now he was about to bear the consequences. He had reached the end of his ability to support the never-ending tensions of imminent heart-failure. He had told his lawyer that he could not go on as he was – life was not worth living. He must know if there were any hope at all for him. He and Lynne had long, anguished discussions about the step he was about to take: nothing less than submitting to an angiagram, the surgical examination of his heart which he had lacked the courage to undergo in 1976. Now he was desperate to gain some relief from anxiety, some reprieve perhaps from the foreshortening of years, months or even weeks left to him. Even certainty, one way or the other, would be a relief.

The cardiac trouble he had suffered in November 1979, during the shooting of *Fu Manchu*, seems to have pushed him to this decision, for in December he sat down and wrote one of those early-morning letters to his wife whose alternating mixture of hope and acceptance of fate combined with his avowal of love produced a profoundly sad effect. 'My darling Lynne, I know, believe me, how difficult I am to live with. With what life, this business and my health have done to me, and my stupid mind, it's quite a feat that I'm able to operate at all as a person. How you have stuck with me these three years, I find difficult to understand – most women would have left two years ago. I apologise for last night's deplorable behaviour. I apologise more than I am able to write. My love for you is so great I swear I think of nothing but you for the most part of the day. I'm trying to tell you as best I can that I just don't know what to do. I'll have the operation and anything else going if it will get me back to normal. I must leave this business soon, as I'm no longer equipped to deal with it as it is. Maybe I'll direct or produce or something.... Thank you for all the kindness, love and consideration you give me and have always given me since we first met. I adore you, my darling Lynne. Forever, all my love, Peter.'

They now decided that Lynne would go to Los Angeles and await him there. In a few days he would be with her and ready for the doctors. Meanwhile he would try to keep his spirits high. There was at least one anticipated pleasure that would help him get through the terrifying void which his life had become.

Early on the morning of 21 July, accompanied by Michael Jeffery, he flew to London in a chartered jet. He was only going to stay a day and a half – but how he was looking forward to the second evening! He was planning to spend it in the company of Spike Milligan and Harry Secombe, his pals from *The Goon Show* days. They were going to have a real bean-feast. There was nothing, after all, to beat the 'good old days'.

THIRTEEN

Not The End

Michael Jeffery was laying Sellers's clothes out on the bed in his Dorchester Hotel suite when he heard Sue Evans call, 'Michael, get a doctor!' He guessed at once that the event they all dreaded had happened.

Rushing to the door of the sitting-room, he took one horrified look at Peter lying in the armchair, his face the shade of newsprint, showing no sign of life. Then he grabbed the other telephone and dialled Sellers's doctor. Sue was already gasping to the hotel switchboard, 'Send some-one up at once – Mr Sellers has been taken ill.' The Dorchester's emergency services went quickly into action. Within a minute, two nurses were in the suite. Sister Bridget Siklos pressed her mouth against Peter's pale lips to pump air into his lungs, while part-time Sister Shirley-Ann Bailey thumped the movie star's chest in an effort to re-start his heart. A few minutes later in ran Dr Arthur Unwin, a physician from nearby Knightsbridge, who had been called by the hotel. Sellers's own physician in London, Dr John Gaynor, was on holiday but his partner, Dr John Creightmore, arrived almost on Dr Unwin's heels and took charge. 'Looks very bad,' said one physician to the other, checking the responses of the crumpled figure in the navy-blue track suit and finding them minimal. Then the ambulance men arrived.

Sellers was loosely and swiftly wrapped in gold foil from neck to toe to preserve his body heat and rushed by stretcher down the back lift to the hotel's ballroom entrance in Park Lane. He was so closely shrouded that any passer-by noticing the emergency would never have recognized him. Michael Jeffery and Sue Evans dashed down six flights of stairs to the hotel's main entrance and got into Peter's car. His chauffeur, Peter Greenwood, followed the ambulance driven by Ken-neth John – whose colleague Eric Talmadge kept vigil inside – as its peremptory siren divided the heavy lunch-time traffic and they screamed along Piccadilly before veering north to the Middlesex Hospital, which is almost opposite the offices of United Artists for whom Sellers had made most of the *Pink Panthers*.

Sue Evans, following in her own car, saw the strikingly efficient way in which the resources of a great hospital close in around a crisis like this, to shield and succour a stricken celebrity and simultaneously to set up a communications system to deal with the huge volume of enquiries from the alerted media of London and the world. At such a time, no one appreciated one pathetic coincidence: Sellers was being treated at the very same hospital where his father had died of heart failure on the operating table eighteen years earlier.

Installed in the duty sister's own office, Sue Evans dialled Elwood Rickless. The lawyer was still at lunch, but he hastened to the hospital when the message was relayed to him. 'For me, it was a chimera, a nightmare,' he later recalled. It was not merely the shock of finding the man he had seen and conversed with only a few hours previously now almost beyond hope: 'I discovered that Peter was lying ill in the same bed, in the same intensive care ward, attended by the same doctor, as a childhood friend of mine who had died there four years earlier following – of all things! – a hair transplant that had been done in sleazy conditions in a London clinic. He was regarded as a rich man, but the only bills I ever received were for about £15 of special drugs. Here was Peter, another man able to raise any amount of money to pay for the finest medical treatment – and yet he was already being given it, free, on the National Health Service. It wasn't costing him a cent! Everyone was acting in that wonderful tradition of battling to save a life, not caring what compensation they'd get for their efforts. This had a great deal to do with Lynne's later resolve to do something to help that hospital.'

Lynne had been woken by a telephone call at about 7 a.m., a time in Los Angeles when one supposes a friend to ring with some gossip or an agent with some proposal that needs a quick reply. Elwood Rickless read her the bulletin put out by the hospital, which was now starting to look like a besieged camp as news reporters and television vans arrived by the minute and crowded its forecourt. 'He remains gravely ill,' it concluded.

As it was too late for Lynne to connect with the Concorde leaving New York for London, she rushed to Los Angeles airport and caught a departing 747 with minutes to spare. 'Although it should have been no surprise – God knows, I knew how ill Peter was – it seemed unreal when it happened. There I was getting our home ready for Peter's arrival the next day – now I was trying to beat the clock and get to my husband before his life ran out.'

Britt Ekland was at dinner in Stockholm when the news came through. She 'dropped everything' and flew to London with her daughter Victoria. On arrival, she was quoted as saying that she would visit her ex-husband only if he asked for her. For various reasons, this wasn't considered likely.

Peter was now on a life-support machine, his condition still grave but stable. He hadn't regained consciousness since his heart first stopped. In newspaper offices the world over, obituaries were being dusted off and brought up to date; television editors were selecting representative clips from Peter's films, haggling with the distributors over the price per foot, chopping up an artist's genius into handy lengths of time to fit the newscasts, the arts programmes, or any handy slot. (How relieved some of them were that this had happened when it did, instead of during a period of heavy programming commitment like Christmas-time. Charlie Chaplin, who had had the bad luck to die on Christmas Day 1977, had to wait five days before BBC television could literally find the free time to celebrate his genius.)

Michael Sellers spent the night at the hospital. Lynne arrived at Heathrow early on Wednesday morning, was met by Sue Evans and, as all airport formalities were instantly waived, she was at Peter's bedside within half an hour.

'He was still unconscious. There wasn't the faintest movement that I could see. But I was told that, even in a crisis like this, people still respond to familiar sounds, voices they know and love. When I laid my hand on his arm and said, "How are you, my darling?" the cardiograph machine began to show his heart was beating just a fraction faster. That encouraged me. So I settled down by his bedside and began talking, talking, talking . . . . .'

The Middlesex Hospital's administrator, David Johnson, announced at midday: 'Essentially Mr Sellers's condition is unchanged. He is critically ill.'

However, for Lynne Frederick, ever the pragmatic realist, this was not enough. She asked the doctors to tell her, quite candidly, just how bad it was. Realizing there was a tough core to her delicate-looking exterior, they were equally frank. One doctor said, 'Mrs Sellers, this may seem a harsh thing to say to you, but let me tell you, it would be better for your husband if he did not make a recovery. He's suffered a lesion that's done massive damage to his brain. He could never again be the man he was. Supposing he recovered physically, it's very, very doubtful if he would be in possession of his faculties.'

Lynne went back to where Peter was lying, that frail invisible thread of life contrasting so strangely with the massive battery of wires, tubes and electrodes attached to his inert form. She gave in to her emotional and physical exhaustion and dozed off in the chair beside him. When she woke up, her head was resting on his arm. She couldn't feel any pulse beat at all, it was so weak, but incredibly the machine said he was still alive. She felt that all that now sustained him was her own presence.

Michael Jeffery later recalled how anxious Sellers frequently was to know where the people on whom he depended could be found at any time of the day or night: 'Just so long as he *knew* where we were – Lynne, Sue, myself – he was all right.' Lynne now felt that somehow, on this occasion, too, he 'knew' where they all were.

It was nearly midnight when the weary group decided to return to the Dorchester and try to snatch some sleep. 'His condition's critical, but he's stable,' the hospital doctors told them. 'Go back, have a bath, get some sleep, we'll call you if need be.'

They went back to the Dorchester, but they had hardly entered the suite – now so oddly cold and empty – when the telephone rang. A voice said urgently: 'Mr Sellers's condition is deteriorating. We think you should return at once.'

They rushed back. As they stepped out of the lift near the intensive-care unit, a hospital official met them and they knew from his expression that they were too late. 'I'm sorry, Mrs Sellers,' he said, in tones of helpless apology, 'he just slipped away from us. His heart gave up for good. We couldn't start it again. There was nothing more to do.'

To the pickets from the media, left on night-watch in and around the Middlesex, the hospital issued its usual terse communiqué: 'It is with very great regret that we have to inform you that Mr Sellers died at 12.28 a.m.'

Lynne Frederick, Sue Evans and Michael Jeffery stood in the room where Peter's spirit had so lately left him. All the unsightly apparatus had now been taken away and they had an unobscured view of him. There was a look of complete peace and contentment on his face.

The next day, 25 July, was Lynne's twenty-sixth birthday; she had planned to celebrate it quietly with Peter in Los Angeles, giving him courage to face the impending angiagram. Instead she was trying to stop the world spinning around her long enough to arrange for his cremation. From all over the world, tributes had poured in: cables, newspaper obituaries (London's *The Times*, in a twenty-four-inch obituary, called him 'a comic genius of the cinema screen'), television programmes (BBC television revised its schedules to repeat a long, sometimes harrowing interview Sellers had done with Michael Parkinson) and even simple, ordinary hand-written notes left at the Dorchester's reception desk by people with names that meant nothing to Lynne but expressing sentiments that showed how much her late husband had meant to the senders.

Among the telephone calls which Sue Evans accepted on behalf of the grief-stricken Lynne was one from Miranda Quarry. The woman who had been Sellers's third wife was now Lady Nuttall by her remarriage to an English baronet. She wanted to convey her deepest regrets. The 'forgotten wife', as some of the media called her, had not forgotten. Lynne was touched anew.

The last rites were arranged for the Saturday morning, 26 July, at the same Golders Green crematorium which Sellers had visited the previous Monday with Michael Jeffery to pay his respects to his parents. As the morning advanced, the summer skies over London darkened to an extraordinary dense blackness and the thirty or so invited guests, who had been asked to enter the chapel by the west door to avoid the waiting crowds, had to brave downpours of tropical intensity. In an ante-room so small that a trio of Bridge tables would have been cramped, the star's closest friends (not all of them famous) exchanged stilted phrases as they waited to file into the chapel for the Church of England service, which was to be conducted by Canon John Hester. This writer sat between Lord Snowdon and Brother Cornelius in a back pew. Nearby was Evelyn de Rothschild. In front were Michael Bentine, Harry Secombe and Dennis Selinger. Graham Stark and David Lodge, with their wives, were two pews distant. Spike Milligan sat across the aisle. Thunder had begun rolling over the rooftops and the atmosphere, already charged with sorrow, became one of intensifying drama.

Theo Cowan, in a streaming raincoat, pleaded with the media people excluded from the service to keep some order. Lines of policemen in unseasonable rain capes contained the patient, soaked crowds of mourners and onlookers, and tried to avoid stepping on the carpet of wreaths and bouquets laid on the paving stones.

Peter's Aunty Ve and Aunty Do were there, too, black-veiled and spectral in the chapel gloom that was now intermittently illuminated by a lightning flash. Suddenly it seemed as if a bolt of lightning had struck the place itself. But it was only the photographers' flashlights going off outside the main door in a sort of synchronized panic in case they missed the figure stepping so boldly and so unexpectedly out of a powder-blue Rolls-Royce. There was a hubbub from the crowd, policemen's voices calling, 'Stand back ... Stand back,' and, as the main door flew open to admit her, people in their pews turned round and gaped as she entered swiftly in an incandescent burst of publicity. Wearing a black suit with a huge floppy bow at the neckline and a dazzling white blouse, Britt Ekland, who had so recently announced her preference for staying in the background, shot a smile at those she recognized and settled into the seat beside an accommodating Spike Milligan.

A few minutes later, Lynne arrived with her step-children. She looked pale and the black dress she wore showed that her usually slim form had grown perceptibly thinner. She advanced slowly up the aisle and, as she did so, she had to pass the pew in which Britt Ekland was sitting. Her eye could not help being caught by that whiter-than-white blouse and, for a second or two, it seemed to everyone in the chapel that she was going to stop and confront the woman whose presence was a disagreeable surprise to her. The moment passed, and the service began.

Canon Hester's address caused no tears to be shed that were not already on most cheeks. It was short and free from cant. 'In life, we can only see the grand design from the back side,' he said, adding with a refreshing gloss on any possible indelicacy, 'if you will forgive the phrase.' From where Peter was now, with the vantage point of eternity, he could perhaps see what had always perplexed him – the whole shape, texture and meaning of his life. And lest this seem too lofty a consideration, Canon Hester brought matters down to earth again with the hope that, in any case, Peter was in a better position to canvass God for the rebuilding of St Anne's, Soho, the canon's former parish church. The listeners chuckled gratefully. The tension caused by 'the rival widows', as the newspapers inevitably called them, was relieved. The lesson was from *John* xiv. 'And now,' said Canon Hester, 'we shall sit and listen to some music that Peter especially asked to be played on this occasion.'

As the actor's plain oak casket began its measured glide into the furnace room, there welled up, unbelievably, almost Goonishly, the jaunty jazz rhythm of Glenn Miller and his orchestra playing *In The Mood*. It was like a scene from *The Magic Christian*, one of those Guy Grand pranks ricochetting mischievously off the surface of astounded conventionality. Actually, it was born out of a *Goon Show* exchange between Sellers and Milligan. 'Any special hymn you'd like to have played when you go?' – 'Yes, *In The Mood*.' – 'Is that in *Hymns Ancient and Modern*?' – 'No, it's in Glenn Miller.'

'I am proud to have been a Goon. I would like to be remembered for that,' Sellers had said to Auberon Waugh, when the English novelist and journalist had conducted one of the last interviews he gave, in Gstaad, a few weeks earlier. He would have been touched to have it confirmed that this was how the public remembered him, too. Amidst the hundreds of wreaths, bouquets and posies hemming the chapel walls outside, many testified to the tenacious hold those days still had on the affections of many people. Harry Secombe signed his card simply 'Neddy Seagoon', and the sentiments expressed by others covered the whole comic gamut of *Goon Show* gag lines: 'Yingtong Tiddly I Po for ever,' said another card. Said Harry Secombe to the Press, 'Bluebottle is deaded.' To millions of people, this said it all.

Some weeks later, a larger and more celebrity-packed congregation, led by Michael Bentine, who was self-consciously wearing a morning coat as the representative of Prince Charles, assembled in the Royal Parish Church of St Martin-in-the-Fields, Trafalgar Square, for a service of thanksgiving for Peter Sellers. Again Canon Hester conducted it with exemplary restraint and even wit; Lord Snowdon, hoarse from what may have been a cold, read the Twenty-third Psalm; Harry Secombe resonantly sang *Bread of Heaven*; and David Niven gave the address, recalling Peter's faults as well as his virtues, but emphasizing the ephemeral nature of the one against the lasting worth of the other.

By this time the media had embarked on the cruel, but inevitable post-mortem that follows any famous person's passing and deals in such matters as the value of their estate and the plans of their surviving partner. This last subject of speculation was shortly resolved when Lynne Frederick became Mrs David Frost, wife of the television interviewer and executive. They had known each other for some years, though the suddenness of their marriage surprised many people and seemed even disagreeable to a few, occurring as it did some six months after Peter's death. By this time the Sellers children had discovered that his will made little additional provision for them beyond the sums of money he had already arranged for them to have. Lynne's remarriage appeared to aggravate their feelings.

Such family disputes are always sad, but there were not a few people who wondered how long Peter would have waited, had he been a widower, before picking up his married life again in that period of loss and loneliness which occurs after all the media commotion is over. Lynne missed Peter with an intensity that may have surprised her and to someone who had been forced to order her own life to stabilize and even prolong his, his death didn't bring relief, only a feeling of purposelessness. Remarriage meant many things to her, including a regained momentum.

The question of how much money Peter Sellers left is unlikely to be answered quickly. 'It's like closing down ICI or Bell Telephone,' said one friend who was peripherally involved in winding up an estate that was distributed in several countries and included many 'bits of the action' in films that range from the immensely lucrative to the dead loss. What is certain is that at the time of his death he was not worth anything like the huge sums glibly attributed to him by gossip columnists whose head for figures can be so dizzy that they often do not know – and sometimes do not care – if they are expressing their guesses in American dollars or pounds sterling. A figure of four million (dollars or sterling, depending on taste) was most frequently mentioned as the value of his estate. It is certainly far less than this for many reasons.

The chief reason is that Peter had an enormously expensive way of life – as has been mentioned, the cost of his charter aircraft in the last year of his life came to around $250,000. When bills of this size, swollen by the backlog of accounts and debts that hadn't yet reached his accountants, are all added up they can make a sizeable hole in any man's fortune. And even in Switzerland rich men have to pay taxes. It is certain that his percentages in huge box-office hits like the *Panther* series will continue to provide an income for years to come. Other people, however, such as agents, take a percentage of Peter's share of the profits, and the profits themselves will be subject to the diminishing returns of public exhibition, with only the *Panthers* providing that 'annuity value' which film-makers seek to create. It is true that he would have earned a fortune from his next two or three pictures; the figures in the contracts have already been quoted. Unfortunately, except for the down-payment on *The Romance of the Pink Panther*, all these carefully constructed deals vanished the instant he died. He didn't die a poor man; but by the standards of his peers he certainly didn't die an immoderately rich one. If the most frequently mentioned figure (in dollars, please) is halved, that sum might not be too far off the mark.

There is no point in attempting a summary valuation of Peter in other ways, as a human being, for instance. He resists summary, as the previous chapters amply demonstrate. He was a man whom some people found easy to like, others extremely difficult, and there were probably only a few people who were able to forgive and love him. Only in the film world, where the fantasy life is built into wheeling and dealing, where greed and ego and occasionally true love of the art all collide, where the most heartless examples of human behaviour are tolerated for the sake of the vastness of the rewards, where true natures are disguised so regularly that they are forgotten even by those to whom they belong, where all things are promised to the star and everything stripped from the fallen one, where fame and wealth look like body-servants but turn into demons who wrench one limb from limb – only in this extraordinary world could the curiously tortured genius of Peter Sellers have been created or tolerated.

'He was the most versatile comic actor of his generation,' wrote David Ansen in *Newsweek*, but when that is said – and most people would grant the truth of it – everything still remains to be said. The range of his interpretation included comedy, but extended beyond it. It touched the heights of absurdity in movies like *Dr Strangelove*, yet included a 'straight' role such as Chance in *Being There*. He was often called a chameleon among clowns; but he did not take on the coloration of his background so much as draw colour from it into a dazzling spectrum of characters. His characters were assembled through his inexplicable talent for extracting elements of reality from the life he knew or could sense, and endowing them with a form that was credible. 'He had absolute pitch for the nuances of human speech in any tongue,' wrote Charles Champlin in the *Los Angeles Times*, 'and it was his unmatched ability to reproduce what he heard that was the soul of his art.' Again this is true, but, like everything else about him, it needs qualifying.

As the greatest comic observers of human life have done, Peter Sellers went from patter to performance. He took the voice with him – the voice which was always his starting-point – and somehow, somewhere en route, he assembled all the other traits of character that couldn't be seen or heard except in his imagination. Gradually he took the performance to the point where even its assembly didn't show.

'His true gift to the cinema was the instantaneous delineation of human oddity,' wrote Dilys Powell in the *Sunday Times*. Part of his surprising delight is the way in which he could prevent the hours of hard mental, emotional and sometimes physical experiment from showing in the performance. He concealed art, like a man who has forgotten where he buried the treasure, but trusts to his instinct to find it again when need be.

He could depict human oddity, too, sometimes to the extent of extravagant buffoonery. He rivalled the great slapstick comics who found their laughs in the dexterity of physical discomfiture. Perhaps his most popular comic creation, Inspector Clouseau, is based on that painful ethic. But with Clouseau, it isn't pride that comes before a fall, nor is it dignity that suffers from it. One senses that it is always in the nature of the character he created so brilliantly, with the bold outline of a cartoon and the detail of a human being, to preserve a life-size fortitude in the face of disproportionate odds. And comedy is a matter of disproportion as well as dislocation of expectations; Clouseau understood both and exemplified both.

Much has been made – far too much, in this writer's view – of the smoke-screen he laid down to cover the tracks of his art, namely that he didn't know who he was. If this were so, then, as one critic remarked, he was a stranger only to himself. The world never really had any problem identifying Peter Sellers, though it's true he wore far more masks than there are in the generic alternatives of comedy and tragedy. But it wasn't concealment: it was transformation. Peter Sellers still showed through. As Stefan Kanfer wrote in *Time*: 'Audiences did not pay to watch the mask: they came to see the man.'

We must believe him when he reported feeling that he was 'taken over' by the characters he played – though whether we should give credence to his belief that he had actually been those characters in past lives must remain a matter of personal conviction or superstition. His own faith sealed the character within him like some flap on a spiritual envelope.

'The art of grown-up comedy has suffered a terrible blow,' wrote Andrew Sarris. His words echo those which Leigh Hunt once set down: 'The death of a comic artist is felt more than that of a tragedian. He has sympathized more with us in our everyday feelings, and has given us more amusement.... It seems a hard thing upon the comic actor to quench his airiness and vivacity – to stop him in his happy career – to make us think of him, on the sudden, with solemnity – and to miss him for ever.'

The great hymn-burst of *Jerusalem* concluded Peter Sellers's memorial service at St Martin-in-the-Fields. As we filed out into the sunshine of the early autumn, it is doubtful if many thought of him as having had a 'happy career' or indeed missed him 'with solemnity', but all of us there, and millions more who weren't, would certainly 'miss him for ever'. The day was 8 September 1980, his birthday. He would have been fifty-five, had he lived.

Epilogue

Ten years after, he is safe . . . safe in memory. The 1980s were six months old when Peter Sellers died. But in the new decade we're moving – speeding – into, his is the name that still evokes laughter and not the puzzled question of 'Who's he?' Others haven't been so lucky. It's surprising the kind of people who have fallen into the gap between achievement and retrieval, particularly when it is a generation gap. I was in New York about a year ago, working as I usually do in the small, quiet hours of the morning, with an ear half-cocked to one of those 'round midnight' radio stations that link a city's insomniacs with discs, news flashes and quizzes, and I heard the disc jockey asking, 'Which group did Paul McCartney belong to before Wings?'

I'm sure that if Peter had been alive to hear that quiz for today's kids, he would have grinned the surprisingly toothy smile that used to appear on his long face when he was genuinely amused at a joke, or simply grudgingly polite to the teller; but he'd have sensed the 'skull beneath the skin' all right. He once told me of an experience that wasn't too dissimilar.

It was when he'd got one of his dearest wishes. He'd managed to meet, yes, actually *meet* one half of his favourite pair of comics. Stan Laurel was alive, not very well and probably on his last legs, but still touring the land that had given him birth, if not world fame. Peter said he was so nervous as well as excited at meeting the dear, dithering Stan – who was actually the sharper partner in the act – that his memory temporarily deserted him and he couldn't for the life of him recall the name of a comedian who had supported Laurel and Hardy in many of their films. Actually, it was James Finlayson, the villainous looking fellow with the squint and the talent for the quick double-takes that shook his pupils like a duple of pinballs into opposite corners of his eyes. Peter groped for the name . . . 'You know him,' he insisted to Stan Laurel, whose visibly poor health more than excused his own memory lapse. 'He used to be in those films with you . . . the guy with the eyes.' A look of slowly dawning recognition spread over Stan's mug – 'just like in the films,' Peter said later, snatching some compensatory recollection from the disaster about to break. 'Oh,' said Stan, 'you mean Oliver Hardy?'

Well, no one has ever said – up to now, anyhow, the tenth anniversary of his death – 'Oh, you mean Peter Sellers?' For one thing, Peter left such a rich stock of material behind – on tape and records and film and TV and now of course on video – that one constantly meets Peter in many media and not just the one that brought him international fame and a fortune that, though modest by present-day standards of celebrity inflation, was, to him, the surest measure of the love people bore him as well as the loot he could secure against the day when that love wouldn't be there.

I originally wrote this book to capture him before affection cooled – and, I suspect, before some people's tempers cooled. For, let's face it, Peter the mime, the mimic, the clown and the actor may have been loved by millions, but some of those he worked most closely with didn't actually like him. He was a wayward genius and could be an intolerant one. He felt the power of creation within him, coursing through him, but resented the lesser folk who treated it, he thought, like bottled water and half expected him to ask them, deferentially, like an obliging waiter, if they wanted it 'with gas, or without?' The fear of being exploited followed immediately on the heels of being loved and enriched. Life for Peter too often became a series of 'tests' he required people to undertake – loyalty tests, honesty tests, artistic tests, friendship tests – so that he could gauge their breaking point. Not that this is uncommon among film folk. Life at the top is tough all right; but it is also suspicious. 'What am I worth to them?' 'What are they worth to me?' The two-way 'celebrity stretch' of that kind makes life a strained business even for stars who look enviably safe and well rewarded. And when the star is a comedian, it may come as a shock to discover that he's not one of nature's philanthropists. It can produce a sharper sense of betrayal and resentment in people than if they uncover the same sort of pathology in one of the screen's 'hard men'.

Peter's need for love was sometimes expressed by his destructive demands for it. His mother, the redoubtable Peg, had given him plenty of love – perhaps too much. From her he learned, early and enduringly, a maxim that he applied to the larger and far less maternal world of show-business – namely, 'Everything comes to him who throws a fit.' Peter threw plenty, as this book shows. But often they were justified: and set against his genius, they were insignificant.

What roles would Peter have played, had he lived longer? Inspector Clouseau, of course. That character was Peter's passport – I won't say 'to immortality'. As well as being a cliche, it's not even a true one. He's remembered for other creations, too, and will be so long as his *Goon Show* eccentricities and his film roles like Fred Kite, or the Indian doctor in *The Millionairess*, or *Dr Strangelove*, remain a part of our cultural collective. But Clouseau was the Peter Sellers creation that travelled best.

I've tried to explain his origins in this book. But one can never explain the universal sympathy, understanding and amusement generated by this bumbling fellow in his slightly outsize Burberry, big moustache and Robin Hood hat. The minute he started assembling Clouseau, Peter gave slapstick a soul; much the same way as Chaplin did when he started assembling Charlie the Tramp. Clouseau was the only character whom Peter enjoyed the luxury of repeating in a film series. Elsewhere, in other films, he always had to be 'different', for he made much of never knowing how to be simply 'himself'. Let's not forget, of course, that Clouseau also sprang from the mind of Blake Edwards, the film director and writer of the first *Pink Panther* movie; but he sprang into Peter Seller's body, and refused to take his leave.

What I most admire about the Clouseau creation is the paradox of a character who played fast and loose with the world's gravity, yet not once lost his own gravitas. Jacques Tati had the same talent: and Peter admired Tati and recalled once meeting him with a catch in his breath. But Tati's M. Hulot was a more solemn fellow. Things going wrong in his vicinity didn't upset him physically, or not often, so much as sabotage him, subtly and meanly. Tati's was the more refined style of comedy, even though M. Hulot owed much to the way that the French see the English; Peter's was a broader caper, even thought his Clouseau owed much to the way that the English see the French.

Going through the letters I received from Peter over the years, I found one that not only has a touching sanity – he could be a vituperative correspondent at times, making Hattie, his loyal secretary, wince as she took his dictation – but it transmits an early tingle of the excitement Peter sensed about Clouseau. It was written from the Regency Hotel, New York, on 23 September 1963:

My Dear Alex,

Quite a bit of news . . . I shall be returning to England on the 3rd, on a Froggy boat, and am very pleased to say that *Shot in the Dark* [the second Clouseau film] is now going to be made in England. With the greatest stroke of luck, Blake

Edwards is directing instead of [Anatole] Litvak. I'll explain how all this happened when I see you, but all I can say at the moment is that yours truly played a very big part in it. Blake Edwards is re-writing the script with Billy Wilder and now we should be all set for a very good time, and a cracking film in the process.

I attended a sneak preview of *The Pink Panther* at the Greenacres Theatre on Long Island, with a big audience. They were showing *Irma La Douce* that night, and there were only about twenty film types sprinkled here and there, and I really mean it when I say I don't think I've ever heard such reaction to a comedy in my life – not even including the early Marx Brothers films. It was so exciting, and I think it should be one of the comedy hits of next year without any doubt. Also it breaks new ground for me, and I am so happy about it as I was rather dreading the occasion.

I have got masses of things to tell you when I see you, and am longing to get home, because I have had New York in a big way, mate. They are all too rude here for me. As can be expected, individually they're fine, especially those people connected with our business, but it's the man-in-the-street – or the woman-in-the-street – because it's the women who run it here. Anyway, never mind.

My dear friend, Peter Bull, opens shortly in *Luther* with Albie [Albert Finney], so let's wish them great luck. I see quite a bit of the Newleys [Anthony Newley then maried to Joan Collins], but aside from that it's one big round of tape recorders and transistorised whaddayoumacallits.

We shall be making *Shot in the Dark* at MGM Boreham Wood, which is where we made *The Millionairess*. I suggested to Sophia [Loren] that she brings over imitation jewellery this time, so that if it's stolen again, there won't be such a hiaitus. [In fact, Sophia Loren didn't appear in *Shot in the Dark*.]

I shall be staying at the Dorchester and will phone you shortly after I get back.

Look after yourself. With all good wishes from your sincere friend,

Peter.*

Peter was planning another Clouseau film when he died. It was tentatively entitled *The Romance of the Pink Panther*. He intended doing it

---

* Peter Sellers's letter is reproduced by permission.

without the mentor (some say progenitor) to whom, as I have mentioned, the Clouseau character owed a great deal – in other words, Blake Edwards. It is well known that each, at times, resisted the other's claim to the credit for Clouseau. But there's little doubt that Peter profited from Blake's judicious discipline; and Blake . . . well, Blake without Peter proved ultimately that he was flogging a dead panther, and, as it turned out, an expensive one. I refer, of course, to the bizarre film starring Peter Sellers as Inspector Clouseau which came out two years after Peter's death.

A significant amount of *The Trail of the Pink Panther* consisted of slapstick scenes that Peter had shot for earlier *Panther* films – 'out takes' as they are called – which were never used because he or possibly Blake decided they didn't fit, or he didn't quite bring it off or for some other reason. Now they were fitted, quite ingeniously, it must be admitted, into a story line involving Clouseau's being assigned to track down the eponymous pink diamond by the very people who have stolen it – in the cop's incompetence, they think, lies their only hope of getting away with the heist.

It is quite a shock at first to see Peter being 'born again'. For a time the grisly sensation of grave-robbing stifled my laughter. But then I found his comedy overcoming such inhibitions. The movie confirmed one thing beyond any doubt: Peter's skill at being able to repeat the same gag several times over and make it seem fresh each time. Not once, but twice, he manages to turn his office into a flaming inferno: first, simply by knocking out his pipe and then by filing away a document without noticing it's burning. On a flight across the Channel, he has a manic struggle trying to sit down on the loo with a leg encased in plaster. The limb's resistance recalls the independence developed by a different limb belonging to another Peter Sellers character in another film – *Dr Strangelove,* whose recalcitrant hand is always seeking to rise in a 'Heil!'.

In all the episodes, Clouseau's dignity remains unrumpled. His recovery from every *faux-pas* simply allows him to jump the better into another one. Thus when he's trying on disguises for size, he demands what he takes to be a false nose: it is the proprietor's wife's own. Without a blink, and torturing his French accent into an apology-cum-eulogy that would set a firing squad's teeth on edge with embarrassment, Clouseau flatters the offended lady into a good opinion of her own proboscis. Pride preserved, dignity saved.

Unfortunately, *The Trail of the Pink Panther* has to be judged as a whole; and it is less than the sum of its sometimes inspired 'inserts'. It did not find a large public. People sensed that the spirit of Clouseau had died with Peter and should have been left buried in the film vaults.

The damage didn't stop there, however. Blake Edwards had already shot a sequel to this ersatz exploit entitled *The Curse of the Pink Panther*. It starred a young and little known comedian called Ted Wass as a detective – not Clouseau – whom the makers compared, a trifle prematurely, to Harold Lloyd. He was no Harold Lloyd; more important, he was no Peter Sellers.

However, the 'curse' was not inapposite in view of what followed: not on a cinema screen this time, but in the English courts of law where Lynne Frederick, Peter's widow, in 1985, was awarded damages of £795,000 (one million dollars at the time) against Blake Edwards' production company and United Artists who had distributed *The Trail of the Pink Panther*. The judge, Mr Justice Hobhouse, disagreed with the defendants' arguments that Peter Sellers's contractual control over film material had ended with his death. His widow claimed that Peter had always refused consent for the use of the 'out takes' in any new *Pink Panther* film. She was also awarded £320,000 interest on the damages award and got an additional £50,000 for the use of clips from other *Pink Panther* movies. (Fortunately for Blake Edwards, the distributors had agreed to indemnify his company against any such eventuality).

If ever there was a case of the widow's might, this was it. Peter, said Lynne Frederick, would have felt vindicated. No doubt about that. Peter was a perfectionist. He was painfully and resentfully aware of the long chain of frustrations between his own inspiration and the people he had to rely on to give it lasting shape in his films. He got immeasurable enjoyment when the act of creation went right: his angsts were mostly engendered by the vigilance he exercised to keep it intact.

Sooner or later, though, as I've remarked elsewhere, the bias of a comic actor seems to turn against comedy in his search for other aspects of humanity to interpret. This was the case with Peter, as it had been with the man to whom he was often compared – in his early days, anyhow. Alec Guinness had also exchanged a 'fun face' for a neutral one. So did Peter in his penultimate film *Being There*, where he played a simple soul who achieves worldly power and influence merely because people project on to his bland features, and read into his delphic words, what they wish to see and hear. Peter often protested – a bit too much, as some thought – that he didn't know who he was. Guinness, as he's confessed in his memoirs, *Blessings in Disguise*, actually didn't know who he was, paternally speaking, anyhow. This loss of 'self' was a huge gain when it came to playing 'others'. Guinness would have relished impersonating an 'utter blank' in *Being There*. But it was Peter who finally gained the distinction he craved, the ultimate refinement, by playing a 'no one' and proving he could still be an actor.

Peter sometimes reminded me of Alec Guinness's worldlier, younger brother, enjoying the good things that success brought him with a flamboyance that would have revolted his staider sibling, who tended to put the temptations of stardom behind him, though always grateful for the percentage point or two of the box-office net, or the gross that his art earned him.

Peter envied Guinness, constantly and secretively. (It was a one-way envy, I think: Guinness would never have succumbed to that sin.) Sometimes Peter was out of the country when a new Guinness film opened. Then the call would come through to me, around one or two in the morning, for, like me, he was an insomniac. 'How is Guinness?' – 'How is he really?' In the early days, Peter was (in his own words) 'emerald with envy' of his fellow actor – 'actor', mind you, not just comic. *Being There* helped close the gap, gave him that taste of seriousness that comics lick their lips over. Had he lived, I believe Peter would have tried to alternate the 'comical-farcical' and the 'humanist-serious,' assuming the public would have let him, which is a fairly big assumption. People know what they like: it's even truer to say they like what they know.

He often told me how badly he wanted to do another film with Stanley Kubrick. Kubrick wanted to work with Peter, too. Both were men driven by private demons. But when the omens are as propitious as the scripts, even demons come out and dance a measure in each other's company. 'What do you think was Peter's greatest gift?' I asked Kubrick, expecting him to say 'impersonation'. He replied; 'improvisation'.

Once Peter was in the character Kubrick's script devised for him, his talent for free-ranging association took over and he improvised a 'life' that expanded to fill the space that Kubrick continuously pushed back, like a magic circle, so that his star kept on expanding to fill it. It was something that had to be witnessed. Kubrick has probably preserved every one of Peter's 'out takes': but you would sooner expect to find a brain scanner revealing the progress of a thought than film footage disclosing the chain reaction by which Peter constructed his comedy.

I'm sorry he's not here to share one posthumous irony. Like most of us, he used to chuckle over the coincidence of history that turned the fictional *Dr Strangelove* into the factual Dr Kissinger complete with his Teutonic accent. George Bush has come to the White House since then: and now it is his dry and slightly rasping intonation which resonates in Peter's impersonation of President Muffley in Kubrick's comedy.

It's been said that Peter's dazzle would have been dimmed in the era of *Monty Python* whose *Flying Circus* up-dated *The Goons'* surrealism for the following generation. I doubt if that would have been true. *The Goons* were 'sound': the *Pythons* were 'vision'. Peter had already cut himself out of the pack by the time *Monty Python's Circus* had landed. He was no longer an exclusively 'funny' man, though his sense of fun, like a divining rod, would have guided him to the humanity in any 'serious' role he played. He would have worked with Kubrick again: both men dearly longed to find the part. He might even have fitted into a Woody Allen-directed film: both men admired each other greatly. How many more Clouseaus (or Clouseaux) he had it in himself to do, we shall never know. He has left no successor; as Kenneth Tynan once pointed out, British cinema never developed another great comedian to match or surpass him. The line on the palm of his hand simply gave out, like the heart inside him; and although a biography such as I have written allows us to see this strange and singular man's whole life, it would be foolish to try and extend it. Peter stays with us: the others go on . . .

His last wife, Lynne Frederick, now lives in Los Angeles. Shortly after Peter's death, with no great fuss, she married David Frost, the television interviewer and programme maker. I spent Christmas 1981 with both of them in what had been Peter's Swiss chalet in Gstaad – though the two-and-a-half storey mansion (with mezzanine) perched on a hill-top stretched the definition of 'chalet' to the point where it resembled an annex to the nearby Palace Hotel. It was a set fit for a film star: but for all the hospitality and generosity inhabiting it that Christmas, the place remained a reminder that the star would never return to it. Perhaps that is why Lynne Frederick moved to Southern California after her marriage to David Frost was dissolved. She now lives in Beverly Hills, married to Barry Unger, a well-known cardiologist, with a family, and, in her spare time, breeds pedigree dogs and takes flying lessons. She has not returned to films so far.

Filmography

The following is a list of Peter Sellers's feature films, including the director, leading players and the date of the first public screening in either London or New York, whichever is earlier.

Penny Points to Paradise. Dir. Tony Young; Harry Secombe, Alfred Marks, Bill Kerr; UK, 12 October 1951.

Down Among the Z Men. Dir, Maclean Rogers; Spike Milligan, Harry Secombe, Michael Bentine; UK, 12 July 1952.

Orders Are Orders. Dir. David Paltenghi; Brian Reece, Sid James, Raymond Huntley, Clive Morton, Donald Pleasence, Maureen Swanson, Tony Hancock; UK, 30 September 1954.

John and Julie. Dir. William Fairchild; Moira Lister, Constance Cummings, Wilfrid Hyde White, Andrew Cruickshank; UK, 15 July 1955.

The Ladykillers. Dir. Alexander Mackendrick; Alec Guinness, Cecil Parker, Danny Green, Herbert Lom, Katie Johnson; UK, 24 February 1956.

The Smallest Show on Earth. Dir. Basil Dearden; Bill Travers, Virginia McKenna, Margaret Rutherford, Bernard Miles; UK, 11 April 1957.

The Naked Truth. Dir. Mario Zampi; Terry-Thomas, Dennis Price, Peggy Mount, Shirley Eaton; UK, 2 January 1958 (US title: *Your Past Is Showing*).

Up the Creek. Dir. Val Guest; David Tomlinson, Wilfrid Hyde White, Reginald Beckwith, Lionel Jeffries; UK, 11 November 1958.

tom thumb. Dir. George Pal; Russ Tamblyn, Jessie Matthews, Terry-Thomas, June Thorburn; UK, 24 December 1958.

Carlton-Browne of the F.O. Dirs Roy Boulting, Jeffrey Dell; Terry-Thomas, Ian Bannen, Thorley Walters, Raymond Huntley, John Le Mesurier; UK, 13 March 1959 (US title: *Man in a Cocked Hat*).

237

The Mouse That Roared. Dir. Jack Arnold; Jean Seberg, David Kossoff; UK, 17 July 1959.

I'm All Right, Jack. Dir. John Boulting; Ian Carmichael, Irene Handl, Richard Attenborough, Terry-Thomas, Dennis Price, Margaret Rutherford, Liz Fraser; UK, 13 August 1959.

Two Way Stretch. Dir. Robert Day; Lionel Jeffries, Wilfrid Hyde White, David Lodge, Bernard Cribbins, Liz Fraser, Beryl Reid; UK, 11 February 1960.

The Battle of the Sexes. Dir. Charles Crichton; Constance Cummings, Robert Morley; UK, 25 February 1960.

Never Let Go. Dir. John Guillermin; Richard Todd, Elizabeth Sellars, Adam Faith; UK, 2 June 1960.

The Millionairess. Dir. Anthony Asquith; Sophia Loren, Alastair Sim, Vittorio De Sica; UK, 8 October 1960.

Mr Topaze. Dir. Peter Sellers; Nadia Gray, Herbert Lom, Leo McKern; UK, 23 March 1961.

Only Two Can Play. Dir. Sidney Gilliat; Mai Zetterling, Virginia Maskell, Richard Attenborough; UK, 11 January 1962.

The Waltz of the Toreadors. Dir. John Guillermin; Margaret Leighton, Dany Robin, John Fraser; UK, 12 April 1962.

Lolita. Dir. Stanley Kubrick; James Mason, Sue Lyon, Shelley Winters; USA, 14 June 1962.

The Dock Brief. Dir. James Hill; Richard Attenborough; UK, 20 September 1962.

The Wrong Arm of the Law. Dir. Cliff Owen; Lionel Jeffries, Bernard Cribbins, Nanette Newman; UK, 14 March 1963.

Heavens Above. Dir. John Boulting; Ian Carmichael, Cecil Parker, Isabel Jeans, Irene Handl, Eric Sykes, Bernard Miles; USA, 21 May 1963.

The Pink Panther. Dir. Blake Edwards; David Niven, Capucine, Claudia Cardinale, Robert Wagner; UK, 9 January 1964.

Dr Strangelove, or How I Learned to Stop Worrying and Love the Bomb. Dir. Stanley Kubrick; George C. Scott, Sterling Hayden, Keenan Wynn, Slim Pickens, Peter Bull; UK, 30 January 1964.

The World of Henry Orient. Dir. George Roy Hill; Angela Lansbury, Paula Prentiss; USA, 20 March 1964.

A Shot in the Dark. Dir. Blake Edwards; Elke Sommer, George Sanders, Herbert Lom, Graham Stark; USA, 24 June 1964.

What's New, Pussycat? Dir. Clive Donner; Peter O'Toole, Woody Allen, Ursula Andress, Paula Prentiss, Romy Schneider, Capucine; USA, 23 June 1965.

The Wrong Box. Dir. Bryan Forbes; Ralph Richardson, John Mills, Michael Caine, Nanette Newman, Peter Cook, Dudley Moore; UK, 26 May 1966.

After the Fox. Dir. Vittorio De Sica; Britt Ekland, Victor Mature, Akim Tamiroff, Martin Balsam; UK, 29 September 1966.

Casino Royale. Dirs. Joe McGrath, Robert Parrish, John Huston, Val Guest, Ken Hughes; David Niven, Orson Welles, Woody Allen, Ursula Andress, Deborah Kerr, Charles Boyer, William Holden; UK, 14 April 1967.

Woman Times Seven. Dir. Vittorio De Sica; Shirley MacLaine; USA, 28 June 1967.

The Bobo. Dir. Robert Parrish; Britt Ekland, Rossano Brazzi; UK, 17 August 1967.

The Party. Dir. Blake Edwards; Claudine Longet, Marge Champion; USA, 5 April 1968.

I Love You, Alice B. Toklas. Dir. Hy Averback; Jo Van Fleet, Joyce Van Patten, Leigh Taylor-Young; USA, 8 October 1968.

The Magic Christian. Dir. Joe McGrath; Ringo Starr, Richard Attenborough, Laurence Harvey, Yul Brynner, Spike Milligan, Roman Polanski, Raquel Welch; USA, 12 February 1970.

Hoffman. Dir. Alvin Rakoff; Sinead Cusack; UK, 16 July 1970.

There's a Girl in My Soup. Dir. Roy Boulting; Goldie Hawn, Tony Britton; UK, 23 December 1971.

A Day at the Beach. Dir. Simon Hesera; Mark Burns, Fiona Lewis, Graham Stark; unreleased.

Alice's Adventures in Wonderland. Dir. William Sterling; Fiona Fullerton, Michael Crawford, Robert Helpmann, Dudley Moore, Spike Milligan, Ralph Richardson, Michael Hordern, Flora Robson; UK, 7 December 1972.

Where Does It Hurt? Dir. Rod Amateau; Jo Ann Pflug; USA, 11 August 1972.

The Blockhouse. Dir. Clive Rees; Charles Aznavour; unreleased.

The Optimists of Nine Elms. Dir. Anthony Simmons; Donna Mullane, John Chaffey; UK, 25 April 1974.

Soft Beds and Hard Battles. Dir. Roy Boulting; Lila Kedrova, Curt Jurgens; UK, 25 January 1974 (US title: *Undercovers Hero*).

Ghost in the Noonday Sun. Dir. Peter Medak; Spike Milligan, Anthony Franciosa, David Lodge, Peter Boyle; unreleased.

The Great McGonagall. Dir. Joe McGrath; Spike Milligan, Julia Foster; UK, 23 January 1975.

The Return of the Pink Panther. Dir. Blake Edwards; Christopher Plummer, Catherine Schell, Herbert Lom, Burt Kwouk; USA, 22 May 1975.

Murder by Death. Dir. Robert Moore; Peter Falk, Alec Guinness, Truman Capote, Estelle Winwood, Elsa Lanchester, David Niven, Maggie Smith, James Coco, Eileen Brennan; USA, 24 June 1976.

The Pink Panther Strikes Again. Dir. Blake Edwards; Herbert Lom, Burt Kwouk, Lesley-Anne Down; UK and USA, 16 December 1976.

The Revenge of the Pink Panther. Dir. Blake Edwards; Herbert Lom, Dyan Cannon, Burt Kwouk, Graham Stark; UK, 13 July 1978.

The Prisoner of Zenda. Dir. Richard Quine; Lynne Frederick, Elke Sommer, Lionel Jeffries; USA, 23 May 1979.

Being There. Dir. Hal Ashby; Shirley MacLaine, Melvyn Douglas, Jack Warden; USA, 19 December 1979.

The Fiendish Plot of Dr Fu Manchu. Dir. Piers Haggard; Helen Mirren, David Tomlinson, Sid Caesar, Burt Kwouk; USA, 13 August 1980.

The Running, Jumping and Standing Still Film, an 11-minute short. Dir. Richard Lester; Spike Milligan, Graham Stark; UK, released 1960.

Index

241